Shared Territory

Shared Territory

*Understanding
Children's Writing
as Works*

MARGARET HIMLEY

New York   Oxford
OXFORD UNIVERSITY PRESS
1991

Acknowledgements: Ever since I first met Pat Carini in the summer of 1982, she has generously provided an ongoing conversation about children and their ways of thinking in and through the world. I hope that this book, filled with the words and presence of Pat, will become part of that larger conversation.

This work has also been furthered by the National Academy of Education's Spencer Fellowship Program (1987–88), and I am very grateful for the research year this fellowship support provided.

I would also like to acknowledge the valuable contributions to this project provided by the Prospect community. Most of all I would like to thank Matthew for being a great, interesting, full of surprises writer and son.

Oxford University Press

Oxford   New York   Toronto
Delhi   Bombay   Calcutta   Madras   Karachi
Petaling Jaya   Singapore   Hong Kong   Toyko
Nairobi   Dar es Salaam   Cape Town
Melbourne   Auckland

and associated companies in
Berlin   Ibadan

Copyright © 1991 by Oxford University Press, Inc.

Published by Oxford University Press, Inc.,
200 Madison Avenue, New York, New York 10016

Oxford is a registered trademark of Oxford University Press

Library of Congress Cataloging-in-Publication Data
Himley, Margaret.
Shared territory : understanding children's writing as works /
Margaret Himley.
p.   cm.
ISBN 0-19-506189-6
1. Language acquisition. 2. Children—Writing. I. Title.
P118.H56 1991
401'.93—dc20   90-47749

9 8 7 6 5 4 3 2 1

Printed in the United States of America
on acid-free paper

Contents

Shared Territory

INTRODUCTION

Situating the Study,
Mapping the Argument

> A work bears forever the gesture and imprint of its maker.
> . . . Glancing through a cookbook kept in the family, the jotted
> amplifications and comments of generations of users brings each
> one briefly into the present moment. . . . From within the rhythm
> of content, word, and gesture, appears the partial visage of a living
> perspective—the cook, the visionary, the economy-minded house-
> holder, the teacher. (Carini, *The Art of Seeing and the Visibility of
> the Person,* p. 4)

> The authentic environment of an utterance, the environment in
> which it lives and takes shape, is dialogized heteroglossia, anony-
> mous and social as language, but simultaneously concrete, filled
> with specific content and accented as an individual utterance.
> (Bakhtin, *The Dialogic Imagination,* p. 272)

> The ideological sign is the common territory for both the psyche and
> for ideology, a territory that is material, sociological, and meaning-
> ful. . . . A word is territory shared by both addressor and ad-
> dressee. (Volosinov/Bakhtin, *Marxism and the Philosophy of Lan-
> guage,* pp. 33, 86).

Works as Shared Territory

The theories of Mikhail M. Bakhtin and Patricia F. Carini present a
challenge to literacy teachers, theorists, and researchers. They both insist
that we start our enterprise from the argument that all actual language use,
from marginalia in a cookbook to a child's first story to book-length
scientific treatises or literary works, must be studied and understood as
both/and: both social and psychological, personal and cultural, unique

3

and normative, public and private, expressive and constitutive. Language is the territory common to the psyche and to ideology. To author text is to author self and be authored by culture. In what Bakhtin calls "utterance" and Carini terms "works"—that is, in the shared territory of actual language use—enculturation is enacted, individuation achieved, and development occasioned.

Bakhtin argues that every bit of language use, even the most casually and conventionally coded daily exchange, both reproduces the repeatable words of others, especially dominant or authoritative cultural voices, yet also expresses an individual accent and an unrepeatable, unique, radically contextualized meaning. For Bakhtin, the self, irreducibly social in origin and orientation, is reciprocally constituted with culture through the shared territory of language. Carini conceptualizes the texts children write (and the sketches and paintings they draw) as works, as particular and personal enactments of transpersonal meaning potentials, as partial and ambiguous evocations of the person who made them—by, through, and within cultural media. For Carini, too, the person emerges out of the deep and continuous, simultaneous and mutual interanimation with the world, and the rich particularity of each person's perspective is enabled by and enacted through larger cultural patterns and possibilities for meaning.[1]

This both/and tension is familiar to those early written language developmental theorists who have tried to move beyond the conceptual limits of an overpsychologized composing process research program, by trying to include the personal and social dimensions of literacy use and learning. In *GNYS AT WRK* (1980), for example, Bissex concludes that learning to write is a process shaped both by cognitive universals and by an individual variation based on personality and personal meaning. And Dyson (1985) tries even more specifically in her research to correlate three variables—"the nature of the individual child, the nature of the situational context, and the complex nature of the writing system itself" (p. 59)—in order to explain written language growth.

Yet all too often we find ourselves reading children's texts *either* as expressive of that particular child's interests and values, as having personal meaning and intention, *or* as evidence of larger patterns of language or cognitive development or literacy learning—but not both.

The both/and premise matters, however, because it offers a richer understanding of the complexity of becoming a writer, and because it participates in arguments for restoring the possibility of human agency and singularity in a postmodern world. If language use can be understood as transformative, surprising, and individualizable, it is neither just totalizing and overdetermined nor merely the private property of rather autonomous subjects. Rather, texts become a messy, whirling orbit, full of multiple and conflicting voices, a site open to reappropriation and individuation and possible communal change (see Schuster, 1985; Bauer, 1988; Schrag, 1986; Smith, 1988).

But it's easier to state the both/and premise than to research it.

This premise requires that we think relationally, not in terms of fixed categories but in terms of border regions which focus attention on dynamic interactions among writers, readers, texts, and language—interactions that somehow allow them to still retain (or develop) their differences. Bakhtin refers to this as ''a drama in which three characters participate'' (1986, p. 122). Texts then become semiotic spaces, or *shared territory,* in which persons compose and express their individuation within, through, and against culture—in which writer, reader, language, even the researcher participate in the meaning. And somehow in this ''dialogic encounter,'' to use Bakhtin's language, each retains its own unity and open totality, while all are mutually enriched (1986, p. 7).

In the following chapters, I take up this project by examining the rich theories of Carini and Bakhtin, by overlapping and juxtaposing them, in order to come up with a possible methodology for doing research—for understanding children as they become writers—that begins with the both/and premise. I end with a documentary account of one young writer, as a way of enacting the theory and as a first effort at using description as both research method and genre. The argument is located at the intersection of development and dialogics:

(1) *Development becomes more explicitly dialogic.* To approach written language development dialogically is to locate new writers historically, as situated within the chain of texts that have preceded them and as oriented toward the subsequent possible responses of readers of all sorts. By learning to write, children become participants in the living dialogue of language itself, and development is the process of assimilation, more or less creatively, of the words of others. Dialogics, then, provides one way to theorize composing as irreducibly and profoundly social.

(2) *And dialogics becomes more explicitly developmental.* In exploring the convergence of Carini and Bakhtin, and in extending their work more specifically into early written language development, we have a partic-

ularly powerful theoretical approach for reading children's texts, for understanding their choices and patterns as writers, and for constructing subjects of study.

To make this argument, I begin with Carini's theories of children and childhood and in particular with her conception of the child as a unique maker of works. Then, through dramatizations and analyses of descriptive talk as knowing and through a reading of Bakhtin, I try to extend, layer, and complicate that opening argument—to relocate her work within a more explicitly dialogic understanding of language use—in an effort to come at the question of children's writing from a complexly both/and theoretical position.

Situating the Study: Rethinking Development

This project is one response to problems that have confronted the field of early written language development research ever since what might be called the cognitive research program, that pioneering strand of work initiated in 1973 by Donald Graves in his investigation of the composing behaviors of seven-year-old children, hit certain limits.

Its findings denied its premises.

As Sowers (1985) explains, the Graves–New Hampshire project initially "was designed to document writing as *development,* that is, the unfolding of the individual according to nature's plan, only incidentally related to instruction and social mediation. Instead, *learning,* or what was provided by the environment, proved to be closely intertwined with developmental data about what and how the child took from the environment for self-generated purposes" (p. 329).

Researchers discovered that the boundaries between the developing child and the actual situational and cultural setting were blurred, permeable, and "bidirectional." Historical definitions of development, with their biological connotations of natural maturation or teleological unfolding, quickly became problematic for analyzing such a messy, often unpredictable or even discontinuous transaction. Even the very concept of cognitive development came to seem inadequately linear, restrictive, a bit impoverished for investigating the complexity of children writing.

But what does development now mean? How can it be conceptualized and described? How might writing researchers actually work with such concepts as developmental reciprocity or bidirectionality or multicausality, when they describe or explain children's composing activities within specific settings and across time? How do they assess what the individual writer brings (e.g., gender, ethnicity, expressive style)? How do they analyze what dimensions of context actually count (e.g., physical environment, the sociocultural, the historical)? How does it all interact? How useful or even valid are traditional definitions of development that still privilege concepts such as sequentiality, end states, causality, and continuity?

The very concept of development has required profound rethinking.

In response to questions such as these, researchers in developmental psychology have attempted answers by turning to multivariate models and multidisciplinary approaches, explicit concern with context, a life-span orientation, and lively debate about methodology and the theoretical bases for definition or categories of development itself (e.g., Cairns, 1979; Lerner, 1983).

In early written language development research, the focus has shifted to the social dimensions of literacy learning. As Gundlach (Gundlach et al., 1985) says, looking at how the social context motivates, supports, and often organizes a child's path of development as a writer has "expanded the unit of analysis in children's writing research from the child's text and his individual composing behavior to a frame that encompasses interaction between child and adult, interaction among children, and the reading and writing activity that a child may observe at home, in a day care center, or in a kindergarten classroom" (p. 3). Writing researchers are now doing ethnographic studies of classroom interactions, case studies of individual writers, and analyses of literacy events in different kinds of communities.

Semiotic approaches to understanding children's literacy learning have also emerged. These approaches define writing as the engaging in a language event, as the orchestrating of multiple semiotic codes, as the negotiating with readers of possible meanings. Studying development from this perspective entails discovering the possibly universal principles of language and language learning that underlie the fine-tuning of those fundamental semiotic processes.

In this project, I, too, start down this semiotic path, but with a twist. By exploring the convergence of Carini and Bakhtin, I come to define writing as a simultaneously cultural and expressive activity, as the making of "works," and I locate written language development within the permeable border regions of child and culture, in texts, in the shared semiotic space that is constituted by and through and within concrete moments of actual language use. I then propose understanding children as writers by dwelling in that space and by reading—carefully, slowly, descriptively, dialogically—the many texts they have written over time and in various settings.

Mapping the Argument

Let me point out explicitly the spatial and temporal metaphors informing this project. To theorize development as irreducibly social suggests working with a dynamic configuration of writer-reader-text-context that tries to trace meaning relationally, interactively, in the process of reading and writing, in the spaces "between." A child's text then may become "a textual space" (Nystrand, 1986), "a whirling orbit" (Schuster, 1985), a drama or performance, an arena or territory, in which the child, readers, and language itself—as Bakhtinian hero—participate actively and across time in the making of meanings.

Perhaps it would be more accurate to say not "the child" but rather "the child writing" or "the child as written into and by the text, read by and through readers," because I am trying to work against the traditional individual-social dichotomy that has been assumed in so much research on development, by getting at the profound, irreducible, and original socialness or otherness of that child. "The child" implies a bounded, autonomous, and centered subject, using language in directly expressive, unmediated ways. "The child writing" suggests, I hope, the person *as becoming and made visible through her engagement in meaningful social activity,* in cultural practices of signification—by, through, and against which she comes to know herself and the many selves she might become.

In so doing, I am trying to locate text as a shared territory, a middle ground between the utterly private and autobiographical and the totally public and conventional, in what Berger and Mohr (1982) call "the social function of subjectivity" (p. 100). I am trying to trace development dialogically (and ambiguously) within those open border regions of child and culture, as enacted in concrete moments of actual language use.

The chapters in this book do not constitute a tightly rendered, or linear, argument, but rather invite readers into a conversation and dramatization, into a shared process of thinking and rethinking together, which depends on the juxtaposing of voices and theories and on the responsive understanding of readers. Indeed, this project is intentionally uneven with respect to voice. I have tried to make room for many voices, at times competing ones, both in articulating and in performing the theory here— voices from theorists Carini and Bakhtin; my own voice woven throughout; the voices of other researchers; the voices of teachers from the Writing Program at Syracuse University and from the Prospect School in North Bennington, Vermont; and, most important, Matthew's voices as he writes across time. The project remains exploratory, rough-edged, and open-ended. So I ask for patience *and for time* to dwell in these voices and theories, to explore their possibilities, to make sense of their many convergences and their contrasts.

There are three basic moments in this argument.

The Child Making, or Texts as Works

The first is based on the work of Patricia F. Carini, an educator and phenomenologically oriented theorist on children and childhood, whose school and archive of children's works in North Bennington, Vermont, has increasingly attracted the attention of many educators and researchers.

Carini characterizes children's projects and products—their drawings and three-dimensional constructions as well as their written texts—as ''works,'' as serious objects of thought, as the objectified workings of the human mind, as artifacts of child-culture interactions, all attesting to the fundamental human impulse to make, build, and narrate our lives. Carini uses the term *works* not to suggest that we all enact some kind of creative or intellectual genius, but rather to emphasize the process of thinking as a common human enterprise, fundamental to our participation within the world, something we all can and do engage in, young and old alike, not just specialists like academics or genuises like Einstein. We are all makers of works, as we jot comments in a cookbook or keep diaries or design table settings or write novels or sketch house plans. When we read a child's story or describe his or her drawing, we are ''reading'' a *particular* and *situated* enactment of cultural meaning potentials. We are ''reading'' that series of moments where child and culture blur and blend, enact and energize each other. Works then become meaningful spaces, abundantly eventful spaces, where we, as writers and readers, can meet at any time, overtime, time and time again, and come to know each other in certain partial ways.

With her notion of the child as maker of works, Carini offers writing researchers an epistemology and a methodology for understanding the development of writing as the development of a practice, or activity, that is both cultural and expressive, simultaneously social and individual.

By carefully and descriptively reading a child's works, by making visible and naming the dialogics of reading, and by locating those works in many contexts, teachers and researchers can come to understand that particular child's unique interests, ideas, accents, ways of learning and thinking. Although children work with common motifs and cultural media, for example, each child explores space, sets boundaries, narrates a story, or dramatizes life experiences in importantly different and particular ways. Each child adds his or her unique imprint, expressive gesture, accent, and intonation and cuts a particular perspective against the natural and cultural world. And for Carini it is this "expressiveness of the person" that explains how we know one another, how we insert ourselves into time and history and setting, and how we come to be and become in and through the world.

In taking the time to dwell in the text, teachers and researchers can also achieve a richer, fuller knowledge of the specific resources of written language and of themselves as particular and situated readers, as they layer text on text and as they describe choices and patterns in increasingly nuanced and finely articulated ways.

The notion of "the child making" tries to move the locus of consciousness from some kind of private space or entity within the person to a visible activity that we can understand to take place within the border regions, the shared territories, of two realities—that of the person and that of the world or culture. It insists, therefore, on a simultaneous and constitutive relationship between the person and the world, a relationship in which cultural practices both appropriate and are appropriated by the person in a continuous, dynamic making and remaking of the world and our humanness. The "old" world, with its thick history, receives and initiates the "new" person, who alters its meanings and opens up yet-to-be-explored regions of possibility.

The Person Speaking, or Language as Hero

The second moment is to turn explicitly to the theory of language developed by M. M. Bakhtin, the Soviet philosopher and theorist. Though not a developmentalist, he, too, is deeply interested in the mutuality and reciprocity between the social and the individual as achieved through language use, a reciprocity based for Bakhtin on the irreducible duality of I/other. Bakhtin usefully complicates and enriches Carini's theory of the child as maker of works by explicitly theorizing the profound socialness of all language use.

A reading of Bakhtin challenges the naive notions of the autonomous subject and the theory of language as expressive realism that are implicit in writing research or curricula that talk about writing as if it were mostly a problem solving matter of a person's finding the right words to convey rather directly and clearly experiences or ideas. He forcefully and provocatively makes the argument that language is not a neutral, pliable medium, readily and somewhat passively available to writers for rather directly fulfilling their referential and expressive intentions. Rather, Bakhtin insists, language itself is active, generative, constitutive, a shared territory, often an embattled one, full of multiple voices and conflicting worldviews.

Language then becomes "hero."

A Bakhtinian perspective therefore argues that learning to write is not a simple, unilateral process in which a child acquires new ways to express private and single-voiced intentions, but rather a complex act of appropriation and resistance (and of being appropriated) in which the child learns the very meanings he or she can have—in which new writers move into new words, into new worlds, into new ways of being.

For Bakhtin, we turn then to the person speaking, to utterance, to the border regions (again) of child and culture, and to concrete moments of actual language use, "anonymous and social as language, but simultaneously concrete, filled with specific content and accented as an individual utterance" (1981, p. 272). And there, Bakhtin implies, we will find tensions between individuating and participating, between expressing and constituting self via text, between the apparently private intentions of the writer and the public and polyphonic possibilities of written language—and the evolving text—itself.

The Child Writing

In the third moment, I bring Carini and Bakhtin together by actually doing a full documentary account of one young writer. Following in the tradition of researchers like Bissex who have studied their own children, this account is based on a descriptive reading of 15 key texts that I have selected from the 160 or so that my son Matthew wrote between first and fifth grades. These works represent the range of themes, genres, expressive choices, and voices in the entire corpus.

This account serves as a first gesture toward actually doing research as a kind of Bakhtinian conversation. It turns description into a way of knowing and a research method, as it invites readers to participate in the dramatization of the account and the shared territory of a child's texts and as it defines the child writing as a semiotic subject of study for early written language researchers.

Description as Dialogic Encounter

In "Deep Talk as Knowing" (Chapter 2), in "A Reflective Conversation" (Chapter 3), and in "A Documentary Account of One Young Writer" (Chapter 6), I explicitly explore the research possibilities of talking together and description as possible research methodologies. To do so, we must begin with a broader definition of knowing than usual. This kind of thinking is both communal and generalist, drawing first and foremost upon the resources of collective thought and community. To think together is to open up another shared territory, a dialogic encounter, where we can meet, know each other, albeit partially, and come to certain kinds of understandings about a shared focus of interest.

The process of description, too, requires redefining. It is not the stripping away of outer layers of meaning to get at some essence or kernel of truth. It is not a psychologized rendering of the text and author. It is not a "meta" or transparent use of language to get at the real, objective meaning of a text or writer. And it is not a way of directly (re)presenting an empirically given reality.

To describe—to deep-talk a child's text—is to layer words on words; to locate the text in various historical, theoretical, and generic contexts; to complicate understanding; to read a text in relation to all other texts written in that genre; to disrupt the pragmatic frame; and to find words to name and evoke the writer's expressive choices within that genre. The process of description then makes a writer "visible" *as a particular social actor* working with cultural themes and shared resources in traditional (given) and unique (created) ways at the same time. The writer comes to be and emerges through, within, and against the shared territory of language use, as a particular person constituted through his or her engagement in cultural activities such as writing. As Bakhtin and Carini suggest, we come to know each other through and within the materiality of the sign, within the shared practices of cultural signification, so that in deep talk and description we come to know the writer (in ways) as a particular enactor of those vast semiotic resources.

In describing Matthew's first story, for example, readers come to know him as he writes himself through, and is written by, the fairy tale genre, as he takes on the archetypal life-and-death questions of coming to the edge of one's resources, as he adds his unique layer of meaning to the textual resources and the cultural themes of the genre. Matthew becomes more and more visible, not as language is stripped away, but as more and more language is added, as his words are embedded contrastively in more and more contexts. Thus, his expressiveness as a writer is named and known, as he is engaged in writing a fairy tale, as he explores a traditional genre, as readers locate his work within varied textual contexts.

It is, finally, in reading a particular work against and within these many cultural contexts that the hand and accent of the person really make themselves felt. This dialogic process of description, therefore, takes place on that large middle ground between the private and the public, the autobiographical and the conventional. By bringing to bear all that they know about language and genre, readers come to name the many ways this particular writer has uniquely accented that language and genre. And in the process, they come to understand more about language, the writer, and themselves.

Language itself, used reflexively, becomes the means for opening up intellectual space; for bringing in complexity and multiplicity of meaning, historicity, etymology, culture, and ideology; for juxtaposing words and worldviews—without the totalizing effect of applied theory and without the fuzzy pluralism of casual conversation. The descriptive process makes explicit use of language as open, unfinished, inexhaustible in further dialogic interaction (Volosinov/Bakhtin 1986, p. 346). Words encounter words: "They may be juxtaposed to one another, mutually supplement one another, contradict one another and be interrelated dialogically" (p. 292).

Again, language is hero.

Reading a student's text, describing it over and over again, layering text on text, experimenting with the right nuances, hearing the different discourses of various readers—all this language use creates a network of meaning, organized not as abstracted or second-order or even totalizing generalizations, but rather as patterns generated by and through the talk. This descriptive knowledge then remains tied closely to the particular student, text, context, moment, group of readers, while opening up into the universe. It is neither uncritical accumulation of practices and beliefs, or Northian (North, 1987) "lore," nor testable in more traditional or scientific terms. It remains disputable—and that potentially is its great value. Descriptive knowledge calls forth a response from others. It forms and informs and reforms through more talk and experience and writing across time and within different settings.

Descriptive knowledge may also be one response to Patricia L. Stock's argument (in manuscript) that the practice of education must begin and end in the ordinary languages and experiences of teachers and re-searchers, that it should lead, therefore, to community, not separation and specialization, and that it should encourage and enable practicing teachers to talk meaningfully with each other.

The Child
Making

1

The Study of Works:
A Phenomenological Approach
to Understanding Children
as Thinkers and Learners

(*Coauthor: Patricia F. Carini*)

The Prospect School:
Making and Learning/Describing and Understanding

Founded in 1965, the Prospect School in North Bennington, Vermont, is a small independent school from kindergarten through eighth grade, located in a sprawling nineteenth-century lodge on a large wooded lot.[1] It is an inviting place, different from the scenes of learning I have known. The small interconnecting rooms and alcoves—filled with scattered tables and chairs, used clothing for drama, papier-mâché dinosaurs, books, children's artwork of all kinds, maps, charts, and aquariums—spread out in labyrinthine ways across all three stories. Sunlight and the smells of drying paint, paste, and old wood flood through the cluttered rooms.

But what really characterizes this school is not the absence of the traditional rectangular classroom with its rows of identical desks or some Summerhill-like romantic expectation about the basic good nature of children that is released in an environment of freedom. Prospect is set apart because of its serious philosophical commitment to *the intensive observation and description of children as the grounding for teaching practice and educational research*. Here Patricia F. Carini has developed a phenomenological approach to understanding children as thinkers and learners—as makers of works—that has significant possibilities for early written language teachers, researchers, and theorists.[2]

What has been set in motion at Prospect is the opportunity for children to work with many expressive media, from paper and pencil to clay and wood, within a more accommodating and flexible time structure than is usual in schools. Carini and her colleagues have created the possibility for children to have an immersed, sustained experience with these media. They then watch attentively as children work with crayon, with written text, with wood—as they think *by* and *through* these malleable cultural materials—reworking their expressive possibilities, adding layers of meaning, and making (partially) visible their ways of knowing the world. A quickness of line is noted, a focus on interiority, an emphasis on spatial relations, an interest in time and history. These expressive choices enact the interanimating relationship of the person and the world and, when carefully and respectfully described, announce to teachers what might really matter to a child in deeply dispositional ways. These understandings not only enhance their conversations with the children themselves about their interests but also widen the context for educational decisions about what ideas or books or projects or media to propose to children as worthy of their interest and important for their educational growth.

This commitment to observation as the basis of educational practice is premised on a specific way of thinking about children, on a belief in the person and learner as a maker of meaning:

> [This] view of the person . . . assumes that learning occurs as the result of the intrinsically human effort to create meaning and order in the world of human experience. Interest and the active pursuit and extension of interest are at the root of learning. Experience needs not only to be taken in but to be grappled with and realized anew, if it is to be deeply understood. Experience actively re-worked and represented becomes accessible to examination and thought. It is out of this formative activity that knowledge grows. (1986a, p. ii)

The educational practices at Prospect reflect this fundamental belief in the critical connection among personal meaning, value, expressiveness, and the formation of knowledge.

With time, and working collaboratively with art historian Beth Alberty, Carini came to characterize the many projects and products that children make as "works," as artifacts attesting to—and profoundly expressive of—the fundamental human impulse to make meaning in our lives.[3] For more than twenty-four years now, Carini and her Prospect colleagues have been collecting children's writings, drawings, and constructions in an Archive that currently contains more than 250,000 pieces. Over time they have developed in action what they call "reflective procedures" for formalizing the processes of observing and describing children and their works.

Carini's approach to responding seriously to children's projects as works is important and intriguing in at least three ways. First, though children work with common motifs and cultural media, Carini notes that all children define space, explore history, tell a story, or enact life experiences in importantly particular ways. By reflectively, concretely, and often communally describing a child's work—a pencil drawing, a written story, a three-dimensional construction—teachers and researchers can come to understand more fully (and always ambiguously) that child's expressive choices, interests, images, positionings, keywords, and ways of learning and thinking, and then use that understanding to support the child's learning.

Second, using Carini's procedures for describing children's texts, readers can achieve a finer, fuller knowledge of the specific cultural resources of written language itself for the making of meaning. The medium, that is, becomes less transparent, more layered, complex, and material, as readers hear others' responses and as they articulate in increasingly refined and nuanced ways the discursive structures, rhetorical effects, and (inter)textual choices in particular writings. Looking at what children have written over several years enables readers to describe and name how these writers have worked and developed across time— that is, what language resources they use, how they work and rework those resources, what changes during that process, and what stays the same.

Third, and most important, by characterizing children's texts as works, Carini provokes a profound rethinking of the philosophical and epistemological questions that inform our discussions of development itself. She problematizes certain traditional assumptions and definitions and offers an alternative methodology for investigating children writing across time. This methodology is based on the phenomenological process of descriptively reading children's texts as works, as locations of actual language use, complexly and reciprocally cultural *and* expressive, social *and* individual.

The ideas underlying Carini's ways of thinking about children's growth and learning are described in three monographs published by the North Dakota Study Group on Evaluation: *Observation and Description: An Alternative Methodology for the Investigation of Human Phenomena* (1975), *The Art of Seeing and the Visibility of the Person* (1979a), and *The School Lives of Seven Children: A Five Year Study* (1982). In addition, I studied at Prospect during the fall of 1987. This chapter also explores ideas from my ongoing conversations with Carini, a reading of her current unpublished papers, and observations of staff reviews and descriptions of children's work as conducted by teachers at Prospect.

The chapter results from a continuing reciprocity in thought and language among Carini, myself, and various readers of this work.[4] At times we have tried in composing this chapter to (re)present the rhythm of that reciprocity, the energetic interplay of thinking and speaking and writing, the inevitable presence of many voices. At other times, my voice recedes, as Carini takes up a thought more historically and reflectively. This roughness in texture marks our effort to stay close to the ways this reciprocity has played out across time, and to incorporate the collage of talking, reflective reworking, storytelling, and "essaying" that has characterized our work together. This chapter also portrays Prospect as Bakhtinian "hero"—a place that brings people together, a time for a particular kind of talk, and an arena of possibilities in which intellectual work occurs and is energized.

The Story of (Everett): Valuing and Preferring/Building and Narrating

Several sections of this chapter present Patricia F. Carini speaking directly based on unpublished essays, notes, and transcribed conversations we had during the fall of 1987. For my questions and comments, I am identified as MH.

MH: Let's begin this discussion with the central place you give to the person as an active agent in the world and with the ways you understand the person as drawn into, extended by, and constituted within that world.

In response to this question, I want to acknowledge first that lots of educational philosophy and theory talks about children as "active learners." My own debt to John Dewey in this respect is considerable.

Looking to developmental psychology, Piaget lends support to that kind of theory when he describes the child's relationship to the empirical world and emphasizes how children work, somewhat like little scientists doing experiments and generalizing the results into rule and law, to (re)discover in rather predictable sequence the logical relationships and principles that order the world. Vygotsky, especially through his concept of the zone of proximal development, also calls attention to the activity of the learner. However, according to my understanding of the major developmental theorists, it's Werner who made the most room for the activity of the person in shaping the world. He accomplishes this by conceptualizing reality as the formation of spheres of significance reflective of the changing powers of the person. For the reason that Werner's structural apparatus is looser, less defined and categorical, he also directs the observer's attention more to the activities of the child and less to an abstract schema for classifying those activities. Still, allowing for their differences, each of these theorists is concerned to establish a model of the activity of the person according to stages end-stopped by mature, adult functioning.

Yet in these theories of development (and others of which I am aware) the emphasis tends to be what I would call mentalistic. This seems to me to be so even when a scholar like Kohlberg inquires into a broader question like morality. But what is more troubling to me are theories of development and of education in which thinking itself is reduced to cognition, and learning to the achievement of discrete skills or abstract, organizing principles.

I want to conceptualize *thinking* as broader than logical analysis or some specialized intellectual set of problem solving strategies. I do that by implicating the body as a fundamental way of knowing the world and by locating thinking in a common human impulse to *value,* to make sense of things, to build, and to narrate the world and our lives. I deliberately widen its embrace to include mind, spirit, will, and imagination. Conceived in this encompassing way, thinking is roomy enough to include persons of all ages, young and old alike. Putting aside models of progressive stages of development, I have been more interested in a closer descriptive look at people, and children in particular, as they "think" the world and themselves—gesturally, bodily, as speakers and makers. In particular, it seems to me that our ordinary works—letters and diaries, handwork, household constructions, drawings, projects of all sorts—are a divining rod to this meaning-making impulse and offer an approach to thinking about thinking in this larger sense of the workings of the human mind.

I do emphasize activity, and, for me, it is "value" that is at its heart. Here my thoughts turn to Whitehead and his understanding that the original and fundamental datum of human experience is not fact or sensation or thing or concept, but a *sense of worth:* "Our enjoyment of actuality is a value-experience. Its basic expression is—Have a care, *here* is something that matters! Yes—that is the best phrase—the primary glimmering of conscious-ness reveals, *Something that matters.* . . . Instead of fixing attention on the bodily digestion of vegetable food, it catches the gleam of the sunlight as it falls on the foliage. . . . The life aim at survival is modified into the *human* aim at survival for diversified worth-while experience" (*Modes of Thought,* New York: Capricorn, 1958, pp. 42–43). Something catches my eye, arouses my caring and attention, and calls me into a world that is public, communal, and peculiarly human.

I am persuaded that the individually felt impulse to worth and to the making of meaning, far from confining each of us to an isolated, personal sphere, extends us beyond ourselves and enmeshes us with others—not only those near-to-hand, but also others who stand at some temporal or spatial distance from our lives.

MH: It would be useful here if you would explain more specifically how these impulses of worth are observable, understandable, as you see them working through the person.

For a child, it seems to me to go this way: there is the love of a medium or an idea or a form that exerts a pull on that child, that results in an intensification of feeling or desire. From my work at Prospect, I am aware that usually there is a clustering, a number of such media, interests, and ideas, that for some significant period of time hold attracting power for a person. To illustrate the attracting power of such a mix of media, interests, and ideas and how these are recognizable in a school and useful in support of a child's education, let me tell you about a child, (Everett),[5] who was referred to Prospect at age nine for the reason that he had not learned to read.

I remember that entering the school, (Everett) was a little wary of conversa-tion with adults—not unfriendly but aloof, watchful—though he was attracted to the materials and immediately chose to draw. What he drew and how he went about it in those first days gave us important insights into his abilities and interests. From a wide selection of kinds of paper, he quickly picked a standard 8 1/2 by 11 sheet. Using a straight edge, he ruled it, as I recall, 4 across and 5 down. He sat for a moment, pencil against his lip, apparently thinking, and then began to draw in the boxes he had created. Intriguingly, he left the first box empty. As I watched, a story unfolded through his pencil—a story of the world coming into being. From water and grasses, dinosaurs emerged, followed by other animals. Dinosaurs disappeared, and apes appeared. The figures were tiny but fully developed, detailed. Drawn mostly in pencil, some were filled in with colored pencil, lightly applied. Finally, in the very last square, a figure of a man appeared.

Figures tended to be executed without lifting the pencil; there was little erasure. Watching, it was plain to me that he was a practiced, confident drawer. It was also plain that what he was drawing was a recreation, a reinterpretation of information and knowledge about evolution absorbed from other sources. The confident manner in which he laid out the page and the minimal erasure and reworking indicated someone with ability to plan and with a grasp of sequence. When I asked about the drawing, he told me it was "prehistory" and explained that it was before there were people.

My observation and (Everett's) drawing became the basis for a collaborative reflective conversation among the school staff, called a staff review of the child. In that review, instead of zeroing in on his deficiencies as a reader, we followed our usual practice of painting as full a portrait of (Everett) as we could. To develop that picture, the teacher who knew him best described him according to five broad headings: physical presence and gesture, disposition, relationships with children and adults, interests and preferred activities, and formal learning. We supplemented that picture with perspectives offered by his remarkable first drawing and the observations of other staff. This multiperspectival description pointed to directions that we might follow in supporting (Everett's) education.

We decided to encourage him to draw on a bigger scale, using a wider range of media, to record what he had to say about his drawings, and to encourage him to compile the drawings into books—which, if he proved willing, could then be shared with the class. The attention to naturalistic detail suggested to us that he might be easily and productively engaged in drawing from life and in observation of plants and animals. Time lines and maps seemed as if they might be useful tools for him to explore. In terms of continuing observation, we decided to try to find out more from him about the sources of his knowledge and information, to pay close attention to his response to novels and poems read to the class, and to explore the extent of his understanding of the mathematical relationships.

In a short time we learned a lot. Conversation with (Everett) and attention to the content of his drawing pointed to an avid and participative use of television. He was drawn to informational and documentary programs, to a variety of dramatic heroes and monsters, and to themes of mystery and the unknown. In reconstructing films, he proved consistently adept at abstracting complex story lines, selecting key images, and employing a cinematic organization to retell the essentials of the plot of such movies as "The Creature of the Black Lagoon." The figure and story of Dracula was a great favorite, and he invented imaginative variations around that theme with enthusiasm.

At the same time, in school he devoured picture and informational books: the Time-Life Series of books about Egypt with special interest in tombs and mummies; Native American legends; myths from all over the world. Time lines showing the evolution of different animal species fascinated him, as did old maps, especially astronomical charts and depictions of planets. Although he was not talkative, we took note of the aptness and precision of his vocabulary and the musical quality of his speaking voice. He was a good singer who quickly knew by heart the songs regularly sung in school. In general, his memory and his ability for close observation were to be counted upon as reliable and as a support for his learning.

As he became acquainted with the range of materials available to him, (Everett) began to use paints, markers, charcoal, and paper that gave him room to expand the scale of his drawings. The idea of compiling his drawings into books appealed to him. With some assistance, he was able to write captions and longer narrative material to accompany the drawings. He was quick to realize that he could use his own books to locate words he wanted. His handwriting, like his drawings, was clear and well formed. Although quiet and unassuming, he positioned himself as he drew in the very midst of the classroom activities. His work was soon greatly admired by other children, and his ideas and drawing techniques and style spread out into the group.

As the early observation and drawing suggested, (Everett) had a sound sense of logic and sequence. He was capable at strategy games such as chess and soon achieved a firm grip on numerical operations and relationships.

Collapsing this story, there are two events that came later and opened up for us another level of understanding of (Everett) and sharpened our ability to teach him. Although we had deliberately avoided a head-on program of reading instruction, we became aware in the late winter of his first year at Prospect that he was reading to himself from his writing. In the early autumn of his second year at the school, he took hold of a class nature project with great vigor. As a collector of natural objects, (Everett) surpassed everyone else in the group. He began to bring in dead animals—mainly turtles, snakes, and birds discovered on wide-ranging bike hikes. He was intent on dissecting these finds, and, suitably garbed in a lab coat and rubber gloves and with tape over his nostrils, he turned the porch into a laboratory for that purpose. Although some of his classmates objected—mostly because these were very dead animals—he was dedicated to his task. He drew the animal parts he uncovered. He looked up information in books. In due time he began to reassemble bones and glue them to paper, carefully labeling each new entry. "The Dissector's Handbook" was created and greeted with wide acclaim. In the course of these investigations, (Everett) broke his usual silence to tell the teacher he wondered where and how life first began and what the things looked like. The interest in the origins of life was affirmed in another way. The teacher noticed (Everett) was carefully maintaining and observing a test tube of water. Some conversation revealed the information that he was trying to start life in the vial on the theory that life first emerged from the water.

It was as if the nature project, shaped by (Everett) for his own purposes, was serving to integrate a number of ideas and interests loosely constellated around the themes of origins, time, the insides or hidden aspects of things, the boundary where the known verges into the mysterious and unknown. At the same time, he was also gingerly easing himself into reading and giving us more opportunities to assist him.

From this sketch of a part of (Everett's) educational journey, I would note that it is the impulse to value, to prefer, to seek worth that is fundamental and educable. This is where education should begin, because preferred, strong interests impel all of us, just as they did (Everett), to press beyond ourselves—into the public arena, into the culture. It is what John Berger calls "the social function of subjectivity" (*Another Way of Telling*, New York: Pantheon, 1982, p. 100), and what I mean about the necessary connection between personal meaning and the formation of knowledge.

From my point of view, then, all children are active learners for the reason that they have common capacities: the power of expressiveness, the capability to make things, the inclination to wonder and to question, the desire to narrate, the ability to give order and meaning, the impulse to value. This is where learning—and development—*do* start. It is where teaching—and inquiry—*should* start.

Rethinking Development

MH: The way you've talked about (Everett) is not the way people often speak when they are speaking from a developmental position. In fact, you have objected to my terming you a developmentalist at all, and so I have referred to you in this project as a theorist of children and childhood.

How do you locate yourself, and what distinctions might you make?

After observing children like (Everett) carefully at Prospect, I stopped subscribing to any notion of "stage theory" or hierarchy, a defining characteristic of traditional developmental thought, or to notions of "progressions," such as from concrete to abstract thinking. I wanted to talk about growth and change in very different terms. Too, developmental theory has been primarily cognitive or mentalistic in its orientation, and although I see cognitive development as a refinement in our thinking, it is not adequate as a full account of us as human beings capable of knowing or "having" the world in many ways. And thirdly, I reject the notion that the end point of development is maturity, in the sense of unchangingness and completion, because then childhood is measured against some definition of maturity that is a standard external to its own activities and leading always to a notion of deficit.

As a school person, of course, I do make common cause with developmentalists, especially with early child educators and advocates for children.

MH: Yet you've been telling us a kind of story about (Everett), narrating a series of events and offering some explanations. Is this a case study?

Actually, it was also a deliberate choice to call the portrayals of children that we do *documentary accounts* in order to distinguish them from the more familiar *case study* accounts and in order to move decisively away from models of causal explanation in development. In a case study, the details and descriptions are often organized in such a way as to link causes with effects, to drive toward a predetermined end, or else they are organized and interpreted according to some yardstick of development or other external referent.

MH: If you don't talk about causality or teleology, how do you describe the relationship of the person to culture and change?

That relationship is, I believe, entirely and at the same time reciprocal, parallel, interanimating, juxtapositional, highly charged. The child is open and permeable, full and intense, and also both impelled and drawn in particular ways.

To give these statements a concrete context, I am going to draw on personal experience. Our son Peter had an ear for sound—for noises and for the flow of speech. A precocious speaker, he asked of nearly every object he came upon—an egg, a spoon—"What say?" He was an apt imitator, both vocally and gesturally. His appetite for stories was enormous. He also drew. When he was between nine and ten, he discovered an NPR program on which literary masterpieces were read aloud. On most afternoons it was on, he listened and drew. He was critical of the reader. His standards were high and particular in this respect. He thought of writing to the station to suggest his teacher as a replacement. Still, he listened. He listened, for example, to all of *War and Peace,* episode by episode, chapter by chapter. Quite probably he mentally tuned in and out, attending sometimes more to his drawing and sometimes more to the story. Who can know how much he understood? Who can know precisely what appealed to him, what kept him glued there for the many months it took the reader to get through that weighty work? Certainly such devotion isn't attributable in any obvious way to Peter's developmental level, to our specific cultural context, or to some other external referent.

I do think from other acquaintance with his attention to stories that even if he didn't always understand this story, he probably assumed he soon would. That is, I expect he was patient with dense or dull patches in the certain expectation that it would soon get clearer or more exciting. It is my strong sense that he not only liked stories, he *believed* in them—in the same way I have known some other children to believe in, to have faith in, numbers. He felt at home in the story world; he wanted to *be* in it. That is a preference, a disposition, an inclination, a passion. In the vernacular, he had a feel for story. I think the genre moved him, made sense to him, was satisfying, was what I would call educationally potent, even when a particular tale eluded or failed him.

His selectiveness in discovering the program, his attentiveness to the reading, is another example of what I mean by valuing. He saw *worth* in doing this even though it was perhaps beyond his understanding. That he listened and continued to listen for so many months is for me evidence of how much it mattered to him, and evidence, too, of the primary place value claims in our lives. Attempts to "explain" valuing, like attempts to "explain" art works, are in my experience inevitably reductionist and diversionary; that is, they carry us away from the *activity* (or work) and its *intensity*. Of course, he did find the program—yet it also seems true to say the program found him.

When I was thirteen, growing up in a small Minnesota farming town, I had a parallel experience. As suddenly as if it were their first appearance on the air, the Minneapolis Symphony Orchestra began one winter Sunday to play for me. I remember my intense sense of personal connection and discovery. Classical music was completely unfamiliar to me. Yet what I heard fulfilled something I had been aching for but couldn't name. I remained loyal to this program even when the music played was, to my uneducated ear, incomprehensible. Not to have listened each week would have felt like a betrayal—of the music and the orchestra and also of myself.

What I wish to emphasize by these stories of (Everett), Peter, and myself is that each child is selective. There is a pattern in the things that catch a child's eye or ear, that matter to him or her, but the selections can't be predicted or explained in any simple way. In fact, the "choice" isn't some intellectual activity, like saying that a child "chose" a word by selecting one from his or her mental lexicon. "Choice" is located in the child's *activity*—or what, after Dewey, I would call experiencing. In experiencing, the child's participation is gestural and emotive, filled with feeling—and not at the distance of a separate mental act. Using those terms, the choice is being made *in* the experiencing of the genre or the language or the line or the stories a child has heard.

Each person marks out a territory, some aspect of language and culture or a medium that he or she is drawn to emotionally, intellectually, and he or she works that territory over and over again, through different media, in various ways, over time and across settings. It seems to me that people incline and move in two simultaneous directions: they return, relish, rework the familiar, nurturing memory; and they press beyond, venture outward into the unknown, exercising imagination. There is, all at the same time, appetite and desire, nourishment and fulfillment, and, as Edith Cobb says, "the promise of more to come" (*The Ecology of Childhood,* New York: Columbia University Press, 1977, p. 28).

To me, what's so interesting about us is our open-endedness. What I can with confidence predict or explain about a person is so limited. With those thoughts, I am again carried back to the person's expressiveness and openness, to his or her impulse to value, to that which puts the person in the way of life and all its possibilities—the animation of nature, the expressiveness of other persons.

Another Way of Looking: Works

MH: This attention to openness and expressiveness is premised on an understanding of the child as person and perspective in the world, always coming into being in complex ways, permeated by time, history, tradition, and memory, yet always engaged in time through the making of personal meaning, through will, imagination, and spirit.

This way of looking at children is based on philosophical claims about the person as a special object of study—as an enduring perspective, expressing unique meaning through the body (as in gesture) and through the body's correlatives (in works and projects). As you have explained in the monographs and in "Considerations of the Lifespan," you want to study the person as a lived and meaningful life, located in personal and epochal time, embedded in nature, profoundly related to the world, and interanimated by other lives in deeply and originally participative ways. It is our coming into being within the world's embrace that offers a starting point for understanding how we come to know and have and become in the world—that is, how we develop.

Could you talk about how that person or perspective is revealed by and constituted through what you call the expressiveness of gesture and works?

Perhaps you might begin by discussing the recurrence of a phrase in your papers—"another way of looking"—and all that that connotes to you about children's projects as "works."

This other way of looking at children derives from Prospect's original commitment to document children's strengths as learners and thinkers, and to take each child seriously as a particular (and complex) subject of study. Looking at works in the context of the child as maker, my colleagues at Prospect and I assumed that the works would express interests, ideas, and sentiments ascribable in important and unique ways to each child. We also expected that the works, like the children who made them, would make sense and hold interest for us as viewers and readers, that they would promote thought in many ways.

Fundamental to this focus on works is a notion of person as the bearer of a unique value and perspective, uniquely situated in the world and in life, and enjoying an individuality and being not interchangeable with that of others. The person cannot, except at a price, be translated or defined in the abstract terms supplied by specialized fields of study. The price of the psychologist's or sociologist's classifications is the sacrifice of the intensity, vividness, unevenness, and wholeness of an individual existence. If something of the particular lingers in the generalization, it is faint and unspecifiable: face, accent, intonation, style, gesture—in a phrase, personal expressiveness—are, of necessity, submerged by abstractions and generalization. Similarly, a poem may be translated into prose, or a painting into geometric forms or a diagram, or either may be generalized as an example of a school or era or theory of art, but only at the expense of losing the work itself and all our pleasure in its expressiveness.

The study of children's works is one way of understanding a child, of coming into contact with that child as a particular, concrete, actual person. For example, Beth Alberty and I, along with twelve other scholars, were struck over and over again as we worked on the Reference Edition at Prospect, with the "presence" of the child in the work, a presence that never ceased to enthrall and enchant us. It is watching what Edith Cobb calls the child's dialectic with the world. In the process of coming to these understandings of what draws a child's attention, what commands thought, what releases will, and what arouses tenderness and passion, it becomes possible to understand in some way each individual child's broad sense of purpose or value of what really matters to him or her.

I start with the idea that a work is more like a subject than an object in that, given a chance, it speaks to another subject, the author or other audiences. Works do that in the making of them, for the children, and then afterward when they are looked at by viewers or readers. There's a public dimension to all of that in that the work stands there, finally, a piece by itself, which has in it the thought and hand of the maker. But the viewer also brings meaning to that thought, and draws more thought out, in ways that are both *coincidental* with what the maker had in mind and also *extensions and additions* to that.

I am reminded as I say this that on several occasions now a group of us has described collaboratively the work of adult artists in the artists' presence. On one of these occasions, a photographer said of the experience of listening to his work described, "Everyone should have this experience. . . . [It is] stunning to see how fragments of other visions clarify one's own. . . . [What is said] is recognized as you hear it. . . . It's not new and it's not foreign. It is a form of memory support—which is what pictures are. . . . It [the description] is both more and less than the picture."

MH: Yes, the first time I attended a Summer Institute (three-week seminars conducted by Prospect each summer), a group did a reading of one of my son Matthew's texts. As is customary in a reflective reading, there was no biographical or situational information given. The readers worked only with the written text, using procedures to be described here in detail later. At the time, it seemed almost magical to me that the Matthew that emerged from the reading was both so recognizable to me and yet so new. Over and over again, references were made to his communal nature, for example, to his pleasure in working in groups and his attention to interpersonal detail. I had never really thought about that before—and it was absolutely right. It was rather startling to meet him that way.

That's exactly what happens whenever we do a description of a child's work at school. Ordinarily we "meet" a child whom we recognize immediately, but it isn't the child we know from the classroom or the child, for example, we encounter when we do a descriptive review. It's another dimension of that person, a deep expressiveness, a broader sweep, as if you cut a plane through a sphere. And then, as soon as it's called to your attention, all sorts of things start to make sense or connect, especially for the classroom teacher.

The Archive of Children's Work: Collecting/Recollecting

Early on, Carini decided to keep the artwork and other projects that children at the school constructed. There was no research design; in fact, at first Carini collected the work that children did not choose to take home with them, even the scraps of paper left at the end of the day in the wastebaskets. Carini explains:

> Mostly I kept these pieces of work because I was overwhelmed with the children's productivity and the beauty and power of the work. I was intrigued, too, with the absence of external motivators prompting the children's productions in the form of directions, cajoling, prodding, or teacher-directed "assignments." The abundant yield seemed instead attributable to substantial (but not expensive or sophisticated) supplies of natural and malleable materials; time to become thoroughly immersed in these materials and to explore their possibilities; a lot of talk, singing, and noisemaking by the children to themselves, to others, and with equal enthusiasm, to the materials; and the respect and value accorded to the children's work, and the products of that work, by the teachers. (1986b, pp. 2–3)

Over time, the value of this casual impulse became increasingly more apparent. "Watching this productive activity," Carini recalls, "tantalizing questions were raised in my mind about what the children were learning and thinking through these primarily expressive materials; about the basis of the choices children made from the wide array of materials available in the classroom; and about the meaning of the works in the context of the children's engagement in making them" (1986b, p. 3). Carini came to appreciate the works as a kind of divining rod to children's interests, ideas, and ways of learning, and then to appreciate the educational implications of studying their work as a basis for teaching practice. As a result, a greater effort was made to collect children's work.

Each classroom, for example, now has an Archive box in it for children to submit works for their own files.

Presently the Archive consists of a twenty-four-year collection of artwork, writings, and classroom records for the approximately 350 children who have attended Prospect since it was founded. The collection, organized by child, is estimated to contain more than 250,000 pieces, including "drawings, paintings, designs, and murals; journals, poetry, essays, stories, and other writings; sewing and other fabric work; prints, photographs, and films; and collage and a limited quantity of other three-dimensional constructions" (1986b, p. 2). By research standards, the collection is rough and untidy, but there is also an unprecedented depth and continuity, a continuity derived from the large sizes of the individual collections (ranging anywhere from 1,100 to 2,500 pieces per child), from the wide range of media used, from the span of years encompassed by each file, and from the supporting documentation such as teachers' narrative records, observations, and other notes.

To make a portion of the collection more widely accessible to a larger community of scholars and educators, and to preserve it in more durable form, Prospect has published a "Reference Edition of the Prospect Archive." Now completed, the Reference Edition consists of thirty-six individual child collections, from eighteen boys and eighteen girls. It encompasses more than 45,000 pieces reproduced in black and white microfiche. No file collection spans less than five years of a child's school life, and some even include home collections or works produced after the student left Prospect. One collection, for example, covers twenty-one years, from ages two to twenty-three. Each edition also includes about 200 color slides of both visual and written work, works selected as representative of the key themes, motifs, and media in the collection. To protect the privacy of the children, pseudonyms are used, and all personal data have been deleted or modified in some way.

Documentary Processes:
Describing and Understanding Children's Work

Prospect has experimented over time with developing procedures or processes for describing children's work in systematic and careful ways. In *The Prospect Center Documentary Processes: In Progress* (revised and updated June 1986a), Carini explains and illustrates three "documentary processes" at this particular point in their ongoing evolution: the

Descriptive (or Staff) Review of a Child, the Reflective Conversation, and the Description of Children's Work. I will talk here about the conversation and description, because they offer a methodology for reading children's texts that I have used in studying early written language development and believe that other researchers might find useful. I have found the processes productive, both for the understanding they enable me to have about children as writers and at the same time for the epistemological problems or tensions they continually raise about the activity of reading and interpretation itself (see Chapters 2 and 3).

I have noted in many studies of early writing development that researchers often have very little to say about the actual texts children write, as if they did not find them interesting or meaningful somehow. The texts are too often read as "evidence" of something else—such as a child's cognitive development, or his increasingly complex composing process, or her desire to compete with her sister. They are rarely read as meaningful in and of themselves, both for the reader and the writer, and as part of a child's effort to make sense of the world, to participate and come to be in that world.

Carini's reflective procedures accord respect to the child's work and allow readers to spend time with that work in ways that make it accessible and hence interesting. Perhaps these processes are less method, more genre—a collaborative way of talking about and describing concretely children's early writing, which produces knowledge in complex, multi-layered, and contextual ways (see Chapter 2). They create a space or arena for knowing, opening up a kind of shared territory, in which a group of participants talk together about a child's work and thereby make visible in ways the expressive presence of the child—the child's hand and mind—as written into and through the work.

In so doing, the processes also enlarge the readers' understanding of the medium involved, and tune them in more finely to the culture, with all its semiotic practices, in which both the writer and the readers are located. The results of these procedures—the juxtaposing and presenting of these recorded descriptions and observations—may be written up later in a "documentary account" or portrayal of the child.

In introducing the processes, Carini explains their overall purpose this way:

> The Documentary Processes depend upon immersion in the focus of interest—a child, a drawing, a setting—and they make available a mode of inquiry with which one can describe and explore a complex human occasion, such as a school or a child's expressiveness, without interference

or manipulation. The child, or the event, is studied "as is," with respect for the integrity and privacy of the person. Regular recording of observations and collecting of children's work gather and preserve events at the Prospect School. The Documentary Processes are a way to re-enter those events in order to grasp, in concentrated form, what occurred at disparate points in time. (1986a, p. i)

The intention of the documentary processes, according to Carini, is to "grasp the person's meaning as it is expressed in the person's interests and in their projects in the world" (1986a, p. ii).

The Reflective Conversation[6]

This is a collaborative procedure, involving perhaps eight to ten people and lasting about an hour, for exploring and disclosing from the perspectives of the group of participants "a range of meanings, images and experiences embodied in a word" (1986a, p. 1). For example, the group may have been looking at a particular child's visual artwork and have noted that the word *bounded* has come up often in the discussion, indicating that a significant aspect of how this artist, (Carly), works is how she defines and uses space to create a strong sense of parts and wholes.

The group may then decide to do a *reflection* on "bounded" or "boundedness" in order to open up the network of meanings, connotative and cultural, that the word offers, in order then to return to the child's artwork in view of that network of meanings. The group participants are asked "to think about and write down their understandings of the word, not in an attempt to define it, but as a way of exploring the contexts in which it may appear, their own experiences with it and the meanings it connotes, and other words, images and ideas that it evokes" (1986a, p. 1). Each participant thereby constructs and reconstructs, in varying degrees of detail, his or her history and relationship with the meanings of the word.

After about ten minutes, each person in turn reads what he or she has noted, taking time to elaborate on these notes in order to clarify and futher enlarge his or her thoughts. These, for example, are my notes on "boundedness":

—energy, contained and formed, bursting, held in
—bound—to leap, leaps and bounds (flying motions)

—Chinese women's feet (restrained, denied growth, checked)
—boundaries = differentiation, marking off this part from that, separating X from $Y,$ creating spaces and difference
—embeddedness—what is bounded is also contextualized; what has an inside has an outside
—artificiality—what creates bounds? constructed out of needs; put bounds on kids, put bounds on behaviors, put bounds on projects
—boundedless = open, amorphous, diluted somehow, yet all-encompassing
—bounds as horizons—the limits of endeavor, vision, knowledge comforting—"given these bounds, I will work the ground within them"; tend to go vertical within bounds, horizontal outside of them
—oppositional word, turns on itself—"Where are you bound?" Where are you headed? Where are you tied down?

The person designated as chair for this conversation listens to each participant and charts or diagrams the ideas, looking for the connections, complementarities, and divergences of meaning among the individual responses. He or she then restates those meanings after everyone has spoken, trying to sketch out the range and the patterns of meanings that have been expressed.

In the case of "boundedness," the chair charted ideas around headings of energy as it is contained and formed yet pushing out; around notions of boundaries as creating space within yet also embedding it in relationship to things outside and contiguous; around oppositions between a place of focus versus a place of relationships; and around images of boundlessness as having a horizontal and expansive moment and boundaries as having a vertical and in-depth movement. He summed up phrases we had used— bounding over the hillside, leaps and bounds, where are you bound? bound for glory, bound to happen, bound together.

We then returned to the slides of (Carly's) artwork with the meanings of "boundedness" in view and focused on the continuity and changes in her use of boundaries across the eight years of artwork.

The outcome of this process, according to Carini, is that the "participants' personal histories, experiences and thoughts are joined with those of others to produce a strong common experience, history and thought connected with the word chosen for their mutual consideration" (1986a, p. 2). The chair offers neither a summary nor a reiteration, but rather a restatement that highlights themes and motifs, using as much as possible the actual language and images offered by the individual participants. The process thus emphasizes equally the unique perspective of each participant as well as the power of collective thought generated through diversity. It also brings into the conversation, through explicit references to cultural events or through obsolete meanings surfacing in this process, the thought of others from other times and settings.

The process enacts and makes visible what Bakhtin calls the "dialogism" of the word, or the ways words carry in them the accents and intentions and meanings of others. During a reflection, the voices of others, both in the immediate group and from the past, are layered in each word, thereby locating the focus of interest in context after context, doing battle with each other, carrying and reflecting conceptual and ideological worldviews (see Chapter 2). The process of description does not reveal some inner truth, but rather contrastively embeds the focus of interest in multiple contexts. It is a reflection on and by and through language itself.

According to Carini, the outcome of the reflective conversation is "a wider, deeper, and more richly textured understanding of the word reflected on, and the meanings that it embodies" (1986a, p. 2). She argues that the process prompts thought, breaks down habituated uses of the word, revitalizes vocabulary, and (I would add) opens up a fuller kind of semiotic space. The person can then return to the description of a child or work both with a richer sense of the child's or work's relationship to multiple contexts and at the same time with a more delimited and refined and nuanced frame, with language sensitive to and evocative of the particularity of the child or work under investigation. As a group, with a more elaborated sense of "boundedness" in our talk, we came to realize the subtle use of boundaries in (Carly's) artwork and her written texts, the particular ways she manages parts and wholes. We "saw" more—and more richly. Her drawings became increasingly interesting to us as a site for thought.

The Description of Children's Work

This process, too, is usually done collaboratively, although it need not be. Paralleling the reflective conversation, "the purpose of the description is to explore and disclose from the perspectives of a group of participants as many dimensions of the work under discussion as possible. . . . A further purpose of the description is to come to some understandings of the perspective of the child who made the work" (1986a, p. 8).

Usually descriptions of a child's work occur as part of a series in which many works by one child, often in different media, are studied. A single piece of work, when closely observed and described, can offer deepened understanding of that piece in its own right, but only a very partial and quite tenuous understanding of the person who made it. Descriptions of many pieces of work by one child, along with staff reviews and school records—when considered in light of one another—provide a fuller, mutually informed, often more complex portrayal of the child.

When several works by one child are to be described, Carini recommends beginning by holding one or more reflective conversations on keywords—words that relate to the medium, perhaps, or to some important theme or motif that appears often in the series.

Following the reflection, Carini asks participants to offer "impressionistic responses to the work . . . as a way of gaining a first acquaintance with the piece" (1986a, p. 91). A written text might be read aloud by several participants, in order to hear it in several voices and interpretations. The designated chair takes notes and reflects on the connections, complementarities, and divergences in these initial and often emotional responses.

Then the first of several rounds of description begins. The chair asks the participants to attend first to the surface of the piece, to the particular elements and noticeable details. For a drawing, for example, a participant might say, "There are three shades of green—the trees are darkest, the grass is lightest, and then there is that sort of olive shade in the man's pants and on what looks like a bird." The point of these early rounds is to get each participant to attend closely to the materiality of the piece and to develop a shared discourse about the literal description. The chair may summarize at the end of each round or wait for a while, depending on the size of the group and the complexity or density of the piece.

Carini illustrates the kinds of aspects of the work that might be talked about in these early rounds:

> *style* ("There is a high horizon line that creates the impression of distance.")
>
> *tone* ("All those shades of brown create an almost somber mood.")

rhythm ("There are a lot of circular sweeps of the brush.")

form ("This drawing is really a kind of map of the insides of things—there are both cross-sections and underground tunnels.")

In later rounds, larger and more inferential statements are made.

As these rounds of description begin to accrue, according to Carini, the patterns in the piece and the hand of the maker become increasingly visible (1986a, p. 11). The outcome of the process is descriptive knowledge, an understanding of the work as a whole—its composition, motifs, images, and ideas—and a sense of the maker's expressiveness, interests, and preferences, as revealed in and through the medium he or she is working with.

An objection might be raised here: isn't this just a group of adults sitting around reconstructing the private mental events that went on in a child's head, and aren't they just guessing about what the child meant or consciously intended?

Carini makes a point of distinguishing between expressiveness and intentionality. She says expressiveness is not more important than intentionality; it is merely the larger, more fundamental, more inclusive piece. Intentionality is more conscious, more "self"-conscious, as when the maker says, "I intend to do this." They are both at work in any given project, but it is the expressiveness that stays across time, that is the glue holding a collection of work together and marking the personal aesthetic.

For example, she called to my attention a certain delicacy of line in the work of a child, (Sean), a line that is present in all his work, spanning both time and media. She described that line as coming right out of his hand, as being the least distant from him. Carini observed that the delicacy of the line has something to do with the way the energy flowed out of him, with the way teachers saw him here or saw him there but never saw how he got there. "Quick," she said, was the single most frequently used word used to describe him in a whole variety of contexts—quick to think, quick to speak, quick, quick, quick. That expressiveness, that quickness, was volatile and open-ended and potential with respect to every medium, every object with which it made contact.

According to Carini, that openness of expressiveness is exactly what we identify as being the person. We do not know each other in terms of traits or behaviors; we know others through their most immediate statement to us, through their expressiveness. Their acts are imbued with expressiveness and so are their works.

Nothing has been more central to Carini's work, nor more easily misread, than the term *expressiveness*. As an educator and thinker deeply absorbed by children and childhood, she has devoted herself to the close observation of children and to the description of their school lives, of their activities, language, and works. Expressiveness is central to this task—in fact, it is central to her understanding of what it means to be human and to know or have the world. Our conversation around this keyword has moved our talk into an essay by Patricia F. Carini, into a fuller account of this concept and its philosophical roots. It is with this essay that I end this chapter.

On Expressiveness: Expressive Fields/Interanimating Lives

For me, "looking" is the embracing idea for "knowing." Looking is at once open-ended (to gaze, to glance, to have a look) and participative: My glance awaits what will entrance it, arouse wonder, reward it with beauty and possibility, hurt it with horror and repulsion, transfix it with intensity and heightened awareness. Given this potency, the human gaze seems to me a way to have a world, to relish it, to value it, and to invent it. Looking is all at once active, receptive, speculative, and evaluative.

How I look at the world is complexly cultural and personal, woven of chosen and unchosen elements. It verges on what I believe is always true of looking: it is, announced or unannounced, a way of knowing so ordinary, so embracing, so familiar that it threatens to escape our attention. As Merleau-Ponty points out, I can change my perspective or entertain several at once, but I cannot be without one. (*The Phenomenology of Perception,* London: Routledge & Kegan Paul, 1962, pp. 406–7).

Because of this interest in looking as knowing, I have been compelled by questions of boundary and bond. How can I, standing here, have knowledge, however imperfect, of something that stands apart from me (or seemingly does so)? What is the nature of the bond between us? Is my knowledge an active force in its configuration? How am I shaped by its presence? Is the understanding of our respective boundaries and the bond between us shaped by a third, more embracing dimension inclusive of us both? Grappling with these questions, all crucial, it seemed to me, to the act of observing, forced me to consideration of such large categories as "world" and "body" and "expressiveness."

For a very long time I have understood the world as foretold in our bodies. If a digression is permissible, I would like to trace the root of that notion. When I was a child in school, I came across the information that the human body is composed of the same "stuff" as the world. It made immediate sense to me. At the risk of reading the past in the light of the present, I think it fell as neatly as a puzzle piece into the mosaic of sympathetic understandings of the world in which I was myself planted and growing. Without pretending to quote my child self of forty-five or forty-six years ago, it was an "oh, that's how it goes" illumination of events, which being altogether daily and familiar were, for that reason, altogether mysterious. In an agreeable fashion it "explained" a vague but undeniable sense of my "fit" with the Northern Plains winds; the inconstant, wayward sky; the heaven-splintering, ear-bursting late summer lightning storms; the sun-dazzled arching leap of a carp breaking the surface of the river; the orderly, industrious domesticity of anthills; the hidden paths of single beetles beneath the foliage of flower borders. I can't remember a time when a point of concentration in nature—the underside of a leaf, a fish's eye, the shadow of a cloud on the grass, the inner recesses of a flower—did not snare me in its rhythms, scale, and design. As I look back now, the discovery of our common chemistry was like finding a hidden vein of sameness running through the profusion of nature's uninhibited variety.

Understandings achieved much later in life feel to me now to point back to that childish intuition of kinship. It is as if it predisposed later intellectual tastes and distastes. Prefigured in that intuition is a suspicion of theories of human nature or our place in nature that make of us a too distinct, separate, and (often) superior dimension of the world. More generally, I have always greeted with caution any position that is premised on original difference or separateness and that leaves unspoken a larger, more inclusive terrain.

Among other things, fixed boundaries separating and isolating events create the problem of getting the fragments back into connection. The ways resorted to for remaking the connection tend to seem elaborate and often unnecessarily so. The reconnecting and the elaboration sometimes seem to me diversionary. For example, if we assume a relatively clear, definite boundary between the infant and the world, something like the Piagetian construct "assimilation/accommodation" is required—but, I would suggest, only if we accept the existence of such a boundary.

More positively, I read in that early sense of kinship an intellectual and aesthetic preference for complex wholes, permeability of boundaries, ambiguity, malleability, circularity, open-endedness, "unfinish." In many ways these are keywords in my vocabulary—as packed as is "looking" with meaning. Discovering, exploring, and reworking ideas like these has been for me compelling in and through the concrete enactment of my inquiries and through conversations like the one you and I have had throughout this project.

Alfred North Whitehead articulated in an altogether satisfactory way the relationship of world and body that I intuited as a child. That articulation continues to ground my way of looking and my work as an observer. For me, that is central. The emblematic statement, the one that riveted by attention, is this: "The Human Body is that region of the world which is the primary field of human expression" (*Modes of Thought,* p. 30).

As I understand that sentence, our bodies locate us as a region of the world, sympathetically, rhythmically woven or housed within it. As a field within this region, the body is intensely and humanly charged with respect to its refinements and details but is nonetheless and more fundamentally a part of the world "stuff" and world animation from which it originates. In our bodies, and more particularly their expressive surfaces (or "field" dimensions), I read our being, our kind of consciousness, and our particular capacities and potentials. Whether I emphasize the more active, expressive dimensions of the body or its more primary, sympathetic substrata, I understand the world to be our dwelling and our medium for being. Although malleable to our touch and vision, it always exceeds us. As I see it, the world, in its profusion, "muchness," and plasticity, calls us to impress ourselves on it and, through our actions and envisioning, to make and remake it. We are attuned to its voice, responsive and open to its rhythms. Whether for good or ill, I notice that wherever there are (or were) humans, nothing in the world remains as it was, untouched. The intimacy of our relationship with the world is crucial to me.

More obviously, our bodies situate us among each other. Through our actions taken together, apart, and toward each other, but always reciprocally, I believe the face of humanity is cast and recast. It seems to me in this respect that communality is the condition for the realization of our most fundamental human capacities: to be speakers and actors, to be makers and keepers of meaning. Through expression, through gestures and works, we disclose ourselves to ourselves and insert ourselves within the expressive field of others. There, in sympathetic correspondence, we complete each other, my gesture continuing and filling in the outline of your expression. Peopling each other's horizons, we are saturated with an irreducible otherness. That is, our individualness includes otherness within its definition. As a dimension of individualness, the presence of others is obscured if we attend to the body as a physical entity or as merely a symbolic site, overlooking its extensive and intensive expressiveness—overlooking, that is, the gestural field that announces our correspondences.

I'm going to turn now to observing and illustrate through examples of children some of what I have said.

Not so long ago, I was watching a group of young children settle in a circle to begin the school day. It is the kind of observation of an altogether ordinary human activity—assembling, gathering in a group—that is useful for the attention it calls to these "peopled horizons" that surround our lives. It calls attention, too, to the gestural correspondences that weave together for each of us a *human* world: a world of rituals and conventions, of boundaries and likenesses, of expectancies and possibilities, of comprehensibilities. Or, stated in other terms, a world that is both safe enough in which to be and to act, and spacious enough for novelty and adventure to be entertained.

I was struck on this day, as I watched the children in the familiar routine of "coming to the circle," that as they approached it, they appeared already encircled, already held within its embracing gesture. I was struck, too, with a look on individual faces that was simultaneously internal (full) and receptive (open). For example, (Anton), angling in from the direction of the cubbies, was gazing somewhere into the middle distance, over the heads of the other children, his mouth slightly open, the look on his face inward or self-absorbed. There was no "space" where he stopped at the periphery of the children already seated. Although no one child appeared to move over, or seemed even to notice him, there was a ripple in the uneven wave of bodies that made an interruption in the half-curve of the line. More than seating himself, (Anton) subsided or sank into that "break" in the wavy line of children—dropping first into a kneeling position and then all the way down, skewing his body slightly to the right as he did so. From all appearances, he was giving no more attention to his body than to the circle. However, just as strong as the look of "fullness" was the strong impression of a sensitive surface absorbing, or being absorbed by, not some particular thing, but something vaguer and yet intense. (Anton) was silent and seemingly unaware of the bubbles of conversation going on around him.

A few moments later (Arlo) arrived, and in some respects the episode re-peated itself. There were differences, too. (Arlo's) face was more contained—the mouth closed, the eyes more downward than up and outward. His clothes fit him more closely. His grip on his book bag was firm in contrast to (Anton), who was loosely holding a few scraps of paper in one hand. The impression was more one of collectedness perhaps than fullness. When (Arlo) got to the circle, he, too, paused by a space not really big enough for him and his possessions, sank to one knee slightly outside the line of children. Without a sound or a backward glance, (Galen) slid a little to the right, closer into the child with whom he was sharing a book. (Arlo) edged forward on his knees, accommodating to the small space by keeping the book bag behind him, but in a way that kept it definitely "attached" to him. Possibly because of the slight downcast of the eyes, inwardness, composure, or boundedness was more accented in (Arlo's) expression than the impression of absorptive capacity.

Another way of thinking about this is that the children's postures suggested that the space, or the circle itself, had substance, was palpable. A younger child, (Nels), coming to the circle, enacted diving into it from the "rim" of children on the periphery, as if the space within the circle was filled with water. Ducking his head forward and holding his hands extended forward around his head in a "prayer" or steeple position, he dived, whispering "splash" when his hands hit the "water," and then crawled with swimming motions to a place on the other side of the circle.

Children in the circle who were looking at books together or talking offered quite a different impression. Instead of looking "full" or "contained," they leaned into each other, words and gestures washing over, dissolving the boundaries of the individual speakers and actors: "Yum, yum, yum . . . berries, let's eat 'em" (motions from three hands plucking food from the book page, sounds of eating and lip smacking). Arms entwined; heads bent together. These clusters formed islands within the larger circle of children.

I want to expand on gesture—its power to unify and conventionalize and its power to transform. I am going to return to (Nels), who in the course of the observation already referred to illustrated both. After the group of children was finally assembled in the circle, the teacher asked who had some news to tell. (Nels) was eager to speak, although, as it transpired, his "news," while riveting, was also of an event that had occurred two years before:

> Astronauts (here his arms went up over his head, hands again in the "prayer" position). . . . Astronauts. . . . I heard there was astronauts going up, up in their rocket (here he rose to his knees, body inclining forward, arms still extended up over his head). . . . And the rocket BLEW UP (here flinging his upraised arms outward). . . . And the astronauts BLEW UP (here he collapsed forward, full-length into the circle).

This performance, like the earlier one of diving, was fluent, the words and gestures apt. In both instances, words and gestures flowed together without interruption or dissonance. It was as if the contexts, the fields—the circle suggesting a swimming pool and the astronaut story—at one and the same time called out the gestures and the words, and also defined and controlled them. The expression was full, complete, satisfying.

I am interested here, as I have been with other gestures, in the spectrum of meaning a particular gesture (or form) can assume: arms extended upward with hands in a "prayer" position can connote the stylized position for diving, the shape of a rocket nose, (drawing now on observations of other children) the top of a tree, or the outlined pinnacle of a skyscraper. Minor but crucial adjustments in the positioning of the arms and hands differentiate the images: to convey the motion of diving, (Nels's) arms extended forward, and the hands were angled slightly downward from the wrists; to suggest the rocket, his arms were stretched high over his head, and his hands were aimed skyward.

Being the diver, the rocket, the tree, the skyscraper, the body echoes and emphasizes the energy, intensity, and "gesture" of these events. The correspondence is intimate and not merely a reproduction of specifiable qualities and properties. It may be that the body "quotes" the object, in a way not altogether different from John Berger's idea that a photograph "quotes" experience and does not translate it, as a painting does (*Another Way of Telling,* p. 96).

There is, though, I think, a radical difference: the body is unmediated in its resonance while the camera and the photograph stand between the viewer and the viewed. A vision is literally embodied. That difference reminds me that analogy, or, as I am inclined to call it, "likening," is a more embracing, more fundamental propensity than either quoting or translating. Our attunement to the animation, the expressiveness of nature to which I earlier referred, is repeated in all its variation in the expressiveness of the body. Mirrored in the body, the world is at once, simultaneous, intensified and transformed. The body is *not* the tree or the rocket, but the body is a "knowing" of them.

Back to (Nels). In the diving position, (Nels's) body and arms were loose and curved; demonstrating a rocket, they were taut and stretched. The child I observed being a tree held her arms curved around her head, fingers flattened against each other, palms not touching; she swayed gently from side to side. The child who was a skyscraper rose up on his toes, stretched very tall, and held his arms high above and tight to his head. He appeared to pull in his cheeks, to hold his breath in the expression of the verticality and height of the building.

Now I'm going to turn this into another direction and talk about another child. The gestural fields of children relate to their gestures in and through works. For me, gestures and works are parallel ways of understanding a child's engagement and expressiveness in the world.

A couple of years ago in the Archive Scholars and Fellows Program, while looking at (Iris's) drawings, we became interested in the recurrent appearance of a curved shape, what we began to call the "arch" form. From its first appearance in drawings done when she was five, it had a characteristically tall, narrow shape and was set at a slight angle. The top was sometimes rounded, sometimes rectangular. We observed it to serve as an entrance—a statement of boundary between inside and outside—and also to connote depth, tunnels, distance, mystery. For example, in a drawing made when (Iris) was six, the tunnel effect is created by repeating arches that decrease in size. At the end of the tunnel, there is a tiny door. Using the same device, but with greater sophistication, (Iris) at age ten inserts a passage of arches within a castle, the last of which, penciled a deep gray, suggests both darkness and a shrouded figure.

Alerted to the form by (Iris's) arches, we began to notice its appearance in other children's works. We were struck that relatively subtle adjustments—of width, roundedness, orientation on the page—profoundly influence the meanings the form verges on. As noted, the narrower, taller, less rounded arches evoke among describers vocabulary around *mystery, tunnel, inner, danger.* In another child's work, broad, low, round arches suggest words like *rainbow, cave, shelter, safety.*

It was borne in upon us, as we explored works made by different children, that this form, like other spatial geometries, assumes a characteristic configuration in each child's work. The generic arch becomes a highly particular arch. Its own dimensions, orientations, and location in the child's works border on large, loosely constellated meanings and correspondences: high, narrow curves bring up corresponding images of closedness, innerness, darkness, deepness, traps, mysteries; broad, low curves invite the corresponding images of openness, softness, nurturance, color, rainbows, security. The interlacing of this form with other elements in the child's work moves along the refinement and the diversification of meanings. In (Iris's) work, the insertion of the arch in castles adds to the element of mystery and darkness. When it appears curved with a red carpet leading from an elegant room (as it does in one drawing), it suggests sumptuousness, a bygone romantic era. In (Meg's) work, the broad, low arch form is usually colored green, depicting a low hill, or banded with color, representing a rainbow. In either case, there is often a "treasure," some small, bounded, encapsulated element embedded within, under the curve. The addition of the treasure and the soft pastel color choices accentuates the benign, secure connotations of the low, hill-like arch.

This simple form became fascinating to us—possibly because it was so simple. Its prodigious capacity for generating meanings seemed referrable to almost inconsequential variations in proportion. It showed up all over the place once we were alerted to it—in nature, in buildings, in the human body, in vegetation. Its ubiquity notwithstanding, we knew from the children's work that the arch in any given person's repertoire of gesture had highly identifiable characteristics.

We tried making arches ourselves. All of us were easily able to vary the curves we drew, but we noted as well a tendency to revert to a particular dimension, orientation, proportion—as it were, a preferred arch gesture. Drawing one arch led to drawing more. We elaborated. We added other elements. Just as in the children's works, the arch began to announce its intentions, to simultaneously expand and bound a pool of meanings.

I was reminded by the exercise of a casual observation of knowing the world through its expressive gestures. Many years ago now, in a laundromat, I noticed a small girl, certainly no older than three, who was watching her mother take the laundry out of the washing machine. When the mother straightened up, she tossed her head back. Her hair, long and glossy black with red highlights, shimmered in the sun as it fell back from her head. The little girl standing behind her caught her breath and whispered, "Oh, rain," while at the same time "shimmering" her hands, held outstretched before her, palms down, in a rhythmic responsive to the motion of the hair as it fell in wavelike motion down the woman's back. A charming episode, but also a provocative one. In one small gesture and two soft words, she illustrated a fundamental and peculiarly human way of knowing the world—by finding likeness in the expressiveness of otherwise different things, in this instance hair and rain. The child's understanding achieved intensity by the simultaneous enacting of that likeness in words and hand gestures. The knowledge gained can be assumed, it seems to me, to be both bodily and verbal.

All of these illustrations—(Nels) being the diver and the rocket; the upthrust prayer position of the hands accommodating the likeness of trees, rockets, divers, and skyscrapers; the arch form making room for mountains, bridges, tunnels, and caves to appear; the rich variation of meanings ascribable to minor variations in a curved line; a small child's understanding of the correspondence between hair and rain—weave meaning from expressiveness.

It is expressiveness in the world that is mirrored in the expressiveness of the body. The expressive power of the body finds the world knowable in its answering rhythms. Expressiveness identifies us with the world. Simultaneously it situates us in an energetic region of intense human activity. That region is profoundly gestural, emotive, saturated with feeling. At the outset, in infancy and earliest childhood, rhythms, inflections, tonal variation, atmosphere, temperature, color, and light exercise a primary claim on being. Life is a dappled experience. We (and many other animals) are primarily attuned to the world through gradations of emotional intensity, variations of rhythm, and distinctions of feeling tone. I am persuaded that for all of us, for all of our lives, these expressive intensities compose a subsong of inclinations, tastes, attitudes, postures, temperaments, which subtly, persuasively, and importantly color and influence our actions, choices, and pursuits.

Giving my close attention to expressiveness has yielded plentiful and useful insights into the ways children learn, think, and come to know the world. That has been richly rewarding for me personally and as an educator. It is unceasingly interesting—and moving—to me to watch youngsters like (Everett) or (Nels) or (Iris) discovering themselves, their own deep interests and preferences, through their active engagement in and through the world.

But expressiveness recommends itself to me for other reasons. I place a high value on both the inclusiveness of our common humanity and the rich, disjunctive, competing, and unendingly novel variations on that common theme. Seeking for a way to conceptualize our humanness that is sufficiently wide and sufficiently descriptive to advance my ability to consider both, and their relationship to each other, has been a preoccupation intertwined with my observations of children. Expressiveness seems to me to offer that large embrace and that descriptive specificity. It calls attention simultaneously to the commonalities that bind humans together and to the diversities attributable to age, to culture, to history—including the plurality of individual meaning and valuing—that challenge and enliven those commonalities.

In terms of its embracing capacity, expression easily encircles children and adults, the unsophisticated and the educated, the afflicted and the privileged, the peoples of antiquity as well as moderns, people on all sides of the globe. At the same time, across cultures and within them, expression points to a visible, observable, describable display of complex variation broadly reflective of local circumstances as well as larger historical and cultural conditions. It calls attention as well to the smaller-scale, but equally vivid, variations that distinguish us as individuals, each a unique embodiment of humanness.

These variations and alterations, communal and individual, are tremendously important. I am attuned to the expressions and expressiveness approved by my particular status, culture, and era. Those gestures that fall outside that range, I find puzzling, perhaps intriguing, or jarring and confusing, or affronting, frightening, and even terrifying. Nothing is more telling in this respect than the strong emotion aroused when a subgroup's inflections and usage—for example, the English spoken by some African Americans—are perceived by an educated or privileged class to threaten the purity of the language. Equally, the fascination of exotic places is at least partly attributable to delight in modes of expression and gestures compellingly different from one's own. Authenticity of expression is a standard by which we have judged a novelist's or artist's portrayal of a unique time or place or person. And more intimately, our responsiveness to other people, especially those closest to us, depends on our recognition of fine gradations and alterations in gesture and inflection.

These few and schematic examples invite others, all confirming the importance of historical, cultural, and individual variations of expression. Cultural anthropology, social history, sociology, social psychology, and the psychology of personality are among the specialized disciplines that investigate these variations or employ them as parameters to define a field of inquiry. It seems to me that style, aesthetics, personality, and culture are ideas that are incomprehensible without attention to variation and alterations of expression.

Still, for all their importance, these variations appear to me contingent and localized in comparison with the common human capacity for expression. The disposition to express, while vague with respect to its specific outcomes and purposes, is as insistent as the body itself and as much a necessity of bodily existence as breathing and eating. The body, in turn, by giving expression location, definition, and particularity, concentrates and intensifies it. Finding a new center of diffusion in each human body, expression, as a unique, individually located impulse, exercises a refreshing and invigorating, unruly and challenging, influence on culturally and historically conditioned conventions of expression and style. By enlarging the human repertoire of expressive possibility, the expressive impulse, individually located, unsettles in marked or subtle ways our common capacities for seeing and knowing the world and ourselves.

At the same time, the conventions of style and expression ascribable in broad terms to an epoch and culture influence and educate individual expression with respect to purposes and outcomes that are both larger and more specific than its own. There is, I believe, a dramatic, unfolding interplay among the common human disposition toward expression, the expressive impulse as it is manifested in the individual body, and the conventional and stylistic influences on expression.

The expressiveness and the diffusion of expression in individual bodies, on which cultural and historical variation rests, is wider and deeper than those variations in still other respects. Expressiveness, in some degree, extends to all living creatures, and not only (as Whitehead points out) to the higher animals. Looked at most broadly, whatever lives is a center of expression, diffusing feeling in the world. Or, as Whitehead says: "Wherever there is a region on nature which is itself the primary field of the expressions issuing from each of its parts, that region is alive. . . . The energetic acitvity considered in physics is the emotional intensity entertained in life" (*Modes of Thought,* pp. 31, 232). By embracing not only humans but the world in all its living dimensions, expression offers itself as a way of comprehending our intimacy with the world. Expression, as much as the chemistry of our bodies, situates us in the world as, to borrow Whitehead's phrase, "a moment continuous with the world" (p. 30).

So far, I have been speaking of expressiveness in spatial or geographic terms—as constituting a gestural field, as situating us both in nature and in the cultural world. We need to turn now to the temporal dimension, and expressiveness further helps us to understand children as learners and thinkers across time. To round out my thoughts on the importance I place on expressiveness for understanding humanness, I am going to pair it with the words *change* and *motion*—words that foreshadow the slant I take on time as a human experience.

In human terms, I take time to be not something we have or possess or only an abstract, physical category, but an enactment. It is interesting to me that just as Whitehead suggests that our bodies are "a moment of the world," Merleau-Ponty observes, "The passage of one present to the next is not a thing which I conceive, nor do I see it as an onlooker, I perform it. . . . I am myself a time, a time which abides" (*Phenomenology of Perception,* p. 421).

We are constantly in motion. As enactors of time, we move along and, like all things that live, change. *Change* is a big, ambiguous word. It means at the same time growth and flowering, loss and decline, death and decay. It means continuing and connecting; abrupt shifts and sharp cleavages; gathering up, reliving, and remembering; opening up and widening out; deepening and interiorizing; making transitions and precarious leaps into the unknown; the dissolution of old bonds and departures, chosen or forced, from familiar contexts. Thinking of ourselves as performing time, as time in motion, I see us befallen by change in all these ways and more.

We find ourselves *in* life, *in* motion, acting *in* the world, thoroughly implicated *in* a peopled landscape, witnessing and gathering up our lives as we live them. Within the wide expanse of possibility that opens up between the ongoingness of life and abrupt deviations of course, we can for different purposes come down either on the side of continuity and connections or that of radical change and discontinuity. That is when, experiencing or recollecting our lives, we can emphasize threads running through time and connecting events, or we can highlight disjunction and jarring moments of dramatic change. It seems to me both emphases are true and each is partial.

Studying children's works, I am aware of these same interplays of change and connectedness. In (Iris's) work, the arch form I spoke of threads through and connects the span of the collection from age five to age thirteen, but itself changes—and, in changing, contrives to change and to complicate the thematic and compositional meanings that it makes possible. I notice, too, that within a body of works, each individual piece claims its own place and singular importance, while at the same time each achieves a different and fuller visibleness and recognizableness within the context of the whole than when standing in isolation.

Equally, the connections among individual works are never simple or unidirectional but always complex and interlaced. The continuities are not, for example, a succession or repetition from work to work of identical elements, so that in (Iris's) work I could substitute the arch in one drawing for the arch depicted in another. Neither are the changes in works merely substitutional. That is, it does not square with the actuality of a body of works to describe the changes within it in terms of the insertion of more sophisticated elements that merely replace or substitute for earlier, less complex ones. When looking at (Iris's) collection of art works, I cannot adequately describe the changes as a progression from simple to more complicated depictions according, for example, to some developmental schema. To do that would require me to overlook or violate the energetic complexity and unbounded volatility of the works. The elements lifted from their dynamic surroundings lose their comprehensibility, are rendered mute and opaque—just as words in a text are silenced, their meanings truncated—if they are divided into separate pieces of language.

I think we can feel these statements to be also true of our lives, our personal meaning: the experience of continuousness with myself does not refer to a repeating element or even the repetition of a complex pattern of elements, and it most assuredly does not conform to some abstract schema of "progress." Similarly, the experience of jolting change is not one of absolute disjunction with myself, nor does it announce a new, improved me to substitute for an earlier, less developed persona. I am ever present with myself as well as ever changing. For the reason that any change alters the "whole," we witness in works and lives a continuous remaking, a remaking that is vague with respect to specific direction and goals but energetic in its renewal of possibilities.

Taking them all together, the connections and the disjunctions, whether in works or in lives, fall together in a fashion that is roughly describable as self-coherent. A body of works is admittedly partial and uneven in its contours, necessarily open-ended, unfinished. A body of works is redolent of the maker, suffused with an unmistakable and unique flavor. Each piece of work, in order to *be,* announces choices foreclosing other possibilities, yet each also opens up new options. Each recollected life is indisputably a "telling," carrying the imprint of the person who bears witness to its interiority, its meaning, its connectedness, its diversions, its fragmentations, its foreshortenings—to all the adventures and befallen-nesses of a lived life. Also, the particular telling inevitably points to silences signifying other tellings, other ways of selecting, that are, momentarily or more permanently, veiled by this version of the life story. At the same time, even in the act of telling, events are leading on, changing and altering the contours of the life being told.

When I said earlier that expressiveness constitutes a gestural region, a field in which our lives are interanimated, change and motion were implied. By explicitly situating expressiveness in the context of motion and change, I have specifically elaborated it as ever moving, ever changing, as inimical to stasis and boundedness. For these reasons, I understand expressiveness to exercise what, with some caution, I am going to call a transforming effect. As I am using it, I take *transformation* to mean essentially what I have been trying to describe: that something continues while everything changes. Characterizing transformation in this way, I am distinguishing it from what I'll call *transmutations,* which are signaled by achievement of a dramatically new form—for example, the caterpillar's reappearance as a butterfly. I wish instead to place the emphasis on the transforming *process,* on motion that by an inward or outward reworking opens the way for novelty to enter. That is, I would focus on the liquidifying of the caterpillar and the reforming within the chrysalis rather than the butterfly. Or to employ another image, the main event for me is the working of yeast on dough rather than the risen loaf.

Expressiveness seems to me to be some such transforming agent—and also a pathway, the trace that discloses the transformation. Understood as a pathway, interweaving human activity, it maps a region in which my intensity of being—my energy, feeling, gestures, valuings—and that, of course, of others, by virtue of their interanimation, accomplish a remaking of the entire human field. I mean this concretely. Expressiveness literally and unceasingly enlivens and energizes surroundings and relationships. Like the air or the sea around us, expressiveness both sustains life and moves it along. Although expressiveness can, like water, be channeled, "domesticated," and turned to useful social purposes, it can also escape those channels, play false that enculturation. Like the air ever stirring around us, expressiveness, possessing its own energy, is unstoppable. Of course, just as we may protect ourselves from the wind, we may shield ourselves from expressiveness—turning away from emotion that is too intense, averting our gaze from another person's expressions of value and meaning. Or we can control or mask expressiveness, deploying it to protect or mislead others. Yet even when we are "expressionless," expressiveness asserts itself, exercising powerful, if ambiguous, effects on other persons, on the human surroundings.

Continuing the analogy with water and air, I would note that akin to both, expressiveness lacks its own form and, like air, is intangible. Just as air and water flow into and fill all the spaces of the natural world, expressiveness fills to the limits all of the spaces of the human world. Continuously playing itself out on this vast scale, expressiveness has an ever-altering, ever-transforming influence on the human terrain—individual, cultural, historical. In this respect, it seems to me that its transforming energy achieves an exceptional level of visibility, potency, and publicness. It is an energy that is less circumscribed and hidden than the action of yeast on dough and less mysterious and predictable in its outcomes than the ever-repeating life cycles of caterpillars.

I believe for me the power of expressiveness is most satisfactorily and aptly conveyed in the image of the unceasing action of the wind on the natural world. As the wind cuts its invisible pathways across the landscape, the changes left in its wake are not always immediately visible; neither are they altogether foreseeable, nor do they achieve altogether permanent or stable results. Expressiveness, the longings and aversions, the strong desires, and the competing values that interanimate our lives exert a similarly continuous force on our lives, on all human events. Like that of the wind, it is a force that is sometimes negligible, sometimes gentle and benign, sometimes rousing and invigorating, sometimes uprooting and destructive. Like the face of the natural world, the contours of human lives and affairs are ever shifting, subject alike to dramatic upheaval and remaking and to slower, less dramatic, but no less relentless sculpting, refinement, reworking.

As I have said, originally I came to ideas like these from attending closely to bodies and gestures, the expressive surfaces of the body. It is observably gesture that transforms the body from an anatomical event to a recognizable presence. After all, in its form, one body, with significant but relatively minor variations, is very like to all other human bodies. It is in tempos, rhythms, the particular emotional intensities that animate the body that we recognize the person we know. These gestures, these tonal qualities, are deeply dispositional and persistent. Knowing someone well, we are remarkably attuned to the most subtle change in expressiveness, to the smallest shrug of the shoulder or flicker of the eye—it tells us everything. Even with all the losses attendant on aging or ill health, I have noticed that gestures—a tilt of the head, a lift of the chin, a glance—familiarly animate the body, keep before us a recognizable presence. At the same time, everything changes. Finding ourselves in novel contexts, we are altered.

Similarly, language is a means of transforming experience and not just a communications system or a substitution for actual experience or an aid to intellectual development. Meanings keep changing. I take a word in, it lives in me with other words, and it is used in new contexts and in new ways, changing and transforming me, opening up new possibilities, intensifying and expanding. The process is endless, ongoing, dynamic, expressively public.

For example, right now we are talking. My words complete your thought; your thought completes my words. I appropriate your vocabulary; you borrow an idea from me. My words fall into a void if you are not there to catch them. We build on each other's words, participate in each other's thoughts. I think, too, of conversations that are rich in meaning but short on words. Something understood bridges, connects. Ellipsis suffices. Thought flows. Little impedes. Or, conversely, sometimes when I am listening hard to someone, am full of desire to catch their meaning but mistrustful of my understanding, I speak the words along with them sotto voce. Tasting the words on my lips, my tongue assists the ear to translate.

Alone, I am the forum for voices and thoughts. Within myself, I converse with multitudes, am peopled by presences, and stand in my own presence. Voices from books read long ago. A felicitous phrase. Nonsense, or words that get stuck in my head. Songs. A poetic line. The rehearsal of a future conversation. The voice of conscience. A relationship-shattering outburst. Stinging words. Words that can't be taken back. A lie. A betrayal of trust. Vexed words. Bringing a troubled thought into the imagined presence of a friend. Language engages us co-responsively, entangles us in each other's life.

Speaking together, we become coconspirators in the making of meaning. Yet each speaker transforms the language, makes it his or her own—and renders it active and, in some degree, unpredictable. Our vocabularies and our meanings miss each other. The expectation of understanding is betrayed. Repeating the words I just said in another voice alters my meaning. My expressive space is invaded, foreshortened, even closed. Or a familiar thought impressed with a new speaker's intensity, animated by an image, taps fresh pools of meaning. Thinking opens up, flows. Without speakers, a language fades and weakens. It awaits a speaker to animate it.

Much of what I have said about speaking seems to me to apply to making and "works." Making things, or something that has been made, creates a conversational space. Included in the circle are a viewer—the maker or perhaps another—and a material—words or a pencil or paint or construction or cooking supplies. In the space created by making things, words flow. A quilt emblemizes the conversational space of a group of women sewing together. A scholarly text delivers the offerings of a company of professors and disputors. A child drawing creates a world on the space of a page. Children drawing side by side fill the air with commentary, carry on a conversation with the activity they are portraying, and cross over the boundaries of another child's drawing to participate in the drama unfolding there. People working together or side by side on a repetitive task establish a common rhythm and, like dancers, complete or echo each other's gestures. My grandfather and my uncle scything grass, chopping wood. No words spoken. The grass whispers. The axes ring.

I notice that works in the absence of the makers retain their presence. A tool, scarred with use, has about it the lingering touch of other hands. My friend and colleague Alice Seletsky describes taking children to a museum. The docent passes around a brick made in Egypt in ancient times. It bears the thumb imprint of a workman. The children gasp, are awestruck. Each reverently places the corresponding thumb on the print. So does Alice.

A work set at a distance from the maker breaks in upon us, the viewers, the readers, and draws us into its domain. In "Speaking Silence," Nemerov likens a poem to a mind which, in the presence of another mind, will recognizably "think" (*Figures of Thought,* Boston: Godine, 1978, p. 103). That is, the poem or any other work, one in paint or wood as much as one in words, by its presence asserts meaning and invites it. Works call out to viewers. They also call out to other works. With great difficulty, or relative ease, they (and we) step across cultural boundaries or historical gaps.

The meaning density and volume of a work change through viewing. Cezanne wondered how his children had grown up. Yet, by its magnetic power, by captivating and concentrating thought, by forcing a held attention, a work (like a word) sets a boundary. Cezanne's children haven't grown up to be Picasso's. Works also reach out to embrace viewers, to draw us together. Friendships are sealed on the strength of a shared book or film. The music of an era, whether it is found tasteful or distasteful by individuals, tends to bind together a generation.

Making works, we negotiate a well-worn and shared terrain. There have been many makers before us. The world abounds in works. Every work shelters other works, harkens back to them, plays its variations within their themes. At Christmas, I cook and bake in the style of my mother and grandmother. Although they are dead, we make a work together. The work changes in my hands, is transformed by my aesthetic. On a grander scale, each painting exists in the presence of other paintings—a testimony not only to the fertility of the human imagination but to painting as a possibility in the human repertoire. The genre, the medium, that calls our hands into action educates us, works us, channels our expressiveness. Seeing your work, my interest is sparked. I borrow from you. Your space for making may be diminished or enlarged (or both) by my presence within it. A motif lifted from your repertoire glances back at you, sweetly or jarringly (or both) from my production. We are copiers and adapters (and forgers) as well as originators and inventors. Because works are public, they may suffer from exploitation and overworking, tending toward stylization, depletion of vigor, diminishment of worth. Works, like words, await new makers.

The authors of "big works" speak to the audience with authoritative voices. Their authority increases the volume of life for us, their viewers and readers. We are invaded by them, taken by storm. It is not necessarily a gentle experience. Expressiveness, our own or another's, is a force, an intensity fully capable of tearing up the cultural terrain, dramatically altering personal lives. As audience to our own thought or another's, we are implicated in the adventure of forming, giving shape, breaking up achieved forms to make way for new possibilities, pressing beyond the boundaries of the already known.

In works, the author and the other meet, not as personalities, weighted down by the biographical details of their lives, but on the level of making and remaking, of creating and recreating, of thinking. Works, small works and large ones, disclose us as makers, as thinkers. In the work, the maker, whether oneself or another, is thinking aloud. The person met in the midst of thought and adventure is not, I think, subsumable by the person who has a dentist's appointment tomorrow, who has trouble learning math, who sometimes disrupts the class, who in her youth felt a sense of isolation within the family circle.

Works make an impress on the world, faint or vivid. The making of the imprint and the imprint itself engage us all and, in greater and lesser ways, affect us all. Works and language, like persons, are not sealed entities. They are mutually animating fields: fields of intensity, charged with feeling; fields of magnetic power, capable of attracting and repelling; fields of possibility, defiant of closure and finish. The public or social dimension that expressiveness confers on speech and works signals the public and social dimension of persons and knowledge.

The urgent necessity of expressing emotional intensity draws us into the public dimension, into language, into cultural media and symbolic systems, into otherness. In talking or drawing, for example, we express and objectify and transform (and always to some extent lose and modify) that intensity into something else—a text, a picture—that then gives us back to ourselves in a new form and with a different intensity. Something identifiable is sustained amidst proliferating variation and dramatic change.

That's why works have been such a key to my understanding of children. It is from these perspectives that I have laid aside traditional developmental categories and turned to expressiveness with its public dimension and transforming power to understand what it is to be human, to change and grow, and also to abide and gather.

2

Deep Talk as Knowing

After studying with Patricia Carini, I began to characterize the Prospect School as a kind of oral culture.

At first it seemed rather odd to talk about Prospect as oral because of the extensive amount of daily note taking and written documentation that goes on. The Archive itself is lined with shelf after shelf of records of staff meetings, notes from summer institutes, papers and published essays, graduate student theses, grant proposals, long narrative records for each student, catalogues for reference editions of the children's files—and on and on. Teachers walk around with paper and pencil in hand. Children are observed, their drawings and written texts described, keywords reflected upon, teacher journals kept and exchanged and at times published.[1]

Yet most of this writing serves to supplement or record talk, and it is talk—a particular kind of deep talk—that is at the heart of this teaching community.

Indeed, all teachers *must* talk. Hurriedly, in hallways between classes, and later over cups of coffee in the teachers' lounge late into the afternoon, they share anecdotes, assess successes and failures, describe specific students, exchange assignments and classroom practices, laugh with each other—and generally come to understand themselves as increasingly more expert practitioners within (and against) a particular teaching community.

And the talk matters. So much so that at Prospect (and now in ways at the Writing Program at Syracuse University), "teacher talk" has become the central educational and epistemological activity, a critical moment for making teacherly decisions about students and classroom situations and even for doing research on student works. Along with Carini, teachers at Prospect have developed what they call "documentary processes" or "reflective procedures" for describing children's works, for doing staff reviews, and for thinking together about keywords or concepts—as the primary activities for supporting teaching practice and for grounding curricular decisions (see Chapter 1).

This kind of deep talk surely serves a teaching community well, but as I explore it further, I would like to consider other questions: Is this deep talk a research methodology? In what ways might the ordinary languages of teachers and researchers engaged in such conversation contribute to the field of composition? What is the value of knowledge that is descriptive and narrative, local (perhaps radically so), and disputable?

Deep Talk as Scene

It was Tuesday, at 1:00 P.M., time again for the seven of us to gather in the seminar room of the Writing Program. Steve, our coordinating group leader, passed around copies of a student essay that one of the teachers in the group had provided. She had requested that we do deep talk on this paper, because she was having trouble knowing what to say to this student when he came to conferences. Somehow she felt she didn't have the right words to help him see what the problems in the essay really were, or to help him imagine the different kinds of choices he could make as a writer.

"I'll start," Bobbi volunteered, and she read the essay aloud to the group.

"Let's begin with you, Lynn," Steve said.

"Well, let's see. The writer begins by announcing directly that he will talk about his biology class and the kinds of notes he takes during lectures . . ."

And so the paraphrase continued, with teachers taking turns recasting small sections of the essay. Then the chair asked us to begin descriptive rounds, where we went through the text again, with each teacher making low-inferential observations about the text.

"The first three paragraphs are very short, no more than two sentences long, with little transition between them."

"The writer uses 'I think' often."

"There are very few subordinate constructions."

At the end of the round, the chair summarized clusters of ideas or themes, using our actual words as much as possible.

We continued describing, moving slowly and tentatively into more inferential claims and evaluative conclusions. Words repeated; patterns emerged; echoes and traces returned over and over again; key questions kept coming up. At the end of an hour, the teacher who has asked for the deep talk recognized that the textual patterns that had been described in this essay characterized much of this writer's work in the course so far, and she felt confident about what to talk about in their next conference.

Deep Talk as Epistemological Process

What I call deep talk is based on the reflective practices developed by Carini and her colleagues at Prospect, where they have enacted the belief that teaching practice and educational research should be grounded in a phenomenological, or descriptive, understanding of each child as a particular thinker and learner (see Chapter 1). The scene above, the documentary account at the end of the book, and "A Reflective Conversation: 'Tempos of Meaning'" (in Chapter 3) all try to dramatize this kind of talking together with enough detail, I hope, to give readers a real experiential sense of this process.[2]

It is, however, easier to do deep talk than to explain or theorize it.

Essentially, this kind of talk asks participants to engage in a process of collaboratively generated meaning that takes place over a relatively long period of time. The purpose is to open up intellectual space, to understand more fully and richly a shared focus of interest—a drawing or written text, a child's school self, a keyword—through language and the power of collective thought.[3]

This reflective or descriptive process enables participants to see and resee that shared focus of interest in view of an ever-enlarging web of comments, tensions, connections, connotations, differences, oppositions. This reading takes place within the permeable and interanimating border regions among writer, readers, language, and culture. Readers note emerging patterns and connections. They locate the topic within multiple contexts, widening the range of its correlatives, as they come to understand it more fully, both in its particularity and at the same time in its relatedness to other texts and contexts.

These reflective processes have definite time and space and procedural structures, empty in themselves, which serve as place holders for a certain kind of epistemic event. At the Writing Program at Syracuse, for example, where we have adapted this procedure, teachers meet in small groups every week, and at times describe together a student text. First the text is read aloud by several participants, in order to hear it in several voices and interpretations. Then participants share initial, immediate responses to the text, with the designated chair taking notes and later pointing out connections, complementarities, and divergences in these original responses. Next the text is paraphrased, and then the first of several descriptive rounds begins, with each participant asked first to attend to the surface of the text, to particular elements and noticeable details (e.g., "The essay opens with a narrative account," "Each paragraph makes a general claim," "The word 'I' appears often"). The point of these descriptive rounds is to hold off quick or habituated understanding and intellectual closure, to get participants to attend closely to the materiality of the text, and to develop a shared (if not common) discourse.

These procedures create an arena for thought, a space for minds to run through time in parallel ways and perhaps to touch for a moment, almost magnetically. Language itself, used reflexively, is the means to expand, deepen, and complicate understanding.

Deep talk takes time and a willingness to listen attentively to the voices of others. It took more than an hour for one group to reflect on the word *development,* for example, so that members could share concretely their meanings, associations, and experiences with this word/concept. There are heavy intellectual demands in this task. Just to sit still that long and listen, really listen, to others is difficult for the uninitiated (or the agonistic).

The imaginative and intellectual richness generated by these reflective procedures results to a great extent from the inevitable raggedness of deep talk—the way this talk points out to the world, comes at a focus of interest over and over again from many varied perspectives, offers tentatively made connections, dropped like little semantic bombs, but not elaborated upon logically and linearly and fully.[4]

Words carry, as Bakhtin might say, worlds within them, and by simply juxtaposing them, those worlds collide, startle, overlap, do battle, and interanimate in generative, at times unexpected, ways. The semantic relationships and semiotic possibilities do not have to be fully spelled out in the linear discourse grammar of syntax and paragraphs, nor smoothed out into a traditionally coherent text. Rather, ideas and multiple voices are allowed to coexist, to "mean" simultaneously, to remain unevenly elaborated, all held together and bounded, in some sense, by time and space and community.

During the process of deep talk, a spoken text is composed, a text that is communal, rough-edged, open-ended, full of convergences and divergences, both personal and collective. Observations, ideas, images, associations, conclusions, references, and allusions come up, layering one on top of the other, interpenetrating in ways, adding on or diverging from what has already been said. All the participants draw upon their personal histories as well as their cultural knowledge, so that the talk expands out into the wider cultural and historical setting. Though grounded in the particularity of a child's text or a keyword, the talk continually pushes out at the edges—pushes, as a participant once said, "into the universe."

For those who have participated in the reflective procedures at Prospect for a long time, of course, each particular instance of deep talk merges in memory with other instances, so that the experience is even further deepened for those participants. It is enriched, that is, by memory and history. For visitors like me, I have noticed a strong impulse to hold on to these (potentially) fleeting moments, to write everything down, to try to remember it all.

At the end of an hour or so, the room feels full of "stuff," and teachers have—in that context, at that moment, through those persons—an enriched felt sense and understanding of the focus of interest, of the community in which they work, of themselves as particular practitioners, and perhaps of an idea or claim to be pursued later in greater detail.

Note takers during deep talk try to take all that stuff into account. David Carroll (1986) points out that "good notes" are better than any complete verbatim transcript, as the recorder is able, in these moments of "collaboration and mutual insight," to capture that "mixture of facial expression, gesture, memory of earlier comments and connections to previous contexts, so that the overall setting of the conversation is both more broad and more subtle than the literal text of the comments" (Appendix A, p. 1). But it's not easy to report on or to reconstruct—write up, (re)produce—the rich understanding composed by and through and during the actual reflective process of the group.

Perhaps this kind of knowing is radically communal and contextual and temporal—and perhaps, or at least initially, spoken.

But certainly deep talk—as a central, generative way of knowing—

serves to create and maintain a particular kind of teaching community at Prospect (and to an extent at Syracuse), with all that the word *community* implies about diversity and difference within a shared enterprise.

Deep Talk as Teaching Community

Cultural anthropologist Clifford Geertz characterizes the Balinese cockfight as "deep play." He analyzes it as an activity with important psychological values for the men involved, but also as linked to the ever-widening social codes of meaning that constitute the Balinese culture itself. The stakes—psychological, economical, social—are high, endowing the sport with great "interest value." According to Geertz, to participate in a cockfight is primarily a way for a man to learn about his own private sensibility, as set against, or shaped through, the ethos of the culture, rather like a Gestalt figure cut across the ground. In fact, "enacted and reenacted, so far without end, the cockfight enables the Balinese . . . to see a dimension of his own subjectivity" (p. 327), a subjectivity that doesn't really come to exist until it is socially organized and enacted. The personal and public merge here. The cockfight is thus simultaneously expressive and constitutive, both of the self and of the society: "In the cockfight, then, the Balinese forms and discovers his temperament and his society's temper at the same time" (pp. 327–28).

So, too, with deep talk at Prospect.

At one level, deep talk could be described rather straightforwardly as a set of procedures or formats—an educational method—for organizing staff reviews of children and for describing their works as expressive of their ways of making sense of the world intellectually and imaginatively. Because this talk remains concrete, specific, and descriptive, it folds directly—and usefully—right back into teaching practice.

During a staff review at Prospect, for example, a teacher will present a large number of observations about a particular child, organized rather loosely under headings such as "emotional tenor" and "modes of relationships." He or she will tell stories and identify key adjectives that this child evokes, and will listen to anecdotes and observations from others. They all reflect together. Slowly the room fills with stuff, and at some point a felt understanding of the child as person or maker of works emerges from this hour or hour and a half of discussion. Connections among observations are made, word choices become more refined, more finely nuanced, patterns form, and teaching suggestions specific to that person announce themselves.

The teachers all have a lot at stake in these discussions professionally. The presenting teacher may come to an understanding of the student that enables him or her to make more thoughtful, more contextual instructional decisions, and all teachers gain a sense of their shared communal purposes and identity. They hear their voices—their standards, their fears, their approaches and theories—within an ongoing and communal dialogue about what teaching is all about.

This kind of "we experience" serves teachers well. Teachers' senses of their identity are not drawn from within but from the social context in which they work. Deep talk not only makes that context more visible but also enriches it each time talk takes place.

It is, of course, a way to introduce new teachers into a school or program, as they hear their voices in chorus, or in conflict, with other voices in the community. As Volosinov/Bakhtin says in *Marxism and the Philosophy of Language*, "The stronger, the more organized, the more differentiated the collective in which an individual orients himself, the more vivid and complex his inner world will be" (1986, p. 88). So deep talk may heighten teachers' individual senses of themselves, by making visible both their points of commonality and their points of divergence.

But more significantly, deep talk is a genre, a particular and recurrent way of using language, that links people to each other and to a context in quite specific ways (Miller, 1984). It is an expectation about who says what kinds of thing to whom, and how—and so it is a way of establishing a particular kind of community.

Genre in this sense refers to what Bakhtin calls in *Speech Genres* (1986) the relatively stable types of utterances that characterize language use in particular settings or areas of human activity—that is, to the particular themes, styles, and compositional structures that shape utterance.[5]

Deep talk has several generic features that both enact and enable a certain kind of community. In terms of tenor, deep talk as a genre insists emphatically upon parity among participants, with the roles of chair and recorder rotated each time, with all participants addressed on a first-name basis, and with each participant given approximately the same amount of time to talk. The role of chair, for example, relates to group function, not power or status. In terms of field, in each instance of deep talk, there is a particular focus of interest for the group: an individual child, a specific work, or a keyword. All talk centers on this focus throughout, as the hub holds together the spokes of a wheel.

In terms of mode, the talk is oral, although both the chair and the recorder, and typically participants, take extensive written notes during the procedure. With participants situated in a circle, the talk moves around the circle, with little or no cross-talk allowed and with each participant making his or her particular set of observations without interruption. The chair then charts key categories and patterns at the end of each round, using as much as possible the actual language of each group member, noting common as well as contrastive points. Each person's contribution counts, in an egalitarian sort of way, set against and within the evolving, ever-widening communal text. So, as a genre, deep talk draws directly and emphatically upon the power of collective thought in a teaching community and upon the rich diversity of its participants, in profoundly pluralistic ways.

The talk deepens, as different and differing discourses layer across time/space upon the same focus of interest, and widens (or destabilizes), as words prompt and play off of other words. And throughout it remains ragged—multivoiced, open-ended, unevenly elaborated, with each bit of text "meaning" simultaneously.

The generic form reminds me of a wheel, with each participant's contribution connected to the hub, or focus of interest, in some way, but also located as a somewhat self-contained bit on the rim of the wheel, in view of, and juxtaposed with, bits of talk from other participants. There is often repetition, with participants repeating—and modifying—what others have said. This creates a sense of echo, trace, otherness, citation, intertextuality. The talk is organized temporally, cumulatively, perhaps associatively, according to what the participants thought of next, with no fretting about logic or sequence or hierarchical importance. The language is concrete, particular, ordinary, descriptive, avoiding generalizations and abstraction, returning always to the focus of interest. Puns and word play come up often, as do possible etymologies of various words, as each group member becomes a rather self-reflective language user, free-associating or picking words with care, frustrated when words don't work right, enjoying nuance and innuendo, allowing language itself to open up new intellectual space.

The pragmatic framework that usually ties language tightly to a particular context and thereby eliminates (or at least reduces) ambiguity and indeterminacy is intentionally loosened here, so that ambiguity and indeterminacy are welcomed as the means of exploring and reexploring, through talk, a rich multiplicity of meaning. Language, ungrounded from a more pragmatic or transactional function, becomes itself foregrounded as a way of knowing.

This process thereby highlights the specific resources of written language itself, as someone notes the use of alliteration or a narrative beginning, as another comments on the persistence of a metaphor or the intertextuality of references. The process fine-tunes each participant's understanding and appreciation of language itself.

Like light through a prism, deep talk disperses a colorful, open-ended spectrum of ideas and images for viewing and reviewing.

Deep Talk as Methodology

At Prospect, teachers may later write up documentary accounts of students and their works, accounts that go beyond deep talk and become full portrayals of children as unique thinkers and learners. These accounts rely on descriptions of their works and narratives of their experiences in the classroom settings, as well as draw connections at times to other writers, other theorists. In Chapter 6, I, too, am experimenting with a documentary account that tries to use description itself as the primary genre for reporting on research, as a written complement to the spoken texts that emerge in deep talk, and as a way of talking about development that reveals patterns, relates to other research, yet remains open-ended and dialogic.

In the fall of 1988 at Syracuse, deep talk centered around students' literacy autobiographies and other accounts of their experiences as writers and readers, as part of a project we (somewhat mistakenly) called "profiling." We met in small groups and described together patterns, keywords, hot topics, the tensions in the studios for both ourselves and our students. In the Rhetoric Study Group, teachers were also reading an excerpt from Henry Johnstone's *Validity and Rhetoric in Philosophical Argument,* and soon activities like these, although not directly related, began to inform one another. This all resulted in a momentary convergence of intellectual energy around the phrase "risk and resistance." Teachers then wrote various and diverse accounts of their actual courses in view of that phrase, keyed by its particular and concrete meaning for us, published in our in-house journal called *Reflections in Writing* (no. 8, February 1989). I would argue that these accounts both give an immediate, specific sense of the real world of the writing classrooms at Syracuse and at the same time theorize about that world in shareable and meaningful ways.

At least, I think the knowledge is shareable and meaningful. That's the tough question: what is the value or purpose of knowledge that arises conversationally and descriptively, that is composed communally in the ordinary languages of teachers, that is so local and disputable?

In what ways can deep talk serve as a research methodology for investigations in early written language development?

What kind of knowledge and understanding might this process provide?

How might that knowledge relate to other research?

Can talk as a process of knowing be experienced, captured, conveyed later in written text?

One day, as we were working together on Chapter 1, Carini casually remarked that she enjoys certain kinds of writing, such as journals, notes, observations, but has found it difficult to write child studies in ways that are true to the experience of knowing that child through the processes of reflection. She listed many worries—a clumsy style, an inadequacy in truly conveying the complex particularity of the person, a constant worry about reductiveness. But basically she felt as though she couldn't leave the edges rough enough, the mystery intact.

I rejected the conclusion that this apparent resistance to writing resulted either from personal limits or from some necessary limitation within the medium of written language itself.

Yet I too didn't readily see possible written equivalents or formats or genres to Prospect talk.

One obvious problem is that in this culture, historically at least, written texts have typically been read as complete, finished products. To put something in writing is to make it permanent, to inhibit the dialogic and hence generative nature of the reflective processes, to restrict the time—to clip, trim, and prune the ragged edges that continue to push out from talk. In an educational climate where new ideas are rapidly turned into technologies as soon as they're available, Carini fears that a written text (or a public lecture) may too readily lend itself to formula, recipe, unthinking imitation, quick adoption, and facile use. Although many educators have encouraged her to disseminate her ideas on education and development more widely, Carini has hesitated to do so, because that means talking to large groups and/or writing for large audiences. In both sitautions, there is a risk of no real dialoguing, no real thinking, no real contextualizing of ideas.

But I hypothesize that ultimately this apparent resistance to writing comes out of a much deeper intellectual resistance to the limits of monologue, to stasis, to decontextualization, and to linearity, with its implications of causality and closure—intellectual and epistemological choices typically (though not necessarily) associated with formal written essays or public lectures.

Louise Phelps (1985) refers to two fundamental moments or "deeply rooted impulses whose conjunctions and opposition construct [the] fundamental rhythm" (p. 245) in her composing life as a writer and theorist. She recalls that she discovered this tension through paying close attention to a phrase she had written in her daybook: "resistance to form." The first impulse is generative: "a desire to link information and feeling into more and more densely connected and layered networks." The second is discurvise: "a drive to formulate meaning in precisely articulated, highly textualized, and rhetorically addressed sequences of meaning" (p. 245).

It seems to me that deep talk at Prospect enacts and privileges that "generative" epistemological moment over and over again through its communal, reflective practices—and quietly but emphatically resists the "discursive" counterpoint.

But I am interested in both epistemological moments, so the questions become how to enact the discursive moment in more dialogic ways, how to experiment with genre, how to write texts that involve the readers.

It was in our reading of Milan Kundera's *The Art of the Novel* (1986) that Carini and I began to see new genre possibilities for writing in ways that might complement deep talk, that might work against the frustrations inherent in many traditional written language genres. Chapter 6 is one experiment with form—more will come.

Now that the *Reference Edition of the Archive* has been completed, for example, scholars involved with Prospect in one way or another are beginning to study how the Archive can serve as a basis for longitudinal, child-centered research into how children learn and think. Perhaps groups of scholars from different disciplines would work together on a file, sharing first an understanding of how that child makes sense of the world, based on phenomenological description, then diverging later into

knowledge informed more specifically by particular disciplinary interests. Or perhaps several files might be described in terms of larger
questions, such as how children define spatial boundaries or write
narratives or make sense of time or draw arches. To join these two
epistemological moments is to take into account both disciplinary and
nondisciplinary kinds of understanding.

To consider deep talk as a research methodology is to begin with a
broader definition of thought than usual, both communal and generalist in
a sense, drawing first (and foremost) upon the profound resources of
collective thought and community. It is a process everyone can participate in—and contribute to. To think, to know, to understand are defined
and enacted at Prospect almost in spatial and temporal terms, as a kind of
shared territory that we all can dwell in together over time, teacher and
researcher, old and young, specialist and generalist. To think together is
to open up an arena, a territory, based on what John Berger calls in
Another Way of Telling (1982) "the social function of subjectivity" (p.
100). In that middle ground between the utterly private and autobiographical and the totally public and conventional, we can all meet and know
each other and come to certain kinds of understanding.

This is a form of thinking together. During reflective procedures like
deep talk, "participants' personal histories, experiences and thoughts are
joined with those of others to produce a strong common experience,
history and thought connected with the word [or child or work] chosen for
their mutual consideration. Thus, the process illustrates with equal
emphasis the uniqueness of perspective each person brings to an idea, and
the power of collective thought generated by this diversity. . . .
Further, [the cultural associations and references] involve participants
not only in the thought of the immediate group but also in the 'thought' of
humanity" (from *The Prospect Center Documentary Processes,*
1986, p. 2).

Furthermore, deep talk is a constructing of knowledge that values
many ways of knowing—spirit, will, imagination, intellect, emotion.[6]
Group participants bring all that makes them human to the project of
understanding how children and their works come to "mean"—
experiences, knowledge, intuitions, memories, related stories. Indwell-
ing, or deep immersion, in a focus of interest such as a student text leads
to an intensification of the experience of that text, the writer, and one's
self. Within that intensification and engagement, as Carini says, "possibilities announce themselves"—as questions to be investigated, claims
to be made, teaching options to be pursued, hypotheses to be tested.

As Bakhtin (1986) also claims, all genuine understanding of an utterance [or work] is necessarily active, responsive, interactive, and dialogic, with meaning located in the space between language users. ''A generative process,'' he notes, ''can be grasped only with the aid of another generative process'' (p. 102). Once researchers acknowledge the personal meaning in children's texts and in learning, they participate in that meaning—they react to it, extend it, read and even misread it.

Research then becomes a kind of conversation.

And knowledge becomes dialogic and disputable. Reading a student's text, describing it over and over again, layering text on text, experimenting with the right nuances, fine-tuning the language—all this language use creates a network of text, organized not as abstracted or second-order generalizations but rather as patterns generated by and through the talk. This descriptive knowledge remains tied closely to the particular student, text, context, moment, group of readers.

Descriptive knowledge is neither uncritical accumulation of practices and beliefs, or ''lore,'' nor testable in more traditional and scientific terms. It is disputable—and that potentially is its greatest value. It calls forth a response from others. It forms and informs and reforms through more talk and experience and writing, across time, within different settings (see Carini, 1975, 1979, 1982).

In an emerging discipline, these descriptive accounts might be useful, because the careful, precise, detailed portrayals of particular people enable others to experience the richness of those people—and so to anticipate it in others. Although the specific description applies only to one child, an in-depth account of that one child's early writing experiences may help others to see the complexity and the individuation involved in the activity of writing for other children. To know one writer well is to know all writers better. Having read one portrayal, a teacher or researcher might more readily see and acknowledge the individualized, meaningful expressive choices another child makes.

Description becomes a habit of mind, a genre, an art of seeing.

We start with talk. We use language together to come to knowledge and richer understandings of a shared focus of interest, of ourselves, of the communities we belong to, and of language itself.

Other Voices

> I give myself verbal shape from another's point of view, ultimately from the point of view of the community to which I belong. A word is a bridge

thrown between myself and another. If one end of the bridge depends on me, then the other depends on my addressee. A word is territory shared by both addressor and addressee, by the speaker and his interlocutor. (Volosinov/Bakhtin, *Marxism and the Philosophy of Language*, 1986, p. 86)

Each word tastes of the context and contexts in which it has lived its socially charged life; all words and forms are populated with intentions. . . . As a living, socio-ideological concrete thing, as heteroglot opinion, language, for the individual consciousness, lies on the borderline between oneself and the other. The word in language is half someone else's. It becomes "one's own" only when the speaker populates it with his own intention, his own accent, when he appropriates the word, adapting it to his own semantic and expressive intention. Prior to this moment of appropriation, the word does not exist in a neutral and impersonal language . . . but rather it exists in other people's mouths, in other people's contexts, serving other people's intentions. (Bakhtin, *The Dialogic Imagination*, 1981, p. 293)

Nor is it possible, any longer, to distinguish in this writing between the personal and the collective: both inhabit exactly the same language, in the way a post card is at once public and private. (Hartman, *Saving the Text*, 1981, p. xxvi)

I play easily with abstractions, spontaneously searching out the general amidst the particular. Working on Woolf required relishing the particular for its own sake, moving to generality only by tracing increasingly complex webs of connections and layers of meaning. . . . I seemed to learn new ways of attending to the natural world and to people, especially children. This kind of attending was *intimately concerned with caring;* because I cared I reread slowly, then I found myself watching more carefully, listening with patience, absorbed by gestures, moods, and thoughts. The more I attended, the more deeply I cared. The domination of feeling by thought, which I had worked so hard to achieve, was breaking down. Instead of developing arguments that could bring my feelings to heel, I allowed feeling to inform my most abstract thinking. (Ruddick, "New Combinations: Learning from Virginia Woolf," 1984, pp. 150–51)

The multiplicity of phenomenal meanings established through and by the participation of one observer over time, or through the participation of many observers, constitutes a community of collectively shareable meaning. (Carini, *Observation and Description*, 1975, p. 10)

Constructivists make a distinction between "really talking" and what they consider to be didactic talk in which the speaker's intention is to hold forth rather than to share ideas. In didactic talk, each participant may report experience, but there is no attempt among participants to join together to arrive at some new understanding. "Really talking" requires careful listening; it implies a mutually shared agreement that together you are creating the optimum setting so that half baked or emergent ideas can grow. "Real talk" reaches deep into the experience of each participant; it also draws on the analytical abilities of each. Conversation, as constructivists describe it, includes discourse and exploration, talking and listening, questions, argument, speculation, and sharing. (Belenky et al., *Women's Ways of Knowing,* 1986, p. 144)

The sense of a word is the sum of all the psychological events aroused in a person's consciousness by the word. It is a dynamic, complex, fluid whole, which has several zones of unequal stability. Meaning is only one of the zones of sense, the most stable and precise zone. A word acquires its sense from the context in which it appears; in different contexts, it changes its sense. (Vygotsky, *Thought and Language,* 1986, p. xxxvii)

In any quarter skepticism about "ordinary language" (the term was used until recently only by the skeptical) is in the end skepticism about ordinary people, be they nonscientists or nonpoets. (M. L. Pratt, as cited by Brodkey in "Writing Ethnographic Narratives," 1987, pp. 25–50)

To abide with something, is to make visible its dwelling place—that is, all of the object's multiple points or relatedness to other things and to the passage of time. Therefore, observing locates the thing in the vicinity of other things and makes visible both its continuities and transformations through time. (Carini, *The Art of Seeing and the Visibility of the Person,* 1979, p. 18)

Language, from its most rudimentary form onward, testifies to a movement of personal being outside of itself. . . . Human being is not contained within itself. The contours of one's body outline a line of demarcation, but never an absolute limit. . . . The other is for each man a condition of existence. The plurality of individuals, the fragmentation of being, appears thus as an original presupposition of lived consciousness. (Gusdorf, "Speaking as Encounter," 1977, p. 125)

A self is defined dynamically as it exists in a relationship between an I and a Thou: "Man becomes an I through a You." (Martin Buber, cited in LeFevre, *Invention as a Social Act,* 1987, p. 63)

Resonance comes about when an individual act—a "vibration"—is intensified and prolonged by sympathetic vibrations. It may occur when someone acts as a facilitator to assist or extend what is regarded as primarily another's invention, or when people are mutual collaborators at work on a task. Resonance also occurs indirectly when people provide a supportive social and intellectual environment that nurtures thought and enables ideas to be received, thus completing the inventive act. (LeFevre, *Invention as a Social Act,* 1987, p. 65)

3

A Reflective Conversation: "Tempos of Meaning"

This chapter dramatizes the documentary process of describing a work (in this case, a first year essay), using a modification of Patricia Carini's reflective procedures. In this project, we were engaged in a highly speculative process, not looking so much for research results or validity, but rather trying to have some actual experience with student writing at Syracuse University across all four years. We looked at three essays from each writer, written across time, in a very rough effort to describe in broad strokes the possible patterns of development across a large group of writers.

We were very limited in the kinds of conclusions we could draw, and this account is given not as a prescription for doing research but as an illustration of one version of the process of descriptive and communal reading, or "deep talk."

To really trace a person's development, readers would need to look at lots and lots of writing, from different contexts, in different genres. They would have to take time to allow for a deeper immersion in the texts, and they would have to return to texts again and again, to confirm and to chart patterns and keywords, to refine descriptive language, to set up contrasts and comparisons, to see what changes and what stays the same.

Given the limits on the number of works and the type of writing we looked at for any one person, we ended up learning in this reading something about writers (albeit ambiguously), quite a bit about written language and text, and a lot about ourselves as a group of evolving readers confronting a great change in writing instruction at Syracuse.

I hope the account demonstrates the complexity of reading student essays and suggests to teachers and researchers some possible uses for descriptive readings as a way of knowing, as a way of forming a teaching community, and as a way of training teachers.

The Context

It was time again for the six of us to gather in the seminar room of the English Department. Jacki, a graduate student in English Education, set up the tape recorder in the middle of the table, while Don, Delia, Marty, and Lib, all experienced writing instructors, settled into their seats, chatting casually about classes and glancing through the packet of twelve student texts we had been working with.

"Who wants to read the next essay aloud?"

"I will," Delia said—and so we began.

Over the next three hours, we read and talked together about three of these student texts, as part of a communal reading process we had been engaged in for several weeks.[1]

It was an odd reading process for us, dramatically communal in ways that both discomforted and exhilarated us as teachers accustomed to reading student texts alone in our offices. We had embarked on it together as a specific response to a particular problem at Syracuse University. In the fall of 1983, the College of Arts and Sciences established an ad hoc committee charged with reviewing writing instruction throughout the college. At that time, students in this very traditional, form-oriented Freshman English program wrote in-class, five-paragraph argumentative essays on (typically) unannounced topics and had to achieve minimum competency (at least two passes) in order to move on to the next three modules: fiction, poetry or drama, and a mini-course. The kinds and amounts of writing in each module were prescribed, and grading sessions and file reviews were designed to standardize the rather formalistic ways teachers were asked to assign, respond to, and evaluate student writing. As part of its work, review committee members wanted a more specific sense of what Syracuse students are like as writers when they enter the university and in what ways, if any, they change as a result of our instructional program.

The theoretical and methodological difficulties inherent in attempting to design a research project that would answer that question completely or definitively awed us, appropriately enough, yet questions kept nagging at us: What *are* our student writers like? How *do* they change? What *are* the effects of our writing instruction?

So I put together a procedure for reading student texts that would at least give us some actual experience with student writing. I proposed working with a group of Syracuse writing teachers and using the phenomenologically based procedures developed by Patricia Carini (1975, 1979) to do a reflective reading in order to compose a descriptive typology (Patton, 1980) cast in the form of a metaphor.

I will here present a kind of "thick description" of the reflective reading that we did of just one of those texts. That is Clifford Geertz's (1973) term for turning a passing event into an "account," for describing, interpreting, and evoking the complex meanings of that event for others to enter into imaginatively.

A Reflective Reading

Background

Our general reading procedure, based on those developed by Carini, provided a specific structure for each meeting:

1. We read a text aloud.
2. Next we went around the group, with each of us paraphrasing a section of the text.
3. We would then continue around the group, making observations or publicly verifiable statements about the text, such as noting the sentence patterns or repetitions of certain words.
4. Gradually we would move into more inferential statements, such as noting an apparent sense of confusion in the writer's use of a literary term or incoherence in the development of a claim.
5. Once this reflection was "completed," usually in about an hour, we summarized features of the text and categorized it based on our working metaphor of driving a car.

In our first meetings, we agreed that a metaphor would provide an interpretive frame for describing and charting texts. Patton (1980) makes the point that metaphors serve as "a way of communicating the connotative meanings of the various categories" (pp. 316–17), when qualitative researchers report results, as long as reification is avoided. We experimented with several metaphors, such as downhill skiing, looking for an activity comparable in some ways to writing, and ended up with driving a car. The driver, with a certain destination or purpose in mind, selects a route along which he or she travels, negotiating the twists and turns and demands of the road. Drivers vary in their understanding of the car itself, of the route, and of the strategies for handling curves or rounding corners.

In a similar way, a writer has a certain purpose which he or she strives to fulfill within the constraints and potentials of the route laid out by a particular genre. Writers also vary in their understanding of the language, of the genre, and of the strategies for negotiating textual choice points. We ended up with categories like "car careening out of control," "commuter," and "rallye driver."

Fundamentally this structuring procedure serves to bring a group of readers from a common community together for a concentrated conversation about some particular focus of interest (Carini, 1979), in this case student texts looked at from a developmental perspective. As the following narrative illustrates, our conversation slips in and out of the rules, takes place in far less linear fashion, and works in interanimating ways, both to reveal and to unpack meanings as well as to constitute them. This kind of reading process proved complex and generative.

And *odd*. At Syracuse, teachers had tended in the past to work alone, in a kind of isolation, and to respond to texts primarily as products for diagnostic or evaluative purposes. But for this reading we didn't have to grade essays or place students in appropriate courses or design instructional plans. Our traditional institutional constraints were loosened, the traditional reading framework redefined, and we had time and space and a communal setting to enter into the various textual possibilities of these student texts, to play with those possibilities, to respond *differently* and (as it turned out) expansively to student writing.

In this particular session, halfway through the project, the text we worked on (see Figure 1) had been written as a diagnostic on the first day of Freshman English, prompted by a question like "Compare two movies you have seen recently and evaluate which was better." The following is based on an analysis of a transcript from the taped conversation.

The Conversation

This session begins, as do all our sessions, by reading the text aloud. This one occasions a bit of eye-rolling snickering, and then outright laughter at the "side sticker" line. After having read a number of these diagnostic essays, the dramatic tone and attempted flair of this one strikes us as funny, almost as comic relief. Reading as a group seems to call forth a fuller and more open response. In thinking about it now, I doubt, for example, that I would have laughed aloud as I read this essay alone.

"First paragraph?" Marty begins the paraphrase. "A narrative, an anecdotal beginning. I think that's refreshing, don't you?'' The essay's narrative beginning startles us, jars our expectations as teachers in this particular program. The student writer either doesn't know about standard academic essay introductions or is willing to risk, to experiment, to entertain.

"Now, this student was waiting in line and tells a story about, you know, first occasions at SU and the lengthy lines, people discussing things, and movies came up in the topic of conversation, and she or he *had* to interject her or his own opinion because they were discussing which were the better movies of the summer probably, that's my guess, or at least which were highly entertaining movies. When the writer had a chance to put forth her opinion, she discussed two excellent movies, and doesn't name them here, but goes on with this interesting narrative. I like the word 'wondering,' as though Judith Crist were ready to speak about the two movies of the summer—and that's the introduction.''

In the course of this paraphrase, Marty concludes that the writer is female, and so "she" remained throughout the discussion. She also constructs a new context/voice for this text: Judith Crist providing a clever and dramatic critique of a movie. In a sense, that intertextual connection begins to accord a certain kind of respect to this writer, to provide a context or frame in which the writer succeeds. Marty raises no objections to a possible decision by the writer to move outside the expected genre and to suggest inventively a new one. In fact, she finds it "refreshing" that the writer shifts the diagnostic prompt and the task in this direction.

The paraphrase, which is actually longer than the first paragraph, reconstructs the (imagined) setting and adds the theme of "first occasions" as a focus.

On the tape, Lib's tone of voice in the next part of the paraphrase is ironic, a bit dramatic, as if she is having fun with this essay and its parody of Judith Crist. "The narrative is continued in paragraph two. The suspense is built in paragraph one, and we finally find out what the two movies are. They are *Airplane* and *Caddyshack,* much to the amazement of the audience. Discussion of the two movies in this group of people centered on the fact that both were funny and both were popular, but also some liked only one of them, and some hated them both. Then we have a transitional sentence here, moving from the narrative introduction into the body of the paper.''

Along with the other readers, Lib enters into the possibilities of playfulness provided by the text, taking pleasure in the effort at suspense and willing to go along with it, despite its artifice and awkwardness—or perhaps because of it.

Lib's paraphrase adds "writing teacher terminology" to our talk about the text, with words such as "narrative," "transitional sentence," and "body of the paper." She also uses the passive voice at one point. I suspect that, indirectly, this use of technical language served to attribute implicitly a kind of competence to the writer, a sense of intentionality and a knowledge of the possible choices and decisions, as if this, too, is how the writer thought of it.

Delia continues the paraphrase: "Well, she goes on to 'transist' to the discussion of *Caddyshack,* which the writer found very amusing, not confusing even though there were lots of things going on at the same time. The actors were fantastic. And there was a gopher in the movie with whom the writer fell in love. And she rates this movie very highly but feels conclusively that *Airplane* is somewhat better."

The reader's addition of the word "conclusively" indicates how the readers are responding to a voice, a strong voice, in the text, cued perhaps by the hyperbolic adjectives, the straightforward sentence structure in the claims, and the many uses of "I." The text creates a strong or loud sense of author and authority.

"Well," Don says, picking up the paraphrase, "then she goes on to the discussion of *Airplane,* and it definitely affects this writer with a knife slashing . . . ?"

"I think she means 'side-splitting,'" Lib adds.

"I wondered if it was a colloquial expression. I never heard of it," Delia says. "Or she might mean 'a stitch.'"

Don finishes the essay, summing up the last line by saying, "This is definitely opinionated, of course, and we get the advice again to see both movies if you're in the mood for a great comedy." At this point in the project, we have seen the opinion disclaimer/advice often, almost as a standard ending, reminiscent to us of the nearly mandatory ending of the elementary school book report that invites readers to read the book themselves and form their own opinions. We have come to see this as a tag ending, a formula tacked on as an automatic conclusion for each and every essay.

Moving into the next phase of the reading, Delia begins to draw inferences. "I like the way it begins. . . . I'm sure the assignment was 'Pick two movies you've seen recently and pick one that is better.'

There's a real imaginative attempt to make it with a narrative. I don't think that I was laughing at this student, but with her. I'd like to meet this kid.''

The focus of our conversation shifts from features of the text's content and tone to the (imagined) features of the context in which it was written. We are now ''reading'' that first day of the fall semester when a student writer, new to the university and having been hit with a diagnostic writing task, had opted to try an imaginative or creative introduction. Aware as writing teachers of the kinds of constraints that operate in those situations, we acknowledge here a respect for a writer who rebelled or at least took a chance, even one that failed in ways. The response also reveals a kind of defensiveness about having laughed, about having perhaps made fun of a student who was new to the university and its ways of talking, who was in transition.

Three years later, I wonder now if that defensiveness also marked a point of identification—that we, too, as teachers in a rapidly changing program, were in transition, moving between paradigms, straddling two worlds, and sensing our vulnerability to the same charge of naïveté as this new writer was.

The body or second half of the essay, as we came to call it, reveals to us that the writer was aware at least in a general way of the conventions called forth by this task—claims, evidence of some sort, argument or opinion. Even in the anecdotal beginning, as Delia comments, ''There's a real tension between the diction and the intent in the opening paragraph, because I think she wants to be humorous and yet is writing 'an English paper,' so there's a little bit of an attempt at high-sounding diction (e.g., 'I refused to listen to the conversation without voicing my opinion'). And yet that works in service of the humor at the same time. And this writer never loses the thread of the narrative. I wonder about the overstatement of her judgment of the movies, giving rise to our somewhat funny perception of nascent Judith Crist. It's nice. There is a whole little setting for the essay.''

We respond here to the multiple voices in the text—to the conversational and comic voice of the storyteller, the more formal or high-sounding voice of the academic critic, the dramatic voice of the movie reviewer, and the strained voice of the new student trying to fulfill an assignment and (presumably) impress the teacher. The essay, basically, pulls in several directions, yet rather than evaluate that as a failure, we are at this point in the reading more than willing to credit the writer with a range or repertoire of voices and a spirit of risk taking and playfulness.

It seems to me now, as I read the transcript and listen to the tape three years later, that we were reading this essay in relationship not only to the more traditional and "duller" responses other students had more typically provided in these pre–Freshman English essays, but also in relationship to the testing context that none of us approved of or valued. The choices this writer made were read as imaginative, perhaps even rebellious, and they were not considered to be a means of avoiding the assignment or to be a misreading of what the task called for. Again, I sense in retrospect a strong identification with the imagined writer. As we constructed her, so we also constructed ourselves.

The readers' conversation now moves into summative and positive talk about the writer's "engaging style," her sense "that an introduction is supposed to introduce the topic and catch the reader's attention," the coherence and logical sequencing of the claims.

"Technically, it's competent," we conclude. "It shows a student with potential. There's a facility here."

"If this writer learns to provide some real concrete evidence, I think she will be well on her way. A pretty good writer."

From initial and somewhat embarrassed laughter, into a playful paraphrase or enactment of the text, we have hit a moment of closure and have moved into a summative evaluation of the writer based primarily on her textual choices as read against the backdrop of the writing-as-testing context. We have invented a writer who in many ways reflects our values and have given her our communal stamp of approval.

But we still have more time, and as our talk continues, we start to raise questions and problems. "But any good review [the genre we had now located this text in] would bring out some details, or discuss why it is a satire at a higher level than *Caddyshack*," Marty points out. "When you make an assertion, then some concrete exemplification makes it stronger. And wouldn't these kids, if they were standing in line, say, 'Do you remember when . . . ?' They wouldn't say generalities all night. Students would get to specifics."

Having agreed in some sense to judge this writer as "pretty good," the readers move into a more critical assessment of the writer's choices here. Even in the terms of her own narrative, there are problems, we decide, with credibility and development.

Another reader then describes the mixing of voices or personas as a problem with control. Another wonders if this strategy wasn't a "cop-out," a clever way to use a fictional audience to get out of the demands her real audience was making on her. Specifics are missing, and that, Don points out, "gives us a sense of where this writer is and how she defines audience."

The writer has been reconstructed now almost as a "basic writer" in the Bartholomae (1986) definition of the term, as a writer pulling on fragments of different voices and interpretive schemes from different discourse communities, producing a kind of patchwork quilt text. She has presented herself as a storyteller and movie critic (and hence as a capable student writer able to work effectively with this task)—but only to an extent. Rather than "imaginative," her choices now seem to us more desperate and defensive.

But, we go on, she was willing to give this task an energetic try. In that way, too, she exhibits two other qualities of the writers Bartholomae describes: patience and good will. Further, we conclude, the task was harder than it looks. In fifty minutes, with no instruction, a student had to identify two movies, preferably ones that were appropriate to talk about in a university setting (i.e., ones that deserve "serious" consideration), draw on a discourse that she may have had limited experience with, and then rely on her memory for details and evidence.

We had been struck earlier in our reading by the ideological pressures in the diagnostic task. When a student elected to compare "M*A*S*H*" and "Perry Mason," for example, she was told by the instructor at the close of the final summative comment "to consider the assignment—i.e., 'of two *good* shows choose the one that is best [emphasis added by instructor].' "

Our conversation continues, circling back to talk about how and why the text *did* work, but now in more text-specific ways. We agree that the text got our attention and respect, that it engaged us, even though it was flawed in many ways. "She does communicate something," Don noted. "A lot of things that have to do with sound—listen, speak, conversation, voices, voicing, silence. Then we move into the interior, into feeling—amusing, confusing, fantastic, love, feel, and hilarious. So on the one hand, it's very fundamental, very basic, using sense perceptions to develop some kind of descriptive essay. But on the other hand, it leads to some sophistication because it drives into the interior of this person for a few, bright moments. It drives into the personality of the individual somehow.''

"Yeah," Lib adds, "and you even hear some excitement—here's a possibility, I'll start this way. Enthusiasm.''

"With a subtle logical structure to it, too," Don points out.

"And the sentence structure seems quite varied, although there are lapses and strange repetitions ('fell fell') in the hurry of writing. But some dependent clauses, like the beginning of the first paragraph, and the verbal at the end of it. I also like the use of 'I' in 'I, of course,'" Marty concludes.

At this moment in the reading, we move back into an appreciation of an imagined writer making effective choices about how to work this assignment. Writer and intentionality begin to dominate our discussion about this text. The writer has a ''voice'' that registers excitement, that sounds personable, that makes the writer increasingly real to the group of readers. The sixteen uses of ''I'' forcefully locate the author's presence in the text. Against the context of the writing situation, and cued and orchestrated by certain textual features, we have constructed a writer whom we like a lot. I suspect now that we would have constructed a very different writer had the context been different—had, for example, this text been a take-home essay in the middle of the semester. Then she might have ''sounded'' sloppy, lazy, careless, indeed taking a clever cop-out.

Again, the readers move into a conclusion and decide that the writer has made some smart choices: She has picked movies that she has actually seen, that *are* similar in certain ways, and that she has (apparently) strong and genuine opinions about.

"But this question of choices becomes curious then," Don argues, "because if we have these students with this option of choices here, what motivates that choice? 'I have read *Anthem* and *1984* last year, and I only saw one movie this summer . . .' So even though the mode of popular discourse is what the student is really in tune with, all of a sudden. 'I'm in college now, higher education, and this *is* English class . . .'''

The tensions return. We are not fully comfortable with this communal decision. One reader commented later that, in engaging in dialogue like this, he often felt a tension among what he saw/read/felt in the text, what his colleagues saw/read/felt, and what was actually being voiced in the group. In this case the group's overtly positive reaction to this text and writer shut down certain critical responses, yet the text was flawed in ways that kept announcing themselves and demanding our attention.

But, again, we want to give this writer a break. After all, we agree, it was the first day of college, the students had been asked to write what was clearly a diagnostic essay for an as-yet-unknown teacher, and the assignment set up mixed messages. On the one hand, it called forth popular discourse of movie reviews (and hence the voice of Judith Crist), yet it was also assigned in the context of an English class and thus also—and conflictually—called forth academic discourse.

And in a sense, this writer provides a bit of both. As Marty says, "She could have done a 'The two movies *Airplane* and *Caddyshack* have similarities and differences,'" but instead she goes with this "wonderful narrative opening." We conclude yet again that she writes forcefully, with humor and playfulness, and perhaps with a sense of confidence and trust—trust that her audience will respond positively to her choices and efforts here.

We speculate that this writer has had experience writing to an audience that has encouraged her. We are dismayed as we further imagine what this writer's response might have been to a "No Pass" stamped loudly across the top of the paper, with the following summative comment:

> The thesis should come in the 1st paragraph—structurally—though you don't follow Baker[2]—you are organized—However, there is no conclusion, the introduction is too long and involved. The development is weak—and you offer little concrete support—be sure to give specific evidence for any generalizations.

It is easy for us at this point, given our frustration with a program that demanded "Baker" before it had even been taught and that rubber-stamped comments and evaluative judgments in this formal and formulaic way, to feel even more identified with and supportive of this "refreshing" writer.

With a bit more discussion, we assign this writer to the "rallye driver" category of our typology, despite the evident problems with development and organization in the essay. This writer, as we have come to see her, convinces us that she is a risk taker, a writer with potential, with a sense, if nascent, of the imaginative possibilities of written language. In terms of the metaphor we are working with, she seems to know how to rev up the car and tackle a complex course, willing to negotiate the twists and turns of unfamiliar terrain, with a certain kind of bravado and flair and ability and confidence.

"This is a definite writer," Marty sums up. "Knows what she wants to say and isn't afraid to say it. She plays. She trusts her voice, she trusts her skills, and she trusts a positively responding audience. And she makes effective choices, given the constraints of the task."

"Tempos of Meaning"

In "Writing Time," James T. Zebroski (in manuscript) discusses the role of time in reading and writing, the effect of temporality on the way a text is defined and hence on the way a text "means." He calls it "the tempos of meaning." He argues, for example, that "The close reader reads an entirely different text in a completely different time warp from the holistic scorer" (p. 19).

And it is *time* that Carini's reflective procedures provide—time for readers to come at a text from multiple perspectives, to engage with and dwell in the materiality of that text, to construct a writer cued by textual choices, to remember one's own writing experiences and to imagine the writer's current one, to read and reread the possibilities presented by the text against the imagined context of the writing situation and against the comments of other readers.

The reflective procedures also create a communal reading. At the end of the project, in fact, readers reported pleasure in this kind of shared time with a text and in the experience of breaking out of the lonely, labor-intensive grading cycle teachers often find themselves locked into. One reader concluded: "The opportunity to discuss writing and teaching philosophies with a peer group was a real treat—it was fun, intellectually stimulating, and educational." Another noted: "For me personally, the reading experience itself was unique and pedagogically rewarding. Although I regularly read papers for the Educational Testing Service [for the College Board and CLEP exams], I have never before analyzed writing so intensively."

Three years later, one reader suggested further that the process of reading as a group provided a more expansive and hence more complex reading: "What was prevalent and popular in the group, among the cacophony of voices, does not gain narrative courage in quiet, secular reading. Do we lose a sense of play? We relocate, in our individual reading, an identity of conventional rhetoric bounded and shackled by audience of self." He speculated that private readings tend to close off an awareness of codes or competing codes and tend to push toward those that match our own.

Reading together also allowed us to invent and reinvent ourselves as a group and as individuals, to make visible the beliefs and attitudes we held, to define our roles in the academic place. "Now," one reader noted, "the writer and the text are less important. I want to know more about those readers"—and what has happened to them during the changes in the new program.

In this particular conversation, as in all of the others, there were various "moments" in the reading, shifts in attention and feeling and focus. The process was complex and multilayered. The definition and meanings of the text changed across and through time, often in conflicting ways. And through our communal enterprise, in response to different texts, and against the context of the changes going on at Syracuse, we constructed and reconstructed ourselves as a group of readers.

Initially the point in the text that opened up space for dialogue was the phrase "side sticker." Unsure of its actual meaning and amused by its location in a first-day college diagnostic essay, we were intrigued and "refreshed" by its use. Its colloquial quality startled us and invited us into the semantic space shared by readers and writers via text (Nystrand, 1982). In our paraphrase, we responded to the text with playfulness and dramatic irony. We shared the words and phrases with each other as if they were lines from a play that we were performing. In a sense, we enacted the essay, and the text became a *script* for us to say aloud, to activate with our emphases, to entertain each other with. We took pleasure in our voices reading the text, enlarging the scene of text and writer at Syracuse.

The text also opened up a space for *us* to be "rallye drivers" of sorts, to be different teachers from the ones we were accustomed to being and to take some risks with our reading.

Yet at other points the text held us out. The last two paragraphs, for example, even over time, did not invite our participation as the narrative beginning had. The more "academic" she tried to be, the less we "liked" her. We commented on problems, envisioned student-teacher conferences in which we would talk about evidence and illustration to back up rather hollow claims. No longer playful, our responses to the text became serious, and we became teacherly. Now the text became a *draft,* a record of an incomplete process in which we wanted, as teachers, to intervene. Possibilities for revision and instruction occupied us, as we entered the text as teachers fretting about the problems a writer presented to us.

This position alternated with one in which the text was defined as a *product,* an example of what a writer could do, and we became judges, evaluating this product as flawed in certain ways, successful in others. We read the text then as revealing a writer's competence or knowledge of written language discourse conventions and genres. It was then that we saw this writer as falling possibly into the basic writer category.

But perhaps most frequently, we read the text as a *sign,* to which we reacted ideologically, taking a socio-political-historical stance in our reading. We were reading all these essays from within a specific institutional setting at a particular time in its history and from a particular point of view. Our reading project was embedded within a larger project that was aimed at reviewing and (we assumed) criticizing the pedagogical and theoretical model of writing instruction that had dominated writing instruction at Syracuse for more than ten years. We were opposed to the basic theory of development in that program, we were opposed to the writing-as-testing pedagogy, and we were opposed to the stultifying overemphasis on form that had resulted in this program. So, "naturally," we read this writer's choices from a point of identification and saw her text as an act of rebellion and as a sign of the failure of the program to make space for divergent writers and for imaginative, risk-taking texts— and, of course, for divergent teachers and imaginative, risk-taking teaching. One reader wondered later "how much resonance of anarchy toward the then-present paradigm flavored [this particular] reading? Were we truly trying to set up relations of power rather than meaning?" Those points of identification, of course, shifted with each reflection and each text and writer, allowing us to read from multiple points of view over the course of the project.

However, overall, in the process of reading together, we did construct ourselves into a rather particular group of readers, a group that came to value expressivity and voice. Having worked in and against a writing program that pushed product, we were refreshed by [or we "re-freshed"] this text, I suspect now, because we were open to a personalized text, to the individualized stance this writer adopted in her response to this writing task. We were enlarging the possibilities of text and writer (and teacher) at Syracuse. In this case, we constructed a writer, a presence or felt sense in the text, and then rewarded her, albeit a bit ambiguously, with our communal stamp of approval, while at the same time we condemned a writing task (and hence a writing program) that demanded a certain kind of conformity and conventionality from its students. This writer became, for us, imaginative and natural—values that were not legitimate in the old program at that time, values resonant with the very impulses and beliefs about language that had originally drawn us into working as writing teachers in the first place. In this sense, the project enabled us, forced us, to recognize more explicitly the position from which we were reading not only the student texts but the overall writing program, too. And it enabled us to acknowledge, in ways, the romantic and empowering mirage of self that was part of the change going on—our selves, the writer's self, the political self.

Three years later, with that romantic impulse played out somewhat and from a greater intellectual understanding of the social aspects of composing, I read this writer now as unaware of the discourse community she has joined, naive, with only a fragmentary sense of the intellectual and discursive demands of the writing task. For better or worse, I am less willing to enjoy this essay or to categorize this writer as a rallye driver. For me, the text has become a different sign, a sign of the problematic tension between self-expression and conventionality that informs first year writing courses. I hear the polyphony in the text—the voice of the storyteller, the nascent Judith Crist, the fourth-grade book report writer, the academic arguer, and the nervous entering student. While I recognize and celebrate that coherence hasn't been achieved through the suppressing or silencing of these multiple voices, as in so many other essays written in the Freshman English paper voice, I recognize at the same time that the voices may be garbled and cacophonous, the tensions not worked through or perhaps even acknowledged.

I wish I had a chance to talk this new observation through with the group of readers, to open up dialogue again, to play out the further possibilities such a reading would enable for understanding this writer, the writing task, our position now as readers, the changing context at Syracuse.

I wish there were more time.

Figure 1. Student Text

As I was waiting in one of the many lengthy lines I have encountered at Syracuse University, a group of students began discussing the various movies they had seen recently. Some movies were thought of very highly by some people, while others detested them. I, of course, refused to listen to this conversation without voicing my own opionion. When I got a chance to speak, I immediately told them that I had seen two excellent movies this summer, but one was slightly better than the other. Everyone stared at me in silence, wondering what which movies I had chosen to discuss.

When I told them I was referring to *Airplane* and *Caddyshack,* a roar of voices arose. Many people agreed that both movies were very funny and that they would even see them again. Others only liked one of the two, and a few hated them both. As the noise began to die down I then decided to tell them which I preferred.

Caddyshack was a very amusing movie. Many different things were going on at the same time, but it was not confusing at all. The actors were fantastic and they contributed greatly to its success. The was also a little gopher in the movie, which I fell fell in love with instantly. As you can see I rated this movie highly, but I fell that *Airplane* is slightly better.

This movie was so hilarious that I came out of the theatre with a side sticker from laughing. Every scene contains something worth laughing at. *Airplane* is a mockery of the many other airplane disaster movies. Other movies may leave you in tears because of sorrow, but this one will have you laughing so hard you'll cry. This is my opinion and I would definitely advise everyone to see both movies if your in the mood for a great comedy.

The Person Speaking

4

Bakhtin:
Language as Hero in Early
Written Language Development

M. M. Bakhtin's name comes up often these days, as literary critic, social thinker, and philosopher of language, with concepts like "heteroglossia," "utterance," "dialogism," and "voice" turning up regularly in articles on composition. Brought most forcefully to our attention by Kristeva and Todorov, his work rapidly achieved prominence among language theorists. "The first recognition in the United States of Bakhtin's status as major thinker came in 1968, when he was included among a group of internationally known theoreticians contributing to a volume of *Yale French Studies*. . . . Less than a mere two decades later, Bakhtin is being hailed as 'the most important Soviet thinker in the human sciences and the greatest theoretician of literature in the twentieth century'" (Holquist, Introduction, *Speech Genres,* 1986, p. ix).

Bakhtin has entered our intellectual tradition.

I have been interested in how this powerful theory of language puts pressure on the premises we have traditionally worked from, often implicitly, in studying early written language development. I have also been convinced that Bakhtin complements (in complex and useful ways) Patricia Carini's approach to understanding children as makers of works. For this chapter, I have focused my reading primarily on *The Dialogic Imagination* (1981), *Speech Genres and Other Late Essays* (1986), and *Marxism and the Philosophy of Language* (Volosinov/Bakhtin, 1986),[1] along with Clark and Holquist's background book entitled *Mikhail Bakhtin* (1984)—and I have read these key texts as a developmental language theorist might.

Reading Bakhtin from this position, of course, results in relocating his ideas into a different context, using his theory to open up new intellectual or methodological horizons for those of us interested in children's writing. There are obvious risks in this enterprise: wrenching concepts out of context, simplifying ideas, applying literary theory to children's writing, or not fully exploring the consequences and tensions of his (arguably) utopic vision of language use and change.

I offer this speculative reading of Bakhtin in order to theorize (and complicate) our conception of the role of language itself in early written language development. I also present his work at this point in the argument as a responding voice to Carini, juxtaposed yet complementary. Bakhtin serves as a cautionary tale, an alternative perspective, a guard against too individualized a focus in language development research. Bakhtin's theory insists that we embed expressiveness and works within social, political, and cultural contexts, and offers a position from which to acknowledge more fully not only the dynamism and generativeness of language use but also the repressive and authoritative power of dominant voices.

I want to play out the theoretical possibilities from Bakhtin for analyzing language as "hero" in early written language development. I also want to speculate about the value (or perhaps even necessity now) in research design of shifting from a psychological object toward a semiotic subject of study. Lastly, I want to consider briefly Bakhtinian concepts such as "understanding" and "outsideness," as critical to constructing a framework for investigating children's writing that takes language use ("utterance" or "work") as its starting point.

Language as Shared Territory

> The utterance is a social phenomenon. (*Marxism*, p. 82)

Historically, according to the argument developed in *Marxism*, theories of language end up privileging either one side or the other in the "individual-social equation." Ultimately language comes to be defined either as a creative medium for individual self-expression or as a normative and stable social system of phonetic, grammatical, and lexical forms. In what Volosinov/Bakhtin calls "individualistic subjectivism," theorists have defined language as "an unceasing process of creation realized in individual speech acts" (p. 48). The source of language is the private individual psyche, as it finds expression for its inner thoughts and images in and through the medium of language, and the linguists' task is to determine the psychological laws that govern this ongoing, endlessly variable creative process. In "abstract objectivism," however, the focus shifts from the idiosyncratic and unique in utterances to those elements that are identical and normative in all utterances. The source of language is the system, and the linguists' task is to determine the linguistic laws that connect signs within any particular closed linguistic system (p. 57). Individual utterances are uncategorizable and fortuitous variations of normatively identical forms. So generally theorists end up studying either individual speech acts or the system of language—but not both.

It's a problem familiar to writing researchers. In *GNYS AT WRK* (1980), for example, Bissex tries to navigate this equation by concluding rather broadly (and vaguely) that learning to write is a process "shaped by more comprehensive patterns of human growth and learning" (p. 200) yet has individual variation based on personality and personal meaning. Dyson (1985) tries more specifically to correlate "the nature of the individual child, the nature of the situational context, and the complex nature of the writing system itself" (p. 59) into an explanation of the process of written language growth. Yet in both studies those connections remain rather unconvincingly elaborated. I know the problem and have had related difficulties in writing documentary accounts of young writers (Himley, 1986a, 1986b, 1988). We find ourselves reading children's texts either as expressive of a particular child's intellectual and imaginative world, as having personal meaning and intention, or as evidence of larger, perhaps universal principles of cognitive development or language learning (e.g., the patterns in invented spelling)—but we have difficulty working both sides of this equation simultaneously.[2]

It is Saussure in particular who has drawn this dichotomy most forcefully, in sharply contrasting *langue* from *parole*:

> In distinguishing language (*langue*) from utterance (*parole*), we by the same token distinguish (1) what is social from what is individual, and (2) what is essential from what is accessory and random.
>
> Language is not a function of the speaker; it is a product that the individual registers passively. . . .
>
> Utterance, on the contrary, is an individual act of will and intelligence in which we must distinguish between (1) combinations through which a speaker utilizes a particular language code for expressing his own personal thoughts, and (2) the psychophysical mechanism that enables him to exteriorize those combinations. (as cited in *Marxism*, p. 60)

For Saussure, linguistic theory is premised upon a deep and insistent opposition between language as social and utterance as individual.

The key—and very complex—move in the Bakhtinian analysis is to collapse this dichotomy by insisting upon the social nature of utterance:

> The speech act, or more accurately, its product—the utterance, cannot under any circumstances be considered an individual phenomenon in the precise meaning of the word and cannot be explained in terms of the individual psychological or psychophysiological conditions of the speaker. *The utterance is a social phenomenon.* (*Marxism,* p. 82)

As Nystrand (1986) sums this argument up, "Bakhtin sought an account of language as neither intention-driven expression nor abstract system, but rather 'the product of the reciprocal relationship between speaker and listener'" (pp. 34–35). For Bakhtin, language becomes utterance and takes on meaning in the social process and in the social context of actual speech communication, in the semiotic territory shared by the speaker/writer and listener/reader, in the space in between two socially organized individuals.

Language, for Bakhtin, is social through and through.

And *social* in Bakhtin means at least three things. First of all, it refers to language as the shared common denominator embracing both the individual and the social, a common territory for constructing both the individual psyche and the social structures of meaning.[3] Language is the third and overarching term in the individual-social equation. Through social interaction and verbal communication, the individual is drawn into public and cultural spheres of meaning, assimilating words and worldviews or ideologies,[4] deriving and nurturing an inner wor(l)d sedimented from the language communication process itself. According to this argument, "the personality of the speaker, taken from within, so to speak, turns out to be wholly a product of social interrelations. Not only its outward expression, but also its inner experience are shared territory" (*Marxism,* p. 90). Subjectivity itself, therefore, has a social dimension and basis.

Furthermore, it is through such verbal interaction that the social is drawn into the particular individual and continues to live and change—as an ongoing part of his or her private inner world and speech. Thus, it is through the shared process of language use, and through other cultural practices of signification, that the social is actualized, and the individual is realized, in what Volosinov/Bakhtin calls "a continuous dialectical interplay" (*Marxism,* p. 39).

Thus, language, for Bakhtin, is neither completely free and creative nor completely totalizing. Indeed, as Bauer (1988) notes with cautious optimism in *Feminist Dialogics:*

> Bakhtin posits a linguistic community in which the norms are always in flux, always open to renegotiation as those conventions are called into dialogic conflict. . . . Language is not merely a prison house; it does not only cage human potential (although it does that, too), but also produces eruptions of force which do not always follow the norms or conventions that language commands. The very language which restricts human intercourse produces occasions for its own disruption and critique. (pp. xii–xiii)

It is the contextualized dialogue—with its situatedness and orientation to otherness—that allows for resistance and change and individuation.

This dynamic diversity in language is characterized as *heteroglossia,* Bakhtin's master trope and the intellectual center for all his projects. The term refers to the unceasing, living diversity and ontological plurality within a language—for example, the social dialects, professional jargons, generic languages, languages of generations and age groups, and so on (*Dialogic,* pp. 262–63). Each language or voice in heteroglossia is grounded in different principles for organizing a view of the world: for example, the Ukrainian language, the language of the epic poem, the language of the student all cut the world up differently and hence intersect with each other in many different ways (*Dialogic,* p. 291). This linguistic diversity reflects and (re)produces the diversity within the culture. In this sense, then, language is an embattled territory, full of conflicting voices and ideologies, full of convergences and divergences and contradictions. Not a passive or neutral medium, language is full of contest for Bakhtin, "an almost Manichean sense of opposition and struggle" (*Dialogic,* p. xviii), a complementing and conflicting of words and worldviews.[5] These various languages encounter one another and exist in the consciousnesses of real people. Thus, to use language—to speak or to write—is always and inevitably to participate in this social, historical dialogue.

Second, all utterances are *social* in that the actual social situation determines the shape, or genre, and hence the meaning of the utterance. Meaning, for Bakhtin, is radically contextualized: "The meaning of a word is determined entirely by its context. In fact, there are as many meanings of a word as there are contexts of its usage'' (*Marxism,* p. 79). Even a simple utterance like ''What time is it?'' will sound like a demand or a request depending on the history and power relationships of the participants, the social setting in which the request is made, and the other utterances surrounding it. It will ''mean'' differently each time.

But concrete utterances also resonate with—and thus implicate—dimensions of the broader cultural milieu. ''The immediate social situation and its immediate social participants determine the 'occasional' form and style of an utterance,'' Volosinov/Bakhtin concludes, but ''[t]he deeper layers of its structure are determined by more sustained and more basic social connections with which the speaker is in contact'' (*Marxism,* p. 87). Each actual language event, therefore, is coextensive with large cultural patterns and networks of meaning: ''Each separate utterance is individual, of course, but each sphere in which language is used develops its own relatively stable types of these utterances. These we may call speech genres'' (*Speech Genres,* p. 60). It is genres, according to Bakhtin, that make speech communication possible, because ''we learn to cast our speech in generic forms and, when hearing others' speech, we guess its genre from the very first words; we predict a certain length (that is, the approximate length of the speech whole) and a certain compositional structure; we foresee the end'' (*Speech Genres,* p. 79).

Third, *social* also refers to the dialogic nature of language and language use, a key concept in Bakhtinian theory. According to the argument in *Marxism,* one problem with traditional linguistics, especially when working from certain psychological theories of expression, is that the private monologic utterance has been taken as the object of study, and it has been treated as an individual act or as the expression of an individual consciousness, with its particular ambitions, intentions, creative impulses, tastes, and so on, separate from its context both situationally and culturally. It stands—and means—alone.

For Bakhtin, however, utterances are always oriented toward others—that is, they are always dialogic in nature. The utterance, he argues, is always directed toward an addressee—toward specific audiences such as a particular friend or toward a more general class of possible readers, and toward a super-addressee, the other who will understand and respond. It is therefore mutually constructed, collaboratively composed, in the space between the speaker/writer and listener/reader. As Volosinov/Bakhtin says, "I give myself verbal shape from another's point of view, ultimately from the point of view of the community to which I belong. . . . A word is [interindividual] territory shared by both addressor and addressee, by the speaker and his interlocutor" (*Marxism,* p. 86). So an utterance is shaped not only by who speaks/writes but also in anticipation of who listens/reads.

Furthermore, a speaker draws words from a shared social stock of words, from words used in other contexts to express others' accents and intonations and meanings. As Bakhtin says, "The word in language is half someone else's. It becomes 'one's own' only when the speaker populates it with his own intention, his own accent, when he appropriates the word, adapting it to his own semantic and expressive intention" (*Dialogic,* p. 293). In fact, Bakhtin talks about the *three* participants in a discourse event: the speaker, the listener, and the language (the "hero") itself, all presented as participating in the making of meaning (see Schuster, 1985). Language then comes populated with the meanings of others, full of echoes and traces, and is not some neutral, pliable medium readily adapted to one's own intentions and purposes. "One's own discourse," according to Bakhtin, "is gradually and slowly wrought out of others' words that have been acknowledged and assimilated, and the boundaries between the two are at first scarcely perceptible" (*Dialogic,* p. 345).

Language use is dialogic, too, in that each utterance, from the single word to a large work of literature, is a response to—and resonates with—other related utterances. So, for example, any particular narrative account implicates other narrative accounts, and this intertextual relationship shapes its length, boundaries, content: "Each utterance is filled with echoes and reverberations of other utterances to which it is related by the communality of the sphere of speech communication" (*Speech Genres,* p. 91).

Therefore, language in Bakhtinean theory is social, a shared territory, in at least three ways. (1) Language is the shared semiotic medium for both the individual and the culture, through which they interanimate each other. "The ideological sign," according to Volosinov/Bakhtin, "is the common territory for both the psyche and for ideology, a territory that is material, sociological, and meaningful" (*Marxism,* p. 33). (2) The meaning of language is radically contextual, shaped not only by the immediate social relations and situation but also implicated within larger cultural and historical connections. (3) Language is always dialogic, addressed historically to the meanings and uses that have preceded it, addressed in the moment to the anticipated responsive understanding of the other. "The word," then, "is [also] a territory shared by both addressor and addressee" (*Marxism,* p. 86).

Written Language Development as Social

Written language development, from this theoretical perspective, can be broadly characterized as a complex social-psychological process of assimilation and resistance, more or less creative, of the words of others, that takes place in and through the shared territory of actual language use and that results in the expressing and constituting of self (or selves). The developing child is no longer constructed as an autonomous, unitary subject, unfolding according to nature's plan, but rather as an irreducibly social subject, nurtured by and oriented toward social interaction and speech communication—that is, toward language in use. To cite Bakhtin yet again: "I live in a world of others' words. And my entire life is an orientation in this world, a reaction to others' words (an infinitely diverse reaction), beginning with my assimilation of them (in the process of initial mastery of speech) and ending with assimilation of the wealth of human culture (expressed in the word or in other semiotic material)" (*Speech Genres,* p. 143).

To learn to write, then, is not merely to acquire a new symbolic means for expressing one's private thoughts and ideas, but rather to learn about, to assimilate, and to come to own (or at least rent) the very meanings one can have. It is also to fight other meanings, to resist, to want words but not finally to have them.

This theoretical perspective challenges the expressive realism and the concept of an autonomous subject that is implicit in much early written language development research. In some research and pedagogy, for example, children are encouraged first to think about experiences from their lives, jot down notes, and generate a text that conveys that experience, while it holds the readers' attention—as if writing were mostly a matter of finding the right words for rather directly, and without mediation, making one's point clearly and effectively. The novice writer, in this account, appears primarily to be discovering new ways to mean, to be exercising his or her expressive and intentional capabilities in a new medium. Thus, this account ends up postulating a relatively univocal and simple relationship of an autonomous writer to a monolithic language through which he or she can come to realize his or her intentions in a fairly direct way (see *Dialogic*, p. 269).

But not a thing that simply articulates the intention of the speaker, nor a direct and single-voiced vehicle for self-expression (*Dialogic*, p. 355), language in Bakhtin becomes a very complex, semiotic process—of individuating and participating, of assimilating and appropriating (and of being appropriated by) others' words. Bakhtin therefore puts pressure on researchers to begin to think much more explicitly about what it means to learn to write—that is, to work in this *particular* medium, as opposed, for example, to learning to draw or do math. He raises questions about what happens to our understanding of language development when language itself is conceptualized as hero, as a dynamic and generative and in many ways determining participant in the language process itself.

But how do we go about describing and understanding such a complexly interactive and reciprocal assimilation process?[6] Can—or should—the parts of the process be separated out for analysis? Is Bakhtin too utopian? to what extent does language control and create a false sense of individuation? How do we study children's texts as particular and meaningful utterances in any systematic way? How do we talk about children's texts as simultaneously social and individual?

I/Other

> Consciousness takes shape and being in the material of signs created by an organized group in the process of social intercourse. (*Marxism*, p. 13)

Basic to Bakhtin's theory of language is his account of the ''I/other,'' an account that rests squarely upon an irreducible duality conceived in terms of the need to share being. We are born into a world populated, even overpopulated, with texts, with the words and meanings and accents and intentions and voices of others. It is through this richly polyphonic, or ''meaning-full,'' world, through the appropriating and owning of others' words, and through the resisting of those words, that the child achieves his or her individuality or personhood. The individual psyche is ''nurtured on signs; it derives its growth from them; it reflects their logic and laws, . . . [it is] a tenant lodging in the social edifice of ideological signs'' (*Marxism*, p. 13).

This is a strongly argued case for a deep mutuality and reciprocity between the individual and the social, enacted over and over again through actual, concrete language use.

Through social interaction and language use, the individual comes into being, in ways that are originally and fundamentally and irreducibly social. An individual's sense of self (or selves) comes from without, through reciprocal relationships with the world and with social experiences of meaning, and not from within, as in romantic accounts of sovereign egos. Clark and Holquist (1984) sum this up by saying that "as the world needs my alterity to give it meaning, I need the authority of others to define, or *author,* my self. The other is in the deepest sense my friend, because it is only from the other that I can get my self" (p. 65, emphasis added).

This self or I/other then becomes less a bounded entity and more an open semiotic process of authoring—a response to the world, an answerability, never whole or complete, always changing, ever permeable and ambiguous. For Bakhtin, "my self is that which through [deeds and works and] performance answers other selves and the world from the unique place and time I occupy in existence" (Clark and Holquist, 1984, p. 64).

Clark and Holquist (1984) claim that "Bakhtin is the only major [postromantic] figure to frame the [I/other] problem in terms of *authorship.* He is distinguished not by his emphasis on the self/other dichotomy as such but rather by his emphasis on the essentially authorial techniques of dialogue and character formation which permit the poles of consciousness to interact while maintaining their fundamental difference from each other" (p. 80, emphasis added). Dialogic interaction bridges the gap between the individual and the social, between the I and the other. So consciousness for Bakhtin always lies, then, in the border zones between the individual's own living particularity, and the abstract and anonymous reality of the social system and language (Clark and Holquist, 1984, p. 91).

But this theoretical notion of the I/other raises lots of difficult questions. How can an individual person be unique and yet also incorporate so much that is shared with others? Is a person the sum of diverse language events? What accounts for our sense of the continuity in the person? How are heteroglot discourses and multiple voices held together in the person? Blurred in deep and ambiguous ways, how can the individual and the social now be delimited? How do they interact? How does this help us to understand actual texts, actual children, actual development? And how might writing researchers work with a theoretical notion of an I/other authoring texts as an object of study?

Studying Language Use: Utterances and Works

> The authentic environment of an utterance, the environment in which it lives and takes shape, is dialogized heteroglossia, anonymous and social as language, but simultaneously concrete, filled with specific content and accented as an individual utterance. (*Dialogic*, p. 272)

Bakhtin describes what he calls the "ideological becoming of a human being [as] the process of selectively assimilating the words of others" (*Dialogic*, p. 341), but he says little about how that process occurs in terms of actual social-psychological development, or how to talk about it in terms of actual children becoming writers. He does, however, direct us to utterance as the unit of analysis to work with. He directs us, that is, to concrete language use and thus to the moment of the authoring process that takes place within those permeable border regions between the individual and the social through language use. It is, for Bakhtin, in the moment of actual speech communication, in utterance, that language is no longer either individual or system but dialogically and simultaneously (and ambiguously) both.

In taking up language use, or actual situated speech communications, as his object of study, Bakhtin turns first to utterance, then to genre.

The utterance is defined as a dialogic encounter or performance among the writing subject, the addressee(s), and exterior texts—and becomes the site of a complex semiotic process in which various textual surfaces intersect. For Bakhtin, the utterance is a "very complex and multiplanar phenomenon" (*Speech Genres*, p. 93), layered with otherness, furrowed with echoes and traces and the words of others, always directed to others. Even when addressed to an object, it is also addressed to the speeches of others about that object. Utterances are thus "dialogic reverberations" (*Speech Genres*, p. 94), linking to utterances that have preceded it and linked to subsequent utterances that might possibly follow. Whereas the isolated sentence may serve as a unit of analysis in studying language as system, when we look at language in use, Bakhtin insists we turn to the contextualized utterance, "constructed between two socially organized persons" (*Marxism*, p. 85).

Bakhtin further argues, "Each separate utterance is individual, of course, but each sphere in which language is used develops its own *relatively stable types* of these utterances'' (*Speech Genres,* p. 60)—and these Bakhtin calls "genres." It is genres that make speech communication possible. We learn to cast our speech in generic forms and, when hearing the speech of others, we estimate its genre from the very first words. We can then predict a certain length, a certain compositional structure, a certain ending. Although genres are flexible and changeable, they have a normative significance for the speaking person by linking the person with the (typical) speech situation.

Carini makes a similar move in defining works as an object of study. She wants to look specifically, concretely, and in great detail at what actual children do *as* they engage in the authoring process with language and other given cultural media—that is, as they make works and as they compose within various media and genre. From this perspective, works, like utterances, then can be defined as both/and—as both social and individual, as culturally and individually expressive, simultaneously and dialogically.

In using Carini's reflective procedures to study a child's work or series of works, readers look at the complexity or various textual planes of this authoring process. They may come to understand the particular child's expressiveness—that is, how that child engages the world, makes sense of things intellectually and imaginatively. In so doing they approach the child from a point of view that is more semiotic than (as least purely) psychological. That is, it is not an effort to reconstruct private mental events that went on in the child's mind as he or she wrote or drew, or to conjure up that child's intention in some conscious, planned sense of the word, but rather an effort to describe a complexly interindividual authoring process, involving writer, readers, and language itself.

As Geertz (1986) argues, texts "are perceived not as independent realities to be fitted together in the name of mechanical or quasi-mechanical, 'such-are-the-facts' explanation; rather, they come as 'seeing-as' elucidations of one another, inseparable moments of an interpretive dialectic, in principle endless'' (p. 377).

Secondarily, and perhaps less systematically, readers also develop a fuller, more finely tuned knowlege of how the semiotic resources of a particular medium itself, such as language, work. And thirdly, through descriptive reading, they come to experience the tensions of this kind of interpretive process. The meaning of the text involves the mutual, historically and situationally specific participation of writer and readers via work. They come to understand their implicatedness in the meaning of the work, as they study the medium, respond to or answer the child's texts, and in the process author a communal text and themselves.

What does the utterance (or work) as a unit of study suggest for teachers and researchers of children's writing? How does this complicate and redefine our enterprise?

First, this position requires that we read in children's writing not just formal features of the language system, not just the presence of the writer, and not just the relationship culturally and historically of this text to other texts, this word to other words—but all of this interactively. Somehow we have to acknowledge and describe and understand the whirling semiotic relations among all three players or participants in the dynamic drama of the utterance. As Schuster (1985) argues, this position redefines the traditional rhetorical triangle, for now the speaker and the listener engage in acts of communication which include the subject (or language itself) as a genuine rhetorical force, one that becomes at times the dominant influence in verbal and written utterances (p. 595). Thus, he concludes, "the three elements of the dialogue speak, listen, and influence each other equivalently" (p. 596). So we have to work with relationships and not categories, with moments and not taxonomies.

Second, children's writing may be studied and understood as full of voices, the traces and echoes of otherness. Language contains the referential and expressive intentions of both the self and other: it expresses both the writer's meaning and the meanings of other speakers, heroes, listeners, usages, texts (Schuster, 1985, p. 596). Those voices at times may dominate, or conflict, or resist, or be appropriated in a struggle that characterizes all language use and that never ceases.

Third, the utterance as the unit of study directs us next to the study of genre and its possible role in individual development. Although each separate utterance is individual, all the various areas of human activity have developed their own relatively stable types, and, though extremely heterogeneous, genres may offer a possible way to study language use across time and within various settings.

The documentary account of one young writer in this book (Chapter 6) is an effort at experimenting with the methods and textualizing strategies necessary for investigating works as this complex authoring process, and to study a child writing as this kind of a semiotic (not purely psychological) subject.

A Semiotic Subject of Study: "The Speaking Person"

> For speech can exist in reality only in the form of concrete utterances of
> individual speaking people, speech subjects. (*Speech Genres*, p. 71)

In Bakhtin, *semiotic* refers rather broadly to the concrete exchange of
signs in society and history (*Speech Genres*, p. 101). What I want to call a
semiotic subject of study is meant as a theoretical notion for describing
and understanding a person as he or she is engaged in the process of the
exchange of signs, in the practices of signification that constitute a
culture—a person writing, for example, or dancing or drawing or
speaking or making a work. Fundamentally, this notion tries to move the
locus of consciousness from some kind of private space or entity within
the person to an activity or process that takes place within the border
regions between two planes of reality, that of the person and that of the
world (see Chapter 3 in *Marxism*). It shifts the focus from the person to
the person acting.

The notion of a semiotic subject insists, too, upon the deep, dynamic,
and continuous relationship between person and the world, natural and
cultural. An individual's thought, for example, moves ambiguously
between these two planes through the shared territory of language:

> A thought that as yet exists only in the context of my consciousness,
> without embodiment in the context of a discipline constituting some
> unified ideological system, remains a dim, unprocessed thought. But that
> thought had come into existence in my consciousness already with an
> orientation toward an ideological system, and it itself had been engendered
> by the ideological signs that I had absorbed earlier. (*Marxism*, p. 33)

The two planes slide into each other, the transition from inner
experience to outer expression less a qualitative leap than a quantitative
crossing over: "the whole route between inner experience (the 'expres-
sible') and its outward objectification (the 'utterance') lies entirely across
social territory" (*Marxism*, p. 90). The individual psyche is oriented
toward, and drawn into, the social and public, in order to expand and
develop and perhaps resist, while the world draws into the private and the
individual in an almost extraterrestrial way in order to stay alive, to
change, to mean across time and in different settings. For Volosinov/
Bakhtin, in each utterance, for example, a living, dialectical reciprocity
takes place again and again between the psyche and the ideological, the
social and the individual, the inner and the outer:

> In each speech act, subjective experiences perish in the objective fact of the enunciated word-utterance, and the enunciated word is subjectified in the act of responsive understanding in order to generate, sooner or later, a counterstatement. (*Marxism,* p. 41)

Language does not merely transmit a person's ideas or experiences but actually transforms them, objectifies them, connects them to larger textual and cultural networks of meaning. "To express oneself means to make oneself an object for another and for oneself" (*Speech Genres,* p. 110). At the same time, utterances are always new, so that language in use is transformed, revitalized, (re)contextualized, layered, by its use in particular contexts by persons with particular expressive and referential aims.

Carini, too, talks about expressiveness—our fundamental and deeply dispositional way of engaging the world and expressing our intensity within it—as what draws us, as semiotic subjects, into the public dimension. The activity, say, of speaking or writing or drawing a picture transforms that intensity into something else, and something of us perishes, as it moves into the otherness of the medium. But then the work gives us back to ourselves in a new form, with a new and transforming intensity. Through cultural practices, we disclose ourselves to ourselves and to others, as we insert and locate ourselves in an expressive field through gesture and work. Culture, then, or what Bakhtin calls ideology, is actualized through the person, as the person is realized through the culture—in concrete acts of thinking and speaking and writing and making.

Because language use takes place within the border regions of person and culture, no utterance or work, with all its individuality and creativity, can in any way be regarded as a completely free combination of forms of language. As Bakhtin claims, "We speak only in definite speech genres, that is, all our utterances have definite and relatively stable typical *forms of construction of the whole*" (*Speech Genres,* p. 78). Yet in each utterance or work, there is both the given and the created: "An utterance is never just a reflection or an expression of something already existing outside it that is given and final. It always creates something that never existed before. . . . But something created is always created out of something given" (*Speech Genres,* p. 120).

Thus, the semiotic subject, the person speaking or writing, is not an utterly free creative agent, individually and idiosyncratically constructing text. In fact, according to Bakhtin, some words and genres are more conducive to reflecting, or refracting, the individual expressive style of the writer than others. Rather, the person speaking or writing is appropriating (and resisting) the forms and words of others, as that person adds his or her expressive imprint and layer of meaning, as he or she uses language in specific settings for particular purposes, as he or she expropriates meanings for his or her own uses—or at least tries.

From the perspective of the child writing as a semiotic subject of study, then, writing researchers want to understand—to read and respond to—children's writing as meaningful cultural and expressive works. We want to study language where it lives and means, as works, in concrete moments of actual language use.

But how?

Research as Shared Territory: "Understanding" and "Outsideness"

> A generative process can be grasped only with the aid of another generative process. (*Marxism*, p. 102)

> Research becomes inquiry and conversation, that is, dialogue. (*Speech Genres*, p. 114)

> In the actual life of speech, every concrete act of understanding is active: it assimilates the word to be understood into its own conceptual system filled with specific objects and emotional expressions, and is indissolubly merged with the response, with a motivated agreement or disagreement. . . . Understanding comes to fruition only in the response. (*Dialogic*, p. 282)

> A meaning only reveals its depths once it has encountered and come into contact with another, foreign meaning: they engage in a kind of dialogue, which surmounts the closedness and one-sidedness of these particular meanings. (*Speech Genres*, p. 7)

If we define the young writer as a semiotic subject, and if we come to see the text itself as a kind of hero, then research becomes dialogic, too, taking place in the shared territory of interactions among writer, reader, and text. As Volosinov/Bakhtin says, "Meaning does not reside in the word or in the soul of the speaker or in the soul of the listener. Meaning is the *effect of interaction between speaker and listener produced via the material of a particular sound complex*" (*Marxism*, pp. 102–3). Research then becomes a complex event or conversation, where readers (and words) encounter and interact with—and come to understand—the living words of others. To study language use, Bakhtin wants a system that doesn't systematize, categories that remain fluid and overflow their boundaries.

The question is, how do we find ways to talk systematically about children writing without stifling the very flux and messiness and ambiguity and interactiveness that is at the very heart of it? Or without saying more about us as readers than about the child as writer (see, for example, Chapter 3)? Or without being too optimistic about the possible creativity and individuation of the process? How do we work with Bakhtin's constant mandate for those studying language use—"resist finalization" (Clark and Holquist, 1984, p. 6)? What are the consequences of that decision?[7]

Two Bakhtinian concepts offer possible principles for our enterprise: "understanding" and "outsideness."

Understanding

Like philologists, for example, researchers can treat texts as objects, as linguistic facts, and therefore exclude any active response to the content or meaning of the text in advance and on principle. Bakhtin calls this "passive understanding" and acknowledges its role in developing linguistics as a discipline. This approach brackets meaning, he cautions, and treats texts like private monologues, as if there were only one speaker who has no necessary relation to others in the speech event or in the culture.

But to understand language in use, to study utterances and works, readers have to respond actively, fully, holistically, says Bakhtin, because "any understanding of live speech, a live utterance, is *inherently* responsive, although the degree of this activity varies extremely" (*Speech Genres*, p. 68, emphasis added). That means teachers and researchers are not so much explaining the child's text as enriching its meaning—by responding to it, by layering text on text, by articulating its relatedness to other texts and contexts, by saying more and more (see Chapter 2). "Understanding is a response to a sign with signs" (*Marxism*, p. 4). The event of the text, then, lies on shared territory, within the boundary regions between two subjects, and becomes an "arena for the [dialogic] encounter" (*Dialogic*, p. 282). Thus, Bakhtin argues that research in the human sciences always takes place as this "special dialogue: the complex interrelations between the *text* (the object of study and reflection) and the created, framing *context* (questioning, refuting, and so forth) in which the scholar's cognizing and evaluating thought takes place. This is the meeting of two texts—of the ready-made and the reactive text being created—and, consequently, the meeting of two subjects and two authors" (*Speech Genres,* pp. 106–7). The person who understands (including researchers) becomes to some degree, and on a special level, a participant in the dialogue of the text itself, completing the utterance, responding to it in tension with it (*Speech Genres,* p. 125). At times, Bakhtin calls this a "conversation." Within that conversation in the human sciences, various disciplines move toward one or the other pole: either toward language (the language of the author, the language of the genre, the trend or epoch, the national language or linguistics) or toward the individualized, contextualized, and unrepeatable concrete event of the text (*Speech Genres,* p. 107). Both poles are, however, unconditional.

Bakhtin distinguishes between explanation, where there is only one consciousness and the text is treated as object, and comprehension, where there are two consciousnesses, two subjects, and where understanding is dialogic to some degree (*Speech Genres,* p. 111). Understanding thus includes comprehension of the author of the work—the other—to some degree, and it "enriches our understanding of the given language as a system as well" (*Speech Genres,* p. 111).

Outsideness

Understanding is one task. The other, according to Bakhtin, is "to take advantage of one's own position of temporal and cultural outsideness" (*Speech Genres,* p. 144). With this concept, Bakhtin is emphasizing not only the need to use one's understanding to make sense of the other people or other cultures as deeply as possible, but also, having done that, to return to the perspective provided by one's own self and culture (*Speech Genres,* p. xiii). Creative understanding, then, does not renounce its own locatedness—in time, in culture, in history.

Bakhtin talks about this principle of outsideness only briefly, specifically in relation to understanding another culture:

> In the realm of culture, outsideness is a most powerful factor in understanding. It is only in the eyes of *another* culture that foreign culture reveals itself fully and profoundly (but not maximally fully, because there

will be cultures that see and understand even more). A meaning only reveals its depths once it has encountered and come into contact with another, foreign meaning: they engage in a kind of dialogue, which surmounts the closedness and one-sidedness of these particular meanings, these cultures. We raise new questions for a foreign culture, ones that it did not raise itself; we seek answers to our own questions in it; and the foreign culture responds to us by revealing to us its new aspects and new semantic depths. Without *one's own* questions one cannot creatively understand anything other or foreign (but, of course, the questions must be serious and sincere). Such a dialogic encounter of two cultures does not result in merging or mixing. Each retains its own unity and *open* totality, but they are mutually enriched. (*Speech Genres*, p. 7)

These principles, along with the rest of Bakhtin's theory, resonate with Carini's theory of childhood and reflective procedures in important ways—by theorizing the position of the reader more explicitly, by relocating descriptive reading as dialogic encounter, by defining a semiotic rather than psychological subject, and by acknowledging the shared territory of writer, reader, and language out of which all meaning emerges.

5

Thinking Seriously about Children Writing: Constructing an Object of Study

> . . . what we are seeing is not just another redrawing of the cultural map—the moving of a few disputed borders, the marking of some more picturesque mountain lakes—but an alteration of the principles of mapping. Something is happening to the way we think about the way we think. (Geertz, "Blurred Genres")

> Anthropology, or at least interpretive anthropology, is a science whose progress is marked less by a perfection of consensus than by a refinement of debate. What gets better is the precision with which we vex each other. (Geertz, "Thick Description")

I started thinking, really thinking, about children writing in 1979, when I dictated words to my four-year-old son Matthew, and he wrote "TBL" (table) and "JRK" (drink) on a paper napkin in a restaurant—in exactly the way that Charles Read's (1975) research into invented spelling predicted he would. No longer were Matthew's experiments with written texts just something to exclaim "Oh, how cute!" over and hang up on the refrigerator door, along with his artwork and Cubs stickers. These texts now meant something.

With Read's results so tidily confirmed, I ventured enthusiastically into the new field of inquiry—early written language development—that had been legitimated by Donald Graves in his pioneering investigation into the composing processes of seven-year-old children. I eagerly read composing process studies (Graves, 1973, 1983); analyses of children's evolving hypotheses about the relationship of talk to print (Clay, 1975; Ferreiro and Teberosky, 1982); ethnographic and case studies of individual writers and particular classrooms (Bissex, 1980; Calkins, 1983;

Dyson, 1982, 1983, 1984, 1985; Gundlach et al., 1985); semiotic and sociolinguistic accounts of early development (Kress, 1982; Harste, Woodward, and Burke, 1984)—and many others. The journey proved intriguing.

Each research study, regardless of its specific focus and investigative strategy, shared a common impulse: to think and talk about children's writing in serious ways. Researchers argued that children's early writing activities and texts had been dismissed for too long as random, deficient, merely skills-oriented, "cognitively confused," cute but not intellectually interesting. Ferreiro and Teberosky (1982), for example, countered the reduction of literacy to "a set of perceptual-motor skills," with their insistence upon investigation at the deeper level of what they called the "psychogenesis of conceptualizations about written language" (p. 17). And in the introduction to *Learning to Write*, Kress (1982) explained explicitly his motivation for applying sociolinguistic theory to children's school writing: he had noted with dismay that teachers found it difficult to see anything of great import or even interest in the texts children produced in their classrooms, and that they had little to say about them, either to the writers themselves or to each other when they discussed these texts in their linguistics classes.

And so, from different perspectives, each study began to map out the new territory, by defining "problem spaces" or areas of scholarly inquiry; by drawing upon the research design, assumptions, and principles from more established disciplines; and by constructing *the child writing* as various objects of study.

Relying on practices and premises from disciplines such as spoken language acquisition and developmental psychology, especially Piagettian, many researchers initially took a structuralist approach and defined written language as a puzzle, a cognitive problem, which young children qua scientists were to solve. The texts children wrote along the way were read as products of increasingly complex cognitive processes, and often researchers employed a kind of componential analysis as methodology, breaking down texts and behaviors into parts and then inferring possible stages of development. Generalizable explanation was the goal.

Yet as learning and social aspects of language development were more fully acknowledged, researchers turned to sociolinguistics, semiotics, and Soviet developmental psychology, especially Vygotsky. This move quickly expanded and complicated earlier constructions of the object of study. Now language was defined as a social semiotic, the child as a social actor, and the text as event. Methodological practices, such as case studies and classroom ethnographies, became messier, more explicitly interpretive, with particular and situated explanation as the goal.

Well, at least that's one narrative about written language development as an emerging discipline.

In this chapter, I would like to play this narrative out a bit, examine the limits and tensions within the premises and practices that formed and informed these studies, and explore various constructions of the child writing as object of study, as we have moved from a cognitive to an ever more social account of early written language development.

As Geertz suggests, this (re)turn to fundamental questions about how we think about the way we think—that is, to questions of methodology—is indicative of a crisis within the human sciences more generally. This crisis has been brought on in a postmodern world by profound uncertainties about adequate ways for describing and analyzing social realities, about authority and grounding for claims, and about formats for writing up research. Indeed, "[arguably] the most interesting theoretical debates in a number of fields have shifted to the level of method, to problems of epistemology, interpretation, and discursive forms of representation themselves" (Marcus and Fischer, 1986, p. 9).

For writing researchers, that means we are required to operate on two levels simultaneously: to provide accounts of how writers compose and develop and to reflect upon our theoretical choices and groundings for such accounts in the first place.

So I would like to talk methodology here, by tracing the choices early written language development researchers have made as the field has emerged, vexing those choices a bit. And I tell this story, with all its limits and (obvious) situatedness, as a heuristic, as one possible rubric in which to locate and juxtapose various research premises and practices. It is an invitation for other narratives, and one response to North's (1987) call for a more rigorous discussion of methodology within composition in general.

Writing as Cognitive Problem Solving

Set against a research and teaching tradition that had long presented learning to write behavioralistically, as a rather mechanical process of acquiring basic perceptual-motor skills, these studies began by insisting emphatically upon a redefinition of learning to write as a process of cognitive problem solving and conceptual development, based on the active (re)construction by the child of the formal principles and structural patterns that organize written language as a linguistic system.

Often working explicitly within a Piagetian framework, many early research studies looked specifically at the development of the formal knowledge or principles that organized a child's composing behaviors. Children's texts, as well as their behaviors, were treated as facts and read as windows on the mind, as evidence or bases for making more formal, inferential claims about mental processes and possible stages or sequences of cognitive development. The object of study here was constructed as that lone, autonomous Piagetian child, encountering a rich print environment, and somehow—mysteriously but naturally—without much direct instruction or adult mentoring, (re)discovering the principles underlying the system of written language.

Language as Puzzle

In the terms of an early metaphor from Dyson (1982), children between the ages of four and seven confront the written language "puzzle" and then need to formulate and test hypotheses about the precise connection between print and talk, to uncover and discover the structural patterns and principles in the written language system. She then embeds early literacy learning within cognitive theory in general:

> From the point of view of cognitive learning theory, children have a strong desire to master their environment (as do all human beings). They select, interpret, and integrate information about the world in order to form a working model of that world. On the basis of their models, they make predictions about how the world works and, when these predictions do not work out, they attempt to solve the puzzlement. Puzzlements, then, cause human cognitive processing to operate with persistence and at maximum intensity. (p. 831)

Children are constructed as "active investigators of written language" who make "independent efforts to make sense of the written language system" (p. 836). The focus is formalistic, with writing defined structurally, as a cognitive puzzlement, as a complex linguistic system that relates print to talk in precise, though arbitrary, ways. The puzzle of written language is how to translate or reformat texts from spoken to written language.

Similarly, in *What did i write* (1975), Clay portrays children as setting for themselves "the task of understanding many arbitrary conventions" (p. 2) by which speech is recorded, and coming to learn how print talks, how letters are formed, how sentences are constructed and messages conveyed. Based on close observation and textual analysis, Clay then constructs inductively a list of principles and concepts, or "internal procedure[s]" (p. 14), which she argues guide children's early explorations through the full hierarchy of written language. "The examples in this book," Clay explains, "try to illustrate some of the insights that a child gains during his first contacts with written language and some of the points at which he can become confused" (p. 2). Development for Clay is presented as linear and incremental, with time serving as a baseline and texts treated rather factually as "*evidence* of a child's development *if* the teacher knows what the child was able to do one or two months previously and how his current product can be evaluated against that earlier work" (p. 2, emphasis added). In this way, even children's scribbles become meaningful, as they are considered directly reflective of an active, self-organized learning and concept formation process—that is, as motivated by an internal impulse toward mastery.

Text as Product

In her case study *GNYS AT WRK* (1980), Bissex, too, looks at her son Paul's texts as products or "*evidence* . . . of changes in strategy, [of] changes in the concepts about printed language that govern strategy . . . [and of] the child's expanding grasp of the complex principles of written language" (pp. v–vi, emphasis added). Language is defined structurally. Her account includes a richly detailed picture of the subtle phases Paul goes through as he wends his way, through his own (re)invention, toward conventional spelling. Again, "misspelled" words—that which had earlier been dismissed as uninteresting error—are now meaningful for researchers and teachers (and parents) as evidence of the systematic and abstract nature of children's invented spelling, and of the strategies and conceptual categorizations they employ as they master the conventional spelling and textual forms of the written language puzzle (p. 35). Bissex, too, relates these particular phases in Paul's reading and writing patterns to broad developmental principles underlying all language learning, to more "comprehensive patterns of human growth and learning" (p. 200).

Child as Problem Solver

This definition of text as cognitive product allowed researchers to construct the child as an object of study as an active cognitive problem solver, to treat language as a structural puzzle, and to describe even children's earliest efforts with written language as serious and significant achievements. As Ferreiro and Teberosky (1982) claim:

> We see children who actively attempt to understand the nature of the language spoken around them, and, in trying to understand it, formulate hypotheses, search for regularities, and test their predictions. . . . Instead of receiving bit by bit a language entirely fabricated by others, children reconstruct language for themselves, selectively using information provided by the environment. (p. 8)

They then describe in great detail the problem-solving strategies of young children between the ages of four and six, and suggest successive levels of progression as these children change their hypotheses and move closer toward adult conventional understanding of the written language system (p. xii). Based on qualitative analysis of children's responses to writing tasks, for example, these authors construct five levels of development in children's understanding of the written language system: the reproduction of features of basic writing forms, fixed forms, the syllabic hypothesis (one letter per syllable), the alphabetic hypothesis (more letters per syllable), and alphabetic writing. Ferreiro and Teberosky point out in particular the originality of the alphabetic hypothesis as evidence of the peculiar, from an adult point of view, but logical rationale in children's responses, as the making visible of "the internal logic of the developmental progression" (p. 271).

For Ferreiro and Teberosky, the "active learner compares, excludes, orders, categorizes, reformulates, confirms, forms hypotheses, and reorganizes through internalized action (thought) or through effective action (according to the level of development). A learner who carries something out according to instructions or a model provided by someone is not, usually, an intellectually active learner" (p. 15). The child is constructed here as an active (re)producer of knowledge, through his or her own "assimilation schemes" (p. 13), not a passive recipient. Furthermore, as Ferreiro and Teberosky argue, there is a progression in the data they observe in their tasks with children that parallels, and makes visible, the development of thought in the child.

In sum, redefining writing as cognitive and conceptual problem solving served to construct a serious object of study—the child as active learner and cognitive problem solver—and to align it with the two established disciplines of child developmental psychology and spoken language acquisition. "Acquiring written language," Dyson (1982) notes, "has assumed all the complexity and intrigue of the acquistion of oral language" (p. 830). And in investigating this acquisitional process, many researchers followed, or adapted, the methods and theory of child psychology developed by Piaget in his study of other aspects of cognitive growth in children.

Facticity and Componential Analysis

In Piaget, the fundamental epistemological move is toward a reliance on a kind of facticity or empiricism, toward the collecting and the categorizing of facts. As Vygotsky (1986) says of Piaget and his method, "his forte is the unearthing of new facts, their painstaking analysis, their classification—the ability, as Claparede puts it, to *listen* to their message" (p. 14). In similar style, Graves (1973) sets out on four phases of data collection, with little theory and few hypotheses, "not knowing where the findings will carry him" (p. 13), but systematically and thoroughly amassing details and observations from interviews with children, observational profiles of writing episodes, data from writing folders, and information for the case studies. Throughout the study, Graves describes in detail how rigorously and systematically he has collected information, a rigor ensured by his efforts, for example, to neutralize his presence in the classroom, or to employ the same language each time (e.g., always beginning a folder interview by saying, "You have many interesting papers here. Will you please pick out the one you feel is the very best?"), or to honor time sequences (such as never allowing more than twenty-four hours to elapse between the recording and transcribing of notes into typed copy). Children's words and behaviors and written texts, then, like their test scores and background demographics, are treated as facts—givens, in a sense—to be gathered and analyzed and componentially dissected and charted, until they reveal their inner meaning and logic. Writing episodes, for example, are first divided temporally into prewriting, composing, and postwriting. These three phases are then further subdivided into various behaviors—such as "drawing use" or "proofreading during writing" or "prewriting ideation"—which are then monitored for their developmental level. For example, a child who reviews a completed text with contemplation ranks higher developmentally than one who shares the text with friends or the teacher.

In acknowledging Piaget's influence on his research design, Graves (1973) quotes Claparede from the preface of *Language and Thought of the Child:*

> This clinical method, therefore, which is also an art, the art of questioning, does not confine itself to superficial observations, but aims at capturing what is hidden behind the immediate appearance of things. It analyzes down to its ultimate constituents the least little remark made by the young subjects. It does not give up the struggle when the child gives incomprehensible or contradictory answers, but only follows closer in chase of the ever-receding thought, drives it from cover, pursues and tracks it down till it can seize it, dissect it and lay bare the secret of its composition. (cited on p. 13)

Given close examination, the facts will explain themselves. In this case, writing behaviors will reveal the logic or rationale of children's developing cognitive schemes and strategies as writers. Behaviors thus are considered directly reflective of thought, and thought comes to be talked about at the meta-level of problem solving, organized knowledge, formal principles, and universal strategies. The meaning of these behaviors is considered to be contained within them, however deeply, and with energy and persistence an investigator/hunter will force that meaning/prey to make itself visible and trappable. By analyzing and breaking things down logically into their component parts, these parts will somehow add up to the meaning of the event in a more schematized, abstracted, and generalizable way.

Clay (1975) also assumes the empirical world will disclose itself upon close examination, so that her task as researcher is to annotate an empirically and directly given reality. "When I observed five year old children very closely during my research on beginning reading I found the early months of schooling crowded with complex learning. . . . I have simply tried to make children's difficulties a little more obvious by organizing the material and annotating the examples of their work" (p. 1). Furthermore, children's texts, like facts, speak for themselves: "With the thought that the children's own work samples might tell the clearest tale I began this book" (p. 1). More like an editor than an author, Clay presents her analysis as a reading, not a rewriting or intepreting. She "simply" collects children's writing samples and says what they seem to imply to her about children's insights during their early experiments with written language.

Although embedded in an ethnographic methodology, with explicit attention directed to understanding early writing from the point of view of children themselves, Dyson (1983), too, refers to observations and interviews as "data collection" designed to help her "gain insight into [children's] perceptions of writing and their reasoning about writing behaviors" (p. 1). Her rigorous and elaborate procedures generate lots of data: "At the eleventh week of observation, I had recorded approximately 36 hours of spontaneous talk, collected approximately 500 written products, made 112 observations of focal children, and written notations on 377 child visits to the writing center" (pp. 8–9). Then she inductively organizes this data into "analytic categories" (p. 9), classifying and reclassifying data under increasingly refined organizers, producing very detailed analytical schemes about writing purpose, writing process components, forms of written products, and language functions. Other researchers also have relied on inductive categorization and a kind of componential analysis as methodology.

Explanation as Goal

As I review these studies, I read a deep tension running through them—between a desire to recreate for readers the rich, detailed particularity of children writing that spending lots of time in classrooms generates and an impulse to reach and report on significant—that is, high-level and generalizable—causal conclusions. Researchers seem drawn into the "drama," as Bissex (1980) describes it, of watching children personally and particularly enacting the large cultural performance of literacy. Yet they are also pulled, as researchers in an emerging discipline, toward generalized explanation. This impulse may arise from a need to legitimate the field or to assist teachers in their daily encounters with student writers by giving them conceptual frameworks or models of some sort, or perhaps to fulfill a certain definition of what research ideally is. I read these researchers as navigating particular paths along the difficult tension between the impulse to describe or narrate and the impulse to explain, often making the epistemological leap of faith that data—when carefully collected, closely read, and fully charted—will turn into explanation.

Tensions and Limits

But listening to facts turns out not to be such a simple process, as evidenced most graphically by how much of Graves's 1973 study consists of pages and pages of uninterpreted information or raw data. The sheer volume of information becomes hard to control or to make sense of and can lead potentially to a kind of intellectual chaos or to generalizations so broad as to be useless. In completing his 67-page case study of one student, for example, Graves comments: "The chief conclusion drawn from the case study of Michael is that many variables contribute in unique ways to any given point in the process of writing" (p. 213).

And explanation as a goal often comes to mean causality or at least sequence, so that researchers try to line up variables or principles in such a way that X explains why and how Y happens—that gender "causes" boys to write about certain topics, that classroom formality or informality "accounts for" the amount of writing children do, that reading particular books "results" in children writing certain kinds of stories. The obvious difficulty with this goal is in identifying and delimiting particular causes out of the rich, complex worlds children actually live in, or in drawing the parameters around literacy events or writing episodes in order to set up temporal and (presumably) causal relations. Perhaps implicitly, too, it always suggests a stage model of development at work, making it then difficult to understand development as recursive, parallel, transformative, surprising, or disjunctive.

In order to provide explanations, researchers have turned at times to broad developmental principles, like "internalization" or "differentiation," in order to organize their data in some way, to pull things together, to enable a sense of closure and conclusion. Dyson (1983), for example, proposes as a tentative hypothesis about the "process of developing control over written language" that "With development, differentiation occurs—distinct and identifiable concepts and processes emerge. Gradually integration takes place as the new learnings both become distinct and fit together with other learnings" (p. 17). With this move, a kind of meta-analysis results, an analysis that may not sufficiently distinguish writing from any other symbolic or discursive activity (Nystrand, 1986, p. 22), or one person or setting from another. In the same way, Moffett and Wagner have challenged meta-process research in reading:

> Recalling, comprehending, relating facts, making inferences, drawing conclusions, interpreting, and predicting outcomes are all mental opera-

tions that go on in the head of a non-literate aborigine navigating his
outrigger according to cues from weather, sea life, currents, and the
positions of heavenly bodies. Not only do these kinds of thinking have no
necessary connection with reading, but they have no necessary connection
with language whatsoever. (cited in Kress, 1982, p. xi)

So generalized explanations of process and development may seem
vague, broad, applicable to all learning and cognition, from chess to
mathematics to navigation.

As a method of inquiry, too, componential analysis presents a problem
with possible circularity. A phenomenon is divided into parts (e.g., a
writing episode into the three temporal phases of prewriting, composing,
and postwriting), and then those parts are assumed to reconvey the whole
but in a more conceptualized or abstracted form. But what determines
decisions about the dividing up? In a critique of this kind of "logical
analysis" as methodology in educational research, Carini (1975) argues
that while these divisions or parts may seem commonsensically plausi-
ble, they are not really testable as such because they are not directly
derived from, or guarded by, any theory. In this case, decisions are not
really shaped by any theory of written language or written language
development, as no such theory has really been formulated yet. The
models, then, are what Carini calls "agreeable schematizations" (p. 2),
directly reflective of the character of current thought, conservative in that
they concretize common sense but also radical in that they are unbounded
by theoretical or testable limits.

Indeed, a reliance on facticity, or a belief that events and objects in the
world will, under close scrutiny, explain themselves, also runs the risk of
obscuring the necessary entanglement at all levels of fact with theory, or
what Vygotsky (1986) calls "the philosophy of fact" (p. 15). From the
social perspective of the 1980s, for example, it would be easy to critique
the then "common-sense" decision that located "sharing [text] with
friends, teacher" at merely a midpoint on the developmental scale called
"Postwriting Behaviors" (Graves, 1973, p. 101). That decision would
have seemed "natural" in 1973, when developmental theory focused on
private cognition and valued autonomy and independence as signs of
mature learning. But theories have changed, and so have the "facts."

And if researchers trust facts, then questions about the historical
situatedness of the writer (and researcher), alternative explanations, the
contextual particularities and peculiarities of the setting, and the theoretical dimensions informing the design of categories just don't come up.

That allows questions about methods to remain underconceptualized, or even invisible—questions such as how we gain or generate knowledge, what we count as evidence (and why), how we interpret or make sense of facts, and in what textual form we report on results.

Finally, in explaining the process of written language development, two words come up often in these early studies: *natural* and *rational*. In the opening pages of his dissertation, for example, Graves (1973) explains the primary pedagogical problem that motivates his interest in children writing in precisely these terms:

> Although writing has high priority in curricular and teaching expectations, it is seldom seen as a spontaneous activity of most children. Whether in school, at home, or in other setttings, writing is rarely done *naturally*—it is seldom chosen as a means for expression. (p. 1, emphasis added)

Graves contends that writing, unlike speech or drawing or mathematical games, is never selected as an expressive activity, because writing ia a remote, complex, and abstract form of communication, dependent on a child's developmentally achieved ability to do empathetic thinking and to work without the interactive support of an audience in view. The teacher's difficult task, therefore, is to provide "*natural* transitions from overt [spoken] to covert [written] communication" (p. 2, emphasis added). His goal is to identify instructional and research hypotheses to support children in approaching written language as naturally—that is, as spontaneously and expressively—as they do spoken language.

Quickly, however, other researchers began to make the claim that in "a literate society, learning to write and read *may be natural*" (Bissex, 1980, p. 200, emphasis added) processes that are shaped by more comprehensive patterns of human growth and learning. And Ferreiro and Teberosky (1982) define "natural literacy" as literacy learning organized by the child and not by a method or teacher, emphasizing the role and power of the "active learner" as he or she formulates hypotheses, searches out regularities, and tests predictions.

Phelps (1988) challenges this notion of the natural myth in sympathetic yet critical ways:

> To say "writing and reading are natural" is essentially to say that, given a literate culture, young humans make sense of written language in much the same natural, effortless, and unconscious way they learn speech. This process is often spoken of as "acquisition" or "development" of literacy abilities so as to distinguish it from formal learning. (p. 108)

In this view, the culture basically—and, I would add, somewhat mysteriously—supports the process of literacy learning by offering meaningful contexts and experiences for written language events that stimulate the learner's own mental (re)construction of the systems and strategies we call literacy. While Phelps gives full value to the myth of the natural, she insists simultaneously on its complement, "the cultural elaboration of literacy into the skilled, crafted, artful, self-conscious and reflexive use of language" (p. 109).

Phelps discusses three sources for the theme of natural literacy in composition research and pedagogy. Both the biological perspective from Piaget (which takes the child as genetically prepared to learn language) and the Romantic perspective (which emphasizes the inherent creativity in all people) generate such child-centered notions of literacy learning, so that there is little or no attention paid to direct cultural instruction and influence. The third source, the contextualist perspective, reverses this and focuses instead on the specific ways children do participate in literacy events and thereby come to learn the codes and conventions of written language. Yet, Phelps argues, across all three variations there is an identifiable core concept—that each person acts "naively, that is, within the natural attitude," so that "the literate environment is to the learner like the sea to a fish" (p. 115).

The problem, according to Phelps, is that this Edenic view of natural literacy abstracts and oversimplifies and idealizes the complex, real relations between individuals and cultures, as expressed and mediated in literacy development. The child in this myth is always constructed as prepared intellectually and socially to learn and as cooperative; the teacher is always portrayed as caring and supportive, nearly always maternal, amply able to create an "at home" context that engenders literacy growth. And literacy itself is defined as a single practice considered equally accessible throughout all parts of the culture because of a shared print environment, so that factors like race or socioeconomic status or gender, for example, don't matter somehow in the acquisition process. Obviously, this tends to idealize and sanitize the process of literacy learning a great deal. Children from various cultures, for example, may find literacy as it is practiced at school alien, incomprehensible, even terrifying, and teachers don't always create benevolent classrooms.

While the natural myth may prove useful in ways, with learners directing their own reinventions of written language codes and structures, especially as they work out principles of print and patterns of orthography, that construction of the child writing may prove inadequate when children's attention turns to forms, to strategic choice, to technique, to meaning, when writing becomes a meaningful public performance, and when the writer becomes a participant in cultural practices of signification that deeply shape his or her possibilities, personally and politically, as a particular member of various cultures.

Furthermore, this construction of the child writing has tended to reduce thinking to rational cognition, and writing to structural principles used to encode (already) known messages. Dyson (1982) describes the value of early writing, for example, as a way for children "to make explicit their current hypotheses about the written language symbol system and, as a direct result of that process, to make their ideas explicit . . . and to revise those hypotheses" (p. 830). The focus in learning is on the structural aspects of written language, as reinvented by the child qua linguist/scientist, and the motivation is a fuller "awareness of the written language system" (p. 833), of the precise ways messages are encoded into specific written symbols. Similarly, Ferreiro and Teberosky (1982) look for the logic and rationale in children's hypothesizing and in their progressions through various stages, or levels, of knowledge. They conclude that "there are two outstanding characteristics in the developmental sequence of solving these problems: the strict consistency children demand of themselves, and the internal logic of the developmental progression" (p. 271). Like little scientists in lab coats, children are constructed as operating within the rigors and demands of the scientific method, mastering language in terms of consistency and logic and rule.

On the one hand, this insistence on learning to write as a rational and conceptual process has worked effectively against earlier depictions of children as merely deficient writers, working from bits of fragmented knowledge about the written language system and being cognitively confused about what they're doing.

But, on the other hand, this construction has also defined learning to write as motivated by a desire for mastery, not meaning. Bissex (1980), for example, argues that at one stage Paul's texts are "pseudo-informative" and a bit fanciful, and that his purpose in producing them seems to "involve competence, mastery, control. He was writing to learn" (p. 16). While she does acknowledge that his practice with particular textual forms relates to his later development as a writer, reader, and person, she defines Paul's basic motivation here as rational.

This tends to reduce children's experiments with texts to cognitive problem solving exercises rather than to see them more semiotically as part of a pattern in a child's meaningful engagement with the world through (and against) its many symbolic media.

Questions of language *use*—meaning, intentionality, effect, context—just don't come up. Concerned with cognitive process, or how a child constructs a text, researchers attend little or not at all to what texts actually say, what they mean to the writer and readers, how they function in specific settings, or what they can do as works of thought that generate further thought.

Again, it is the rich particularity and meaningfulness that researchers (like Bissex) saw when they spent time watching the "drama" of an actual child becoming literate and using writing and reading in particular and meaningful ways that put pressure on researchers to rethink in deeply fundamental ways how they had defined *the child writing* as an object of study. There was a surplus of meaning that a cognitive research program alone just couldn't account for or even readily address.

Writing as Social Interaction

The basic epistemological move, then, was to expand the focus of early written language studies, in order to deal more fully and more explicitly with writing as a meaningful and social activity. In explaining the significance of this shift, Sowers (1985) concluded that the Graves–New Hampshire project initially "was designed to document writing as *development,* that is, the unfolding of the individual according to nature's plan, only incidentally related to instruction and social mediation. Instead, *learning,* or what was provided by the environment, proved to be closely intertwined with developmental data about what and how the child took from the environment for self-generated purposes" (p. 329). The boundary between the child as writer and the situations in which that writing took place—between the inside (cognition and "development") and the outside (situation and "curriculum")—began to blur in complex ways, raising new and challenging questions about literacy learning and bringing in new decisions about methodology.

The social setting, no longer just a quiet backdrop in the drama of children writing, had became a significant part of the action itself.

Working within Piagetian or Vygotskian frameworks of development, researchers began looking carefully at the social context as it motivated, supported, and often organized children's particular paths of development as new writers. Children's texts were read as sociolinguistic or semiotic means of acting in the world and communicating with others. Researchers began to investigate the way literacy events actually occurred at home and in classrooms, the way writing and reading were presented at home formally and informally, the way specific family interactional patterns helped to explain the choices new writers made (e.g., identifying with a mother who writes children's stories, competing with an older sister), and the way different children in different settings interacted with writing instruction and experiences. The object of study became a far more situated child, embedded in specific interpersonal relationships and specific social settings, learning to use writing to act via text in those relationships and settings.

Language as Social Semiotic

The earlier structural definitions of language as cognitive puzzle, focusing particularly on orthography, are rethought and expanded into more functional definitions of language as use, addressing the actual texts children produced as texts, as linguistic ways of acting in the world and participating in real language events:

> Language varies according to the topic, the persons involved, and whether it is written or spoken. . . . Children learn naturally to make adjustments in their language by having many opportunties to be present in different kinds of settings where language is being used. Successful language users adjust their language to meet the demands of the setting in which they find themselves. (Harste, Woodward, and Burke, 1984, p. xvi)

With language defined as psycholinguistic and sociolinguistic activity, the child's early writing could now be read as both intentional, or meaningful, and interpretive.

Kress (1982), for example, argues that research into written language development had paid scant attention to language itself, having focused too exclusively on "mechanical" matters like letter formation and spelling, not looking carefully at children's texts as texts. To fill this gap, Kress begins by redefining learning to write from a functional perspective—as the learning of genre—and then applies sociolinguistic theory to the close reading of school texts written by children between the ages of six and fourteen. His ambitious goal is "to provide a methodology for looking at children's writing which will apply to all types of texts written by them" (p. xii), to make visible the rich syntactic and textual complexity of those texts so that readers can see something of value in them, and then to draw inferences about children's conceptual operations and knowledge as they handle the textual structures of written language such as cohesion, paragraphing, and the development of thematic material. In *Learning to Write* (1982), Kress analyzes children's texts in order to hypothesize about the ways children use graphics and meaning as they move toward an adult conception of the written sentence, about textual development within narrative and factual genres, and about the cognitive implications of their uses of different conjoined sentence patterns.

Although sharing the goals of the cognitive research program—that is, although wanting to identify generalizable stages—Kress reverses the traditional Piagetian perspective and argues that "the process of learning to write represents one instance of social learning, where pre-existent norms are imposed on the individual" (p. 2): "The most potent factors in the child's learning to write are the models of written language which the school provides and which it encourages the child to emulate" (p. 85). No longer a natural or biological unfolding, development has now become socialization, with big cognitive and political implications. Learning cultural genres "represents the child's socialization into appropriate and accepted modes of organizing knowledge, of knowing, and the modes of presenting perceptions and knowledge to others" (Kress, 1982, p. 123). These genres are "not neutral in their cognitive, social, and ideological effects" (p. 11), and as the child comes to control the genre, the genre comes to control and constrain the child's creativity. Language use, for Kress, is not a simple act of self-expression or the mere encoding of preexistent thought, but actually "contributes to and shapes the meaning intended by the speaker/writer" (p. 5). He argues, therefore, that schools explicitly study and teach the genres that will most impinge upon the later lives of students, so that they can control and organize language for their own purposes (p. 13).

By defining language as social semiotic, Kress locates the child writing in the culture, dramatically drawing researcher's attention both to the linguistic richness of children's actual texts and also to the role of written language itself, as a particular symbolic and discursive medium, in the developmental process. Written language is defined both as an agent of socialization into cultural ways of knowing and as a means, not a result, of cognitive growth. If the cognitive research program focuses rather exclusively on the individual's private and semiautonomous solving of the written language puzzle (what the child brings), Kress tries to correct, perhaps overcorrect, that imbalance by emphasizing a functional definition of language (what the setting imposes) as socialization and by reading texts as instances of social learning.

Interested also in situating the learner socially, Harste, Woodward, and Burke (1984) reject emphatically the cognitive research program's model of development as stages that all children progress through as they move into a conventional, adult understanding of the written language system. They replace *stage* with *strategy*. Invented spelling, for example, is not for them a stage toward conventional spelling, but rather "a specific instance of a more generalized strategy called 'functional writing,' which is rooted firmly in the psychological limits of human cognition and memory" (p. xi). They claim that both adults and children use basically the same strategies for participating in language events, although with more experience people "naturally" come to fine-tune those activities we call reading and writing. So, fundamentally, a child reading a McDonald's billboard is doing the same thing as an adult reading *War and Peace*—exploring and expanding the communication potential of written language. "We have no evidence," they conclude, "that children's psycholinguistic and sociolinguistic strategies are qualitatively different from the kinds of decisions which more experienced language users make" (p. 69). At all ages, then, language use and language learning are continuous processes, with self-correcting devices built into them.

Like Kress, these authors turn to a theory of written language use, in their case semiotics, in order to elaborate more particularly what learning to write means as a discourse-specific developmental process. Researchers begin here to work from more sophisticated theories of written language, as they attempt to construct possible—and still universal— stages or strategies of development. As a result, language itself assumes a kind of agency in the developmental process and must be accounted for in understanding how and why children become writers.

Texts as Event

No longer a bounded entity or product, no longer the result of private cognition, texts now are read as semiotic events that take place in specific settings, that engage writers and readers, and that are determined by the context in which they occur. Text production no longer means print production per se but refers to the activity of public participation in literacy events, the place holding and signing of one's own meaning in particular settings, the "search for text in context, the negotiation of meaning . . . the risk of taking one's current best shot, and the fine-tuning of text with text" (Harste, Woodward, and Burke, 1984, p. xi).

Child as Social Actor

As Harste, Woodward, and Burke (1984) explain, "psycholinguistic processes have their genesis (socially) in the literacy demonstrations made available to language learners as they encounter members of their interpretive community engaged in the psychological and sociological actions associated with literacy" (p. 49). Literacy learning is rooted in and shaped by the ongoing social context and by the child's meaningful transactions with print in that context. As an object of study, the child writing is constructed now as an actor, motivated by a desire to partici-pate meaningfully in those contexts, to communicate and to act via written text. And texts are read not merely as evidence of cognitive operations and mastery but as instances of children acting in the social settings they find themselves in, as they become increasingly able participants in various literacy events and language communities. In a way, this is the semiotic version of the myth of the natural, as the process of literacy learning is still idealized and sanitized, but now with universal strategies as the explanatory goal.

Gundlach et al. (1985), on the other hand, argue for an even more situated object of study, one that takes into account the real social foundations of early written language development in terms of a particu-lar child's actual relationships to particular people. They argue that people, not just print, serve as resources in the child's early literacy learning by providing the motivation to learn in the first place (p. 53).

These authors contend that the object of study in early research has often been misread, so that the "image of the child constructing, more or less on his own, a personal representation of the principles underlying the structure and functions of written language" (pp. 2–3) has been turned, by some educators, into the notion of the child as an autonomous literate learner, thereby making invisible the actual social organization that underlies and shapes the child's experiences with print in very particular ways. Ethnographers, for example, have pointed out that children's interests in print don't emerge naturally at all but result from the particular ways a particular community presents literacy to its children at home and at school:

> Research and theorizing instructed by this line of criticism have, in effect, expanded *the unit of analysis* in children's writing research from the child's text and his individual composing behavior to a frame that encompasses interaction between child and adult, interaction among children, and the reading and writing activity that a child may observe at home, in a day care center, or in a kindergarten classroom. This shift of focus from studying the child's solitary composing operations to investigating the social contexts of the child's early writing activities has not reduced the interest or even the mystery of the young child's composing processes, but it has led researchers to think more carefully about the role of adults and older siblings in the child's learning. (p. 3, emphasis added)

In this version of the social research program, then, investigators would study the ways adults collaborate with children in reading and writing, trace cultural patterns in families' literacy habits of including children (or not) in particular kinds of reading and writing activities, and focus on the details of the kinds of social interactions that surround literacy at home and at school.

The "three [case] studies we report here," Gundlach (1985) explains, "are attempts to place careful observations of an individual child's writing activity, observations much like those Bissex made of her son's early writing, in the broader social contexts to which recent ethnographic studies have called attention" (p. 5). They look at the human interaction in the context of the young child's early writing activity. In the first study, for example, they report on the role of four-year-old Jeremy's parents in supporting his "pretend writing" and encouraging his substantial use of "the cultural materials of writing, both to please and entertain his parents and to make contact with them while he pleases and entertains himself" (p. 5). In the second study, they observe that Jill's seven-year-old sister Nina "often plays an influential role in Jill's writing projects, serving alternately as a model, a coach, a competitor, and a co-conspirator" (p. 5). And the third study analyzes the composing and dramatizing activity in a preschool setting, as children dictate their fantasy narratives to the teacher and dramatize them with their classmates.

These contexts, these authors claim, provide support rather like a small-scale culture in which children who cannot yet read or write independently might nevertheless develop an understanding of the character and uses of written language. Here children encounter models of writers, are often invited to join in the literacy activities these writers are doing, and discover among those experienced writers an appreciative audience for their own early efforts. Their point is that all early writing takes place within a context of actual social relationships with people who matter:

> It was in the context of relationships with parents, siblings, preschool teachers, and neighborhood friends that the children we observed engaged in their early experiments with writing. It was in the course of participating in those relationships—maintaining, expanding, and redefining the power relations in them—that Jeremy, Jill, Nathaniel, and others found reasons for trying to write, for accepting help when it was offered, for seeking help when it wasn't offered, and for rejecting help altogether. (p. 53)

Gundlach et al. (1985) do not want to discount the significance of cognitive operations or to minimize developmental constraints. They do, however, want to replace that image of the "autonomous child encountering a rich print environment and, on his own and in ways mysterious to the adults around him, reinventing the system of language" with a picture of "a child experimenting with written language as a way of participating in important human relationships" (p. 53). The child's desire here is not just for mastery and control over the structures of written language per se but for the ability to use written language as a means of participating within settings and relationships that matter to the child.

Interpretation and Relational Analysis

When Harste, Woodward, and Burke (1984) started off, they were self-declared positivists, with expertise in experimental design, but they claim that during the course of their study they moved into what they call "child-as-informant" research. They tried to identify and explicate the language and language learning principles embedded in literacy stories, to make theoretical and curricular sense out of them, to interpret them. That is, the patterns in these language stories did not "speak for themselves, but in transaction with us and with the history of literacy which we bring to the setting" (p. xix). The epistemological stance has become more explicitly interpretive, with children's texts treated as a canon to be explicated in a dialogic way, and with accounts of literacy events documented fully enough so that readers can contribute their own ideas and interpretations.

Indeed, most of these studies engage in a kind of hermeneutical inquiry, to use North's (1987) term, in that they put together a collection of texts, authenticate them in some way, and then analyze the relationship of the texts to each other, to the writers, to people and events in the context. Harste, Woodward, and Burke collected, compared, and contrasted language stories and looked for key patterns and differences among them. They acknowledge explicitly their own situatedness in this endeavor, the theory from which they read these stories, the "set of beliefs" they were acting from. In explicating these stories and lessons, that theory or set of beliefs was in turn articulated, modified, and developed over time. Gundlach et al. and Dyson go into the homes and classrooms of actual children, reading not only the texts children wrote but also the setting as a kind of text, drawing detailed pictures of each child's literacy learning, and using theory (e.g., Vygotksy or Erikson) or other research to make connections or draw conclusions or frame explanations.

Situated Explanation as Goal

In the process, research has become less universalized, more localized in its goal. For example, Dyson (1984) in her later work looks at the specific, and potentially conflictual, interaction "between the child's construction of written language and school literacy instruction" (p. 6) through a close analysis and case study of one child. In combining the point of view of developmental psychology with the perspective of developmental sociolinguistics and ethnography, Dyson talks about literacy learning in terms of "child/curriculum contrasts" (p. 11) by attending to both sides of the interaction. She investigates possible mismatches between a particular child's efforts at constructing knowledge of written language and a specific teacher's expectations based on her commonsense and curricular notions of language learning goals. Dexter, the case study child, often interprets writing tasks differently from his teacher—as, for example, when he interjects a personal context into certain assignments and therefore follows out a different set of purposes for himself. In privileging the role of the child in literacy learning, Dyson concludes that when these mismatches occur, children become confused, unable to incorporate "floating bits of knowledge" (p.

47) into their understanding of written language and creating an ever greater gap between the child's world and the school's.

In "Individual Differences in Emerging Writing," Dyson (1985) argues even more explicitly for reconstructing the object of study in literacy research. She, too, contends that early researchers focused too narrowly on particular aspects of learning to write (e.g., letter formation or orthographic rules) and recommends focusing now on the individual child qua writer as the unit of analysis. In particular, she argues for attending to the child's purpose and intentional framework as well as to the setting in making sense of their choices as beginning writers:

> . . . the nature of the individual child, the nature of the situational context, and the complex nature of the writing system itself all interact in written language growth. . . . By intensive comparative study of individual children, we can gain insight into the complex, interrelated variables involved in development. (pp. 59–60)

Dyson presents detailed portrayals of three young writers, linking composing process behaviors and choices with each child's "dominant purposes for writing to themes, patterns, and intentions which defined her as an individual" (p. 117). From this "there emerged a picture of Tracy as a constructionist, Rachel as both a pragmatist and dramatist, and Vivi as an eager investigator" (p. 119). Attending to individual variation, according to Dyson, allows researchers to gain "insight into both the nature of the writing system itself and the process of learning to write" (p. 122). With the particular child now as object of study, his or her "patternings of the writing act highlight varied aspects of the intricate writing web" (p. 122). For Dyson, the child is "in control of the kaleidoscope we call written language" (p. 122), and it is through comparative studies of individual children's literacy learning processes that we will come to understand more about written language itself and about the complexities of becoming literate in this culture.

And so the object of study, for many researchers, has become more complex, more embedded in setting and culture, and more situated and individualized—and the possible explanations for how children become writers more far-reaching, more varied, more transactive. The myth of natural literacy undergirding the cognitive research program, with its idealized child and teacher and its definition of written language as a singular linguistic (structural) system, is countered here by close, detailed ethnographic attention to the intractable complexities of actual children, with real interests and motivations and even problems, in many diverse communities and contexts, encountering in specific settings a range of people and a plurality of literacies.

The kind of knowledge generated in this kind of research differs from the kind of decontextualized and causal explanations we somewhat (still) stereotypically assume follow from scientific investigation. Causal claims are replaced by interpretive explication, large numbers of subjects by small ones, and the authority of the experiment itself by the authority of the experimenter himself or herself.

Tensions and Limits

Like light through a prism, attention to the social aspects of literacy learning has opened up a complex spectrum of issues and possibilities for researchers. This expansion from a psychological to a social or contextual model is, according to Phelps (1988), an inevitable intellectual move in a developing discipline like this one.

Much is gained. Language itself is taken seriously, as a specific symbolic system and as an agent, or hero, in the developmental process itself. Questions of meaning and use arise. The child is no longer just a lone scientist uncovering structural patterns and regularities driven by a desire for cognitive mastery, but an active participant in meaningful and public performances of language use. Development itself has become a complex transactional process, full of surprises and disjunctures. The object of study has become a lot messier to deal with conceptually and theoretically, both in defining that object and in deciding upon approaches to explaining or understanding it.

Lots of intriguing questions have also emerged.

What does *social* really mean? Ironically, this key term remains somewhat underconceptualized still, as several composition theorists have noted. They claim that *social* has been defined too behaviorally as a concrete setting or situation in which (typically) members of a dyad interact together, such as a teacher or parent and a child. This definition fails to take into account more abstract yet powerful social influences on composing decisions, such as culture, institution, and ideology. Researchers also still assume that what's "out there" rather directly and concretely "comes in," so that they remain predisposed to stage models and continue to privilege sequence and causality over recursiveness and transformation.

Relying on Vygotsky, Zebroski (1989) further pushes our thinking about what an object of study might look like, by proposing a social subject that challenges the autonomy and essentialism of the child writing:

1. the self is ontologically social, coming into existence only in community;
2. the self is constructed by others;
3. the self is permeable and porous, extending into others, finding self within otherness;
4. the self is dynamic, multiple, many-edged;
5. the self is semiotic, in that language "speaks" the self;
6. the self is refined and developed through play.

If we accept the concept of *social* too easily, Zebroski warns, we may end up defining it merely as individuals doing group work or collaboration, rather than exploring the concept for its rich, demanding theoretical and pedagogical implications. Social factors, then, are not just tacked on later but are at the very ontological heart of our being and becoming. We are only beginning to think through how a social subject might transform the very fundamental notions of self, writer, community, and writing that have informed our investigations (see also Chapter 4).

What is the role of language as agent or hero in development? Recent scholarship in the humanities and social sciences, especially postmodern theories of discourse, have put great pressure on language researchers to rethink the determining, perhaps overdetermining, effect of language use. Learning to write becomes defined as a constitutive act, in which language appropriates the writer rather than the writer using language for his or her own private intentions. Discourse-specific questions emerge about the nature of the complex transaction of child and language. How natural or socially imposed is it? How individualized? And life-span developmental psychology suggests that we study literacy learning as a lifelong experience, deeply interwoven into personal, aesthetic, intellectual, and critical strands of the developing person.

How can readers and researchers read children's texts and make sense of such a complex phenomenon? What is the goal of research then? Is it theoretically sound, or even logistically manageable, to add on social factors to explanations of the developmental process whereby children become literate in this culture?

The situatedness of the writer requires that we also take into account the situatedness of the researcher. Consider the hot theoretical debate going on in interpretive anthropology for a discussion of the problems of how to report adequately and legitimately on social realities (e.g., Marcus and Fischer, 1986). These issues have also been explored in Chapters 2 and 3, demonstrating both the potentials and the problematics of reading and of reporting on the writing experiences of others.

Let's take a homespun example. I have collected texts for one young writer from first through fifth grade and want to trace his development as a writer across all five years and across many settings (in classrooms, at home, with baby-sitters, at friends' houses). Just consider the possible range of social factors I might take into account if I were to try to explain in any detail and in any thoroughly causal way his early choices as a writer. He has had five different teachers and diverse opportunities and assignments for writing, from story starters to rules for a clubhouse he built with friends. In fact, his first real text was composed one day when he had to sit through a composition class that I was teaching, and he used crayons and a large sheet of paper to compose an adventure story while students in the class worked on argumentative essays. His major project in second grade was a self-initiated mystery story that he wrote in lieu of short daily entries in a journal his teacher had assigned. In third grade, he often wrote with friends at school. He read a range of books and watched more movies than I can remember or recount. He's an only child in a highly literate environment, with reading and writing a visible part of the daily routine. And so on and so on and so on.

What social factors are relevant? Beyond scattered observations and anecdotes, how do I collect all this information? Given my position (mother, composition teacher, phenomenological researcher), how will I decide what counts, especially causally? If I look first at his texts and trace the patterns out, don't I risk committing the fallacy of affirming the consequent and forgetting that things can be explained by any number of assumptions or theories or factors? In a similar way, Mailloux (1989) argues that any account that uses context as constraint on literary interpretation risks becoming unworkable. "Either it must simply name 'context,' 'situation,' or 'circumstances' as a constraint and not elaborate any further," he explains, "or it must carry out an infinite listing of all aspects of context and their interrelations, that is, bring everything in. . . . [It] must either never begin the process of specification or never end it" (p. 11).

In sum, we have lots to talk about—theories of the social, the position of readers and researchers, the problematics of too narrowly defined causal explanation as a goal in research, and the powerful agency of written language itself in the developmental process. In this book, I have been developing alternative claims about studying writers as they emerge across time and within various settings: I have been arguing for language as hero, text as shared territory, the child as maker of works, dialogic encounter (or descriptive reading) as method, and understanding (not explanation) as the goal of the research.

All these claims will be brought to bear in the next chapter as I attempt a particular form of "deep talk" in relation to the work of Matthew Himley—and as I present a documentary account from the construction of *the child making* as subject of study.

A Child
Writing

6

A Documentary Account of One Young Writer: Matthew Writing

This documentary account traces the child-culture dialogic encounter that takes place through language use, through the actual making of texts, for one child from first through fifth grade. It is an effort at doing research from the theoretical position argued for through this project: language as hero, text as shared territory, the child as maker of works, dialogic encounter or descriptive reading as method, and understanding as the goal.

Following the tradition of researchers like Bissex, I have collected and studied the writing my son Matthew did both at home and at school over this five-year period of time. From the 160 or so texts he wrote, from warning signs on his bedroom door to story starter assignments from school, I have selected 15 key texts that evoke the range and the pattern in the entire corpus, and completed descriptive readings of these texts, organized both chronologically and thematically.

In exploring a written counterpart to deep talk and describing as a way of knowing, this documentary account is an experiment in method and genre.

As illustrated in Chapters 2 and 3, to read descriptively is to slow down and ambiguate the reading process, to come at a text over and over again, to layer words on words, to disrupt meaning, to locate the text in multiple and changing contexts. This kind of reading loosens the pragmatic frame, opening texts up to ambiguity and multiple meanings, and moves slowly and carefully and respectfully (and always partially) from outsideness into otherness.

That is, to describe is a method to make explicit both how social the text is and how individual it is—*both* to enlarge and locate a text within multiple cultural and historical (con)texts *and* to note the patterns of its particularization—all at the same time, all within the shared territory of the text itself.

In the first sections of this account, I describe Matthew's texts much the way it happens orally in deep talk. I ask readers to read these texts aloud, to lend their voices to them, as Matthew has lent his voice to us. The experience of reading the texts aloud is necessary. Especially in the first two sections, I offer lengthy descriptive rounds, and I move slowly. These descriptions contain repetitions, traces, and echoes, and they typically stay at the level of description for a long time, allowing textual specifics and patterns to emerge as they do in deep talk. As I work more directly from within a Bakhtinian perspective, I do less actual description and present Matthew's texts either alone or with more explicitly interpretive and argumentative speculations.

I have resisted conventions of biography such as photographs or detailed background information, because it is not "Matthew" but "Matthew writing" that we are studying.

I want readers to start from Matthew's texts, to read them as works, and to take them seriously as objects of thought which are capable of generating further thought among readers. I also want readers to hear the voices of earlier readers who have described, responded to, and thereby enlarged these works. Most importantly, I want readers to think, feel, dispute, reread, challenge, and further enlarge the possibilities of meaning and understanding.

This kind of research report, therefore, asks a lot of patience from the reader—patience to dwell in the text, to move raggedly toward closure and argument, and to participate responsively in the process itself. The account differs from the child studies completed at the Prospect School and from the earlier accounts I have published. This documentary account intends to make its argument (and to lead to what Bakhtin calls "responsive understanding") in uneven ways, through detail, description, dramatization, and argument.

Reading Across Time: "Deep Talk"

In this section I explore the particular ways Matthew has been drawn across time to the semiotic resources of written language, and look at commonalities amid proliferating diversity in his expressive choices as a writer. I want to evoke here his unique and distinctive accent as a writer, in what Carini calls "the personal aesthetic." It is a way for readers to meet "Matthew writing."

This opening section is also a way to demonstrate in detail the process of description, or deep talk, as a way of knowing. The descriptions of texts I and II follow the structure of rounds of Carini's reflective methods for understanding children's works (see Chapter 1 for a full explanation) and are based on a transcript of an actual descriptive reading of these texts completed by the members of a collaborative study group at Prospect Summer Institute II, 1985.

I want to acknowledge and thank the participants: Kate Guerin, Susan Jacobson, Rhoda Kanevsky, Judy Mintier, Ellen Schwartz, Alice Seletsky, and Betsy Wice.

Text I (1st grade, fall 1980, about age 5 years, 10 months)[1]

Wose oepon A tim tHeR Wer to litl Boys
tHeR Nams WR Matt and Matt
tHeR Moms anD DaDys weR lost
tHey HaeD to spenD tHeR oewn mone to Bi
FoeD sou tHEy coDe Eat BRaKFist anD lonch
anD DinR Wone Day tHeR
moms anD DaDs cam Home
tHey astD Hoe tHay Got FOD
How Do you think witH MaNe
DiD you Ha eNOF Mone   yEs We weR
amost   owt   inam GlaD you DiD Not Di
we amost DiD saD Matt Himley

[Once upon a time there were two little boys.
Their names were Matt and Matt.
Their Moms and Daddys were lost.
They had to spend their own money to buy
food, so they could eat breakfast and lunch
and dinner. One day their
Moms and Dads came home.
They asked how they got food.
"How do you think? With money."

"Did you have enough money?" "Yes, we were
almost out." "I'm glad you did not die."
"We almost did," said Matt Himley.]

Paraphrase of the Text

The tale, set initially in the past, opens with the conventional fairy tale
beginning of "Once upon a time." The main characters are introduced,
with a play on doubleness, as the boys have similar names. Somehow the
parents have gotten lost, and the boys have to take care of themselves
with their own money. The writer lists very specifically each meal that
they have had to provide for themselves.

In that ambiguous time of "one day," their parents collectively return
and are curious about how the boys got food. Their response is a bit fresh:
one or both of them ask a rhetorical question and give the firm answer that
they got food "with money," of course! The parents then ask if they had
enough money, and the boys respond that they had "almost" run out of
resources. The parents express relief that the boys didn't die, and Matt
Himley replies that they "almost" did.

The exchange between parents and boys has an edge to it, and leaves
lots of questions unanswered, like why the parents went away in the first
place and why they didn't leave any money.

In sum, this story about two competent boys starts out conventionally
in the fairy tale mode and with the fairy tale convention of the children
being in charge of their own lives. The parents return and, in a curious
way, ask how they got food and if there had been enough money. The
boys' response has a flippant edge to it. The tale ends happily, with the
normal order of things (apparently) restored.

Descriptive Round 1

The boys are presented as "little," though they will be shown in the
course of the tale to be behaving in adultlike ways and with the economic
resources that adults typically have. There is the possibility of humor and
a touch of self-awareness in the writer's decision to say that their names
were Matt and Matt. The fourth sentence is quite long—nineteen
words—and it, too, is a bit humorous, with the formal listing of each

meal, as if to say that they were at the limit of their patience with this situation. The tone of the first three lines is rather matter-of-fact, which contributes to the ironic quality of the fourth line.

The story is told straightforwardly and factually (as established by the many uses of the verb "were") and in predictable order in the first half. Then the "one day" breaks the orderliness, gives the sense of lots of time having somehow passed, and enables the reader to recognize more fully that the boys have been abandoned in a sense. Initially the reader doesn't know how serious the crisis is—or could be.

Lots of information is packed economically, and implicitly, into the first four lines. With no elaboration, the characters are introduced, the situation established, and the boys' response summed up. There is also a rather precise focus: here are two boys all on their own in the wide, wide world, but the writer focuses on only one aspect of this experience, the question of food and money. There is a vague sense of a whole background setting that lies behind the reported events, but a background the story leaves unexplained. Time, too, remains ambiguous, though phrases such as "one day" and "almost did [die]" suggest the possibility of a lot of time (and trouble) having passed.

Summary of Round 1

The story might be characterized by its opposing specificity with vagueness. On the one hand, the story starts definitely, has a predictable beginning, lists meals specifically, focuses on food and money in concrete detail, consists of actual dialogue among characters, and twice makes use of the qualification "almost." Yet on the other hand, many things remain unspecified, even unclear: the fact that the boys have the same name, the question of how they got to be where they are, the background and location of the events, the sense that the boys know how to act like adults, the curious actions of the parents, and the ambiguous time frame.

Descriptive Round

There is an easy conversationality in the language, as in the "Moms and Dads" line. The words sound like something people would say. There is also a rhythm to the story, a bit of swing to the prose, as in the parallel delineation of each meal and in the "said Matt Himley" line, which reverses the expected order of a tag line. The word "almost" is used twice, adding to the quality of self-awareness, as if the writer knows this is a kind of funny tale. The boys have been pushed to the edge, and Matt Himley wants to rub it in a little with the last line, in a dramatic but playful way.

In a way, this tale reverses the abandoned children stories, as it is the parents here who get lost. There is also a bit of uncertainty about who these parents are, leaving their kids, but little sense of their being mean or evil, just off doing those mysterious adultlike things somewhere else.

The theme, ultimately, is profound—about life and death. Reasonable explanations don't exist for the possibility of death, but there is a haunting sense of coming to the limit of one's resources, of being pushed to the edge, and of "almost" going over that edge.

The doubleness of the two boys is a typical convention in adventure stories (e.g., Hansel and Gretel), where children don't have grown-ups and where benign adults are in the background somewhere but don't interfere.

The writer expresses real interest in the issue of money and food buying, and he gets right to that issue, without doing the background details. He focuses quite intensely on needing and having resources for surviving in the world.

The story can be read and reread, as there is enough substance and suggestiveness to engage readers' interest. Although the names are specific, the theme and events resonate with universal concerns of food and money, concerns that can readily be read as symbols of resources for survival more generally. It is also easy to hear the voices in the text, to read the lines of dialogue aloud and hear the inflection and rhythm that go with them. The story ends evocatively with an open-ended line, adding to the sense of this tale being a small piece of a larger scene.

The story lulls the reader, with its rhythmic quality and its specificity. It makes the reader want to participate, as evidenced in the ways readers (in this session) repeated the dialogue out loud and played with it, especially the last line.

The story teases, too. It's a "typical" adventure story, but with twists. No explanation is offered about how the boys got the money or the food. There is a feeling that there is more to the story than is being told. The short sentences that don't spell everything out add to this sense of ambiguity. The phrase "come home" is ambiguous—from where? The boys' adventure, ironically, takes place at home, in a normal world abruptly reversed by the parents' mysteriously getting lost, and these unexplained disappearances and reappearances add a dreamlike quality to the tale.

Summary of Round 2

Oppositions structure and animate this story. There is a sharply focused event rendered against a vague and mysterious backdrop. Precise explanations and exact explicitness about names and meals, for example, contrast with all the unanswered questions about plot and the vagueness of the backdrop to these events. The logical understanding of how the world works which is suggested by the use of the connector "so"—that is, the possibility that events in the world can be known and explained—works in tension with the mysterious, unknowable, and finally unaccounted-for disappearance of the parents. The writer's use of normal, ordinary, everyday language, as in the listing of the meals and in his dialogue, is set off against the haunting and dreamlike quality of the text as a whole.

In an almost classic way, the writer explores profound questions of life and death, cause and effect, the coming to the edge of one's knowledge and resources and almost dropping off the cliff. There is a kind of comforting (and discomforting) circularity to the story. Life does return to normal—people are reunited; the crises pass; relationships, authority, and normalcy are reasserted—yet things are somehow both the same and different.

The story thematizes children searching ambivalently for independence but not quite being there. It takes a surprise, a transformation or reversal of the normal world, to enable them to assert this independence, but then they are ready to return to the constraints and safety of that normal world.

The writer demonstrates lots of knowledge of the medium and genre he is working with. Without meandering or false starts, he positions himself as a distant or omniscient narrator and later as a character. The narrative structure of the story is tightly symmetrical and tightly rendered, with a strong sense of wholeness, boundedness, and closure. He constructs a text world, populates it with two main characters, sets up a problem, and proceeds logically to resolve it within its own terms. Once money and food are raised in the beginning, it is the working out of those details that moves the story forward. In a sense, this is a "when/then" text: when this kind of event occurs, then these kinds of things follow.

The writer uses conventions of the fairy tale genre and adventure stories but works them around real-world, concrete concerns like food and money. He uses dialogue to great effect. Readers can hear, too, the "voices" of the teller of fairy tales, the factual or distanced narrator, the concerned parents, the children alternately sarcastic and scared, proud and angry. And all the elements of fictional narrative are here: generic structure, some formal and fairy tale language, adventure story content, characters, direct and indirect dialogue, crisis and resolution, and several narrative stances.

The text is pulled along by the rhythm of the syntax, the demands of the genre, the logic of the text world—*and* the expressiveness of the writer.

In this text, we can begin to read the particular and unique ways Matthew will come specifically to appropriate the semiotic resources of written language. We can begin to see his expressive textual choices and hear his particular accent and intonation.

Text II (5th grade, May 1985, age 10 years, 5 months)

1999

"They finaly did it," I whispered
to myself as I woke up to see the
city in crumbles. The bomb must have
landed about 80–90 miles away since
I was only knocked down and
bruised up. I was looking at a huge
black cloud to the west when my
heart stopped. Where was my mom?

Since the house wasn't damaged
very much I went inside to see
what I could. then I just remembered
that my mom said that she was
going to the grocery store. I went into
the garage to get my bicycle. the
wall of the garage must of sheltered
it because it was almost exactly
like I left it. And then I set
out to find my mom.

When I got to the grocery
store everyone was up and around.
When I saw my mom I was very
relived. She was sitting against the
magazine rack, with one eye open
and one eye closed. We hugged and
kissed for a while. And the with
our hands around each other we
went home.

Paraphrase of the Text

The story starts in the middle of the action. The narrator looks up and sees the city in ruins. He realizes the damage is from a bomb and estimates its distance. The "they" is vague, but the word "finally" suggests an expectation. He "whispers," and that's odd, since he's alone. It is interesting how he is knocked *down* and bruised *up*. The word "crumbles" suggests a gingerbread house or city. The narrator sees a black cloud in the west, and this terrifies him, because he doesn't know where his mother is.

Apparently the home is not damaged, and the narrator goes off to find his mother. Interestingly, the city is in crumbles, but the house isn't harmed very much. In the midst of all this commotion, his taking the bike strikes a rather normal note. The garage, the bicycle, and the grocery store are quite normal, too.

At the grocery store, everyone is "up and around," which suggests minimal damage and injury there, too. The narrator ends the story by answering the question of what you do when this happens: you put your hands around each other and return home.

In sum, this story begins in the middle of something, with a boy alone and asleep, who whispers to himself. There is a bomb in the distance, which has knocked him down. Though the city is in crumbles, those things the boys needs—his house, his bicycle—are intact, sheltered by the wall. The store, too, and Mom are all right, only slightly injured. Then there is a happy-ever-after kind of ending, a return to a damaged but intact world.

Descriptive Round 1

The opening sentence may come from children's storybooks, but the word "crumbles" and the phrase "knocked down and bruised up" make the writer's own voice evident. There is rhythm and parallelism in the prose, almost a singsong swing to the phrasing and an alternating of long and short sentences. While the quest is heroic—"I set out to find my mom"—the language is direct, colloquial, and simple. The "one eye open and one eye closed" line creates a dreamlike atmosphere, in the middle of the rather normal setting of a grocery store, during the quite extraordinary moment of a bomb explosion.

The story is complete and self-contained, although there is a whole other story behind it and many unanswered questions. Was it a nuclear bomb? What will their life be like now? What's happening in the rest of the world? An entire background scenario is implied.

The main character does a lot of reasonable explaining. He calculates precisely and mathematically the relation of damage and distance. In the second paragraph, in two long sentences that sound believable and rational, he assesses and explains the limited damage to the house and bicycle, using logical language like "since" and "because." There is a kind of interplay between certainties and uncertainties, between the tangible and known and the unexpected and unknown. The character also comes up with a plan and acts; he doesn't feel lost nor does he just sit there, waiting for more events to happen to him.

The language is both sophisticated, as in the word "sheltered," and simple, childlike, and conversational.

Structurally, the story is constructed in three tightly symmetrical parts. Each part has an ending that not only concludes that part but also marks a transition into the next one. The parts are all about the same length and have a specific focus and setting—waking up to the explosion, surveying the damage to the house, and going to the grocery story. Yet the story coheres through the quest for Mom.

Even though the city is in crumbles, those things that belong to the character remain intact. In a sense, the story is about things changing rather dramatically yet still staying the same. They return to the shelter of a not very damaged house. There is a wholeness and circularity to the story, as he ends up where he began—in a world that is the same but different.

The phrase "up and around" is frequently used for people who are in the hospital recovering from an illness or surgery, as a sign of their return to well-being. Its use in this story carries with it that upbeat sense of a return to normalcy, of restoration, even renewal.

Although the story starts off with something very frightening, the writer quickly brings the tale to what matters to him—to Mom and shelter. He zeroes in on the heart of the matter. Though the story is about war, perhaps even nuclear war, the writer focuses quickly on what is important to him, on the details of ordinary life.

Summary of Round 1

This story takes place in 1999, right on the edge of a new century. It is a heroic quest of a child who obviously has a lot of strength. The normal is set dramatically against the extraordinary, the rational against the unknown. There are lots of concrete, everyday, normal things in the story: bicycle, garage, house, grocery story, magazine rack, Mom. Perhaps even nuclear war, seen so often on TV, seems normal now. And there are lots of events that can be logicallly explained—for example, the little damage done to the bicycle. Yet all this incontrovertible normalcy and reasonableness is set against a dramatic backdrop of war, disaster, and potential chaos.

Descriptive Round 2

There is a strong feeling of symmetry in this text, with its paragraphs constructed almost equally in length. The last two sentences have such classic qualities to them, with echoes and traces from texts in other contexts, moving the story beyond itself in some ways, into universal moments of reunion and closure.

The phrase "almost exactly" in the second paragraph suggests that the character really wanted things to be the same, but they were not quite so. It resonates with the "almost" and "almost did [die]" in text I, because in both there is that sense of coming to the edge of the world.

Both texts are about life and death, cause and effect. Both have implicit why questions—Why did the parents leave? Why did "they" explode the bomb?—which are never answered and remain part of the ultimately unknown backdrop. In both there is order out of chaos, or at least a potential chaos. Things could fall apart completely, but they haven't. Normalcy is restored—and no one dies.

The narrator works with a clear sense of focus and tells the story directly, consistently, without meandering or getting sidetracked.

The boys in both stories are quite purposeful: you have to eat, so you get food; you have to find your mom, so you set out to do so. They are competent and ready to take charge of things even in dangerous situations. It's a kind of wish state for children—a world in which they can take care of not only themselves but even their parents.

Texts I and II seem rather like vignettes—small, self-contained portraits drawn sharply and completely and purposefully, but always with a fuzzy, complex background and lots of unanswered questions behind them. The word "almost" links the focused event with the fuzzy background, by always keeping things open just a bit, always teasing about possibilities that might occur, always threatening to disrupt the happy ending and the return to normalcy, always challenging the logic of that normal and safe world. Even the "one eye opened and one eye closed" line suggests imagistically the possibility of "almost"—of almost seeing everything but not quite.

Summary of Round 2

Text II, like the first story, has symmetry and rhythm and the classic children's story theme of children searching for their independence but not quite being there yet. It takes a transformation—parents disappearing, bombs exploding—to enable the boys to show this independence, and there is a confidence that they can handle the basic things, like food and shelter. Despite the extraordinary events, there are enough ordinary words in both stories to show readers that the stories, and the characters, are believable.

The voice of the writer is mostly simple and colloquial, with sophisticated words interjected now and then. He sounds direct and purposeful and focused, as he draws the boundaries of the story and works through the logic of that circumscribed text world. The prose invites reading aloud, with its hint of ambiguity and playfulness and rhythm. Although there is little descriptive language, each text is emotive and evocative.

The stories are ultimately life-affirming, despite the disasters, shaped by oppositions between precise and focused versus vague and implicit, between grounded and concrete detail versus fuzzy background, between rational explanation versus (potential) chaos and lack of control.

"Precise" as a Keyword

In the description of the first two texts, a word that emerges often is *precise,* referring to Matthew's listing of meals, his mathematical-like calculations, his tightly structured rendering of texts, his care with word choice. Following Carini's procedure for doing a reflective conversation on a keyword, I offer here an instance of deep talk on the word *precise* as another method, through language itself, for understanding Matthew's expressive style as a writer and maker of works.[2] We can then trace this feature as it appears and reappears in various texts and forms throughout the documentary account. This open-ended process unpacks the multiple associations, connotations, uses, tensions, and cultural contexts in which the word turns up, and thereby provides a reading on the range of *precise* as one feature of Matthew's expressive style:

—acute, acuity, cutting, incisive, to the point (or pre = before)
  a kid is likely to force a parent into precision with imperatives or commands like "you didn't tell me not to!"
  precision cars and machines—move smoothly, no noise, not calling attention to themselves as they fulfill their functions

—precision drill, precision tooling, precision haircuts
  precise measurements
  exactitude
  associations with parts and machinery, as when trying to be precise about gapping spark plugs (if the gap is wrong, the car won't start)

—the chalk line on a two-by-four snapped for a straight line
  Gillette razor blades for a clean shave
  a figure skater's blade cutting designs in the ice
  the swing of a pendulum, the tick tock of a second hand
  two objects meeting in one space and time
  measured, inspected, recorded, analyzed, sharp, shiny

—clipped, a "proper" word, like Mary Poppins, prim and proper Brits
  concise, no useless syllables
  careful, calculated, organized, clean, planned, exact
  something that can be pinned down, known
  "make your writing more precise" = say what you mean, don't get off the subject

hair in place, clothes pressed, right for the occasion

—incisive, sharp, cutting, incision
exact place, placed exactly
of a definite time and place, to the point, of a point
precision tools, delicate machinery, do exactly what they're sup-
    posed to do, nothing more, nothing less, just right for the job
"precisely," like no other word would do
intelligence, a skilled mind or hand is precise

—something that operates exactly as is said without variation, neat
predictable, consistent
"it worked with precision"
what is the difference between concise and precise?

—accurate, not erring
cutting wood in carpentry, material in sewing
legal language, like "what was the precise moment that such and
    such happened?"
an architectural drawing of a building
making an appointment to arrive "precisely" at nine
saying exactly what you mean

The word *precise* opens up into concepts of measurement, definiteness,
delicacy, and exactness. It suggests a skilled and disciplined hand behind
a quick, clean movement, like a surgeon performing an incision or an
architect planning a building. It relates to punctuality, temporality, what
happens in an instant. If there's more time, there are more variables, and
things get messier. *Precise* is caught most sharply in the image of the
figure skater cutting a careful and exact design across the ice, a skill that
requires training, discipline, control, and exactitude.

Language as Hero

In this section I look at four versions of a story Matthew wrote in second
grade over a three- to four-week period of time. Version 1 was written in
school. Matthew's second-grade teacher presented the assignment to the
class by putting this title on the board: "The Day the TV Disappeared."
She then initiated a class discussion about how much television the
children watched, what their favorite shows were, and what they'd do if

parents limited TV-watching time. Version 2 was written later that day at the baby-sitter's house, on a large sheet of drawing paper that he had carefully lined first. Version 3 was written at school over a three- to four-week period of time, in lieu of journal entries on mostly assigned topics. The final version, 4, was written in his journal on the back page of the story. Matthew apparently worked independently on versions 2, 3, and 4, not sharing them with his teacher or classmates at all.

In this section of the documentary, I want to trace the moments of microgenesis—the ways language itself, as Bakhtinian hero, pulls Matthew's development as a writer forward by opening up new semiotic possibilities for him. I want to trace, that is, the ways the story tells itself—through certain key words, the requirements of the emerging genre, the syntactical patterns and rhythm, the resources of spoken language, and the many "voices."

A shorter version of this analysis, focusing primarily on Matthew's expressive choices, appeared as an article entitled "Disappearing TVs and Evolving Texts" in *Language Arts,* March 1986, pp. 238–45. I again want to give special thanks to Rhoda Kanevsky as chair and Alice Seletsky as secretary of a reflective reading of this text, with special attention to version 3, during Prospect Summer Institute II, 1982.

While building from a descriptive reading, this account moves the argument into more specifically theoretical directions. I do not recreate the descriptive rounds but extend that reading into Bakhtin and into questions of child-culture dialogic encounter.

Text III (2nd grade, fall 1981, age about 6 years, 11 months)

[1] The Day the tV Disappeared

Once opon a time I	[Once upon a time I
was playing Atare and	was playing Atari and
My tV disappeared I	my TV disappeared. I
did't now what to do	didn't know what to do.
I ran to my mom I	I ran to my mom. I
said the tV disappeared	said, "The TV disappeared.
What shode I do?	What should I do?"
My mom said com down	My mom said, "Calm down.
shod I cole the poles I	Should I call the police?" I
said yes!	said. "Yes!"]

The basic crisis of the story has been provided by the assigned topic: what if the TV disappeared? The teacher intended her second-grade students to assess how much time they spent (or wasted) watching TV and to consider what they'd do if their parents restricted this viewing time. But Matthew takes off in a different direction.

Perhaps it is the word *disappear* itself that engages Matthew's interest, that matters to him, and that ultimately draws him into the process of composing and recomposing this text over time.

Disappear does, after all, suggest a provocative range of semantic possibilities. As an agentless verb, it directs attention to a potentially magical vanishing process, and it raises the question of a quest, as one goes about solving the disappearance and coming to understand how it happened. The verbs "do" and "know" come to figure prominently in all the versions of the text.

Given its centrality to the story, readers might do a reflection on the word *disappear:*

—The word calls to mind transformations, shifting realities, visible and invisible elements, magical powers.

—A question that follows is whether or not what has disappeared is retrievable, whether it will reappear of its own will or power, whether a larger power (magic, fantasy, justice, perhaps just persistence) is needed to reinvoke it.

—Another question concerns what has caused the disappearance, whether it's a real-world or magical cause, and what forces control it.

—Search is also involved, for the thing that has disappeared, for control over events.

—And search also suggests a challenge, a journey to understanding why the disappearance has occurred, a quest to restore order.

This kind of reflection offers a possible point of entry into understanding the text, its meanings and its making, by more fully locating *disappear* in a larger and larger semantic network. The word *matters* to Matthew, in the way Carini talks about in Chapter 1 when things in the world become valued, create an intensification of feeling within us, engage our interest, resonate for us, and draw us into public spheres of meaning.

And video games such as Space Invaders enact a kind of magical disappearance in a way that can be mesmerizing, as rocket ships disappear from the screen at the pushing of a button and in the twinkling of an eye. The possibilities of discontinuity are everywhere in the world of videos, which then may become emblematic of that quality of discontinuity in the world itself.

After the narrative crisis is set up in the opening three lines, the flow of information—that is, the way the text is developed locally—reads like the transcription of a spoken language dialogue. The unit of text, more phonological than graphological, as well as the absence of periods, supports the interpretive possibility that the writer relies on spoken language resources for text generation.[3] It is as if he were transcribing voices that he hears in his head, with boundaries left unmarked, because the boundaries are conveyed auditorily in terms of intonation contours rather than graphically in terms of periods. The writer may hear the boundaries as he writes, while the reader may have to subvocalize to locate and recreate them. While the question mark and exclamation point do point to the writer's beginning use of what Cazden (1982) identifies as "easier" graphical signs, the text consists primarily of single clauses, or intonation contours, or "voices," that tumble unmarked down the page.

The text's overall development remains rather tenative, with no clear genre form emerging as yet. The "once upon a time" fairy tale beginning, the use of the simple past tense, and the fictionalizing construction of Matthew as "I" all mark the text as narrative, but the dialogue suggests also a play or a script. This text is clearly a beginning, a start, with only a vague form and no developed direction.

---

[2]

Once opon a time I was	[Once upon a time I was
playing Atre and my tV disaperd	playing Atari and my TV disappeared.
I did't now wath to do	I didn't know what to do.
I went up sars to tell	I went upstairs to tell
my mom she said to com	my mom. She said to calm
down but wath shod I do	down. "But what should I do?"
do you want to cale the	"Do you want to call the
poles yes! do you now were	police?" "Yes!" "Do you know where
the phone is of cors then go!	the phone is?" "Of course." "Then go."
Ok. 911 I diyld heloo plese	"OK." 911 I dialed. "Hello, please.
my tv disapered I said my	My TV disappeared," I said. "My
adres is 8201 plese come over	address is 8201. Please come over."
wele be over in a sekint	"We'll be over in a second."

ding dond were is the tv said the	Ding dong. "Where is the TV?" said
poles it was ther so wath	the police. "It was there." "So what
hapend I don't now then I	happened?" "I don't know." "Then I
don't well we can't find it	don't." "Well, we can't find it."
the end	the end]

Apparently attracted to the imaginative possibilities suggested in the first version, Matthew begins again. The first two sentences replicate exactly the first two lines of the first version, while the indirectly quoted speech in the embedded construction in the fifth line summarizes a bit of dialogue from the first version. The texts build on each other.

Consider the collection of voices here: the detached, more public narrator explaining the crisis; the excited young Matthew questioning his mother about what to do; the more official, older Matthew doing "reporting to the police" discourse; and the policeman voice inadequately responding to the situation. There are now seven conversational turns in the section about calling the police, compared to three in the first version. The writer relies heavily on the imagined interaction among the characters—their voices—to figure out where the plot's going, what's going to happen next.

Several effects follow from this reliance on spoken dialogue within a narrative framework. One is concrete, dramatic immediacy: the reader is drawn into the narrative in a very intimate way, as perhaps the writer himself is. The dialogue also creates a sense of process, of ongoingness. And the writer begins to develop the narrative possibilities through the characters—through their voices, their implied worldviews, their differing knowledges—as he identifies what each character may be able or likely to contribute, their respective speech acts, their perspectives on the situation. The writer separates out his point of view as the narrative "I" from other points of view.

It is through a refraction of voices—like light through a prism—that the narrative opens up and that the text world deepens, differentiates, and takes on form and imaginative possibilities.

In writing out the conventional version of the text, I have noted a textualizing strategy, and I have spaced the third version of the story in parts in order to emphasize it. Matthew has invented a kind of paragraph: he indicates an external action (e.g., dialing the phone, the doorbell ringing) and follows that action with the dialogue, or speech act, relevant to that action. These bits of clues about the action and setting seem like nascent exposition, or perhaps even stage directions, as the text does now resemble a script.

Perhaps this textual strategy allows him to keep the action going without getting slowed down by the details (and cognitive demands) of fuller exposition; if so, he thereby successfully balances his intention to develop a long story with his still limited writing resources. He may also be taking the reader's needs into account, by providing the key clues that enable the reader to follow the shifting scenes and actions—an emerging sense of how to actualize the principle of reciprocity in discourse (Nystrand and Himley, 1984).

The global structure remains embryonic. The crisis has mobilized the narrator into action, and he has called in the police, but as yet the dialogue goes in circles, with the writer unable to formulate—through his characters' voices—a plot or particular plan of action.

These "voices," however, take off in the third version.

---

[3]

once upon a time
I was playing atere
and my tv disaperd. I
didint now becase I went
to get some thing to jrink
I went up stars to tell
my mom my mom sad com
down but I can't I said
then sit down Ok but wath
shod I do do you want
to cale the poles yes!
Ok do you now ware
the phon is yes. in your
room right right go!
Ok

911 I cald helow
my tv disaperd my
adjres is 8201 plese come
over we wile be over

[Once upon a time
I was playing Atari
and my TV disappeared. I
didn't know, because I went
to get something to drink.
I went upstairs to tell
my mom. My mom said, "Calm
down." "But I can't," I said.
"Then sit down." "OK, but what
should I do?" "Do you want
to call the police?" "Yes!"
"OK. Do you know where
the phone is?" "Yes, in your
room, right?" "Right. Go!"
"OK."

911 I called. "Hello.
My TV disappeared. My
address is 8201. Please come
over." "We will be over

in a sekint Ok	in a second." "OK."
Ding dog	Ding dong.
wers your tv it was	"Where's your TV?" "It was
right ther I said so	right there," I said. "So
wath hapend I don't	what happened?" "I don't
now I will get my mom	know. I will get my mom."
ok said the poles man	"OK," said the policeman.
mom the poles man are	"Mom, the policemen are
here I will be down in	here." "I will be down in
a sekent ok now whres	a second." "OK." "Now where's
the tabl thats wath	the table?" "That's what
wer thriing to find out	we're trying to find out,"
said the poles man	said the policeman.
I went to get some	"I went to get some-
thing to drink I got a	thing to drink. I got a
cup and some pepsie	cup and some Pepsi."
is anething gone now	"Is anything gone now?"
I said no but I might	I said, "No, but I might
now were erve thing is	know where everything is
gouing wher! there is a rodber	going." "Where?" "There is a robber
that has a mashen near riglin	that has a machine near Ridgeland
park shod I cale a frend	Park. Should I call a friend
that livs near riglin ok	that lives near Ridgeland?" "OK,"
said the poles man	said the policeman.
383-8377 I didl	383-8377 I dialed.
hi matt can I come	"Hi, Matt. Can I come
over I will call my mom	over?" "I will call my mom."
ok	"OK."
771-7044	771-7044.
hi matt	"Hi, Matt."
ya yes you can I will	"Ya?" "Yes, you can." "I will
be over in a sekent ok	be over in a second." "OK,"
said matt	said Matt.
ding dong	Ding dong.
hi matt	"Hi, Matt."
what do you want to do	"What do you want to do?"
well first I shod inter	"Well, first I should intro-
dose thes peple this is capten	duce these people. This is Captain
tom from the poles stashan	Tom from the police station.
now this is why he came here	Now this is why he came here.

my tv disaperd and capten
tom might now wher it
is gohing wher said matt
to riglin park want to go
ther ok yets go
but one thing I cant
play ok well yets go
ok capten tom yes can
we ride in the cope
car I ges - sow ok

after they got ther
Matt Himley said were
dose he lives right
over ther Ok don't run
ok I will go first
get down yes sear don't
calle me sear call me
tom ok tom get down
ok

ding dong yes hide tom
my name is matt his
is to so what we have
ben waking for days do you
mind if we have a bite
to eat no! get out
hold it said tom
your comeing with me thanks, matts
and margret. your the wone that
shod get tanks. then thanks
you can go home now ok

matt can you come over
now for real I will aske
yes I can then come
on! Ok! what do you wont
to do yets play space invader
and kill um Ok yets go
7777 big score time to go
By matt by. boy am I sacked

My TV disappeared and Captain
Tom might know where it
is going." "Where?" said Matt.
"To Ridgeland Park. Want to go
there?" "OK." "Let's go.
But one thing, I can't
play." "OK." "Well, let's go."
"OK." "Captain Tom?" "Yes?" "Can
we ride in the cop
car?" "I guess so." "OK."

After they got there,
Matt Himley said, "Where
does he live?" "Right
over there." "OK." "Don't run."
"OK." "I will go first.
Get down." "Yes, sir." "Don't
call me sir, call me
Tom." "OK, Tom." "Get down."
"OK."

Ding dong. "Yes?" "Hide, Tom.
"My name is Matt. His
is, too." "So what?" "We have
been walking for days. Do you
mind if we have a bite
to eat?" "No! Get out!"
"Hold it," said Tom. "You're
coming with me. Thanks, Matts
and Margaret." "You're the one that
should get thanks." "Then thanks.
You can go home now." "OK."

"Matt, can you come over
now for real?" "I will ask . . .
Yes, I can." "Then come
on!" "OK! What do you want
to do?" "Let's play Space Invaders
and kill 'em." "OK, let's go."
7777 Big score. Time to go.
"'Bye, Matt." "'Bye." Boy, am I
sacked.

matt! matt! wath. time to
get up. Tuf luck! by Im
gonag to scoole fine

lunch time. what ear we
haveing soup be down in a
sekent. did any thing disapear
the pot! the tabl and the stove
the sink the flor - evrething
(the machine is gonging crazy)
yets get out of hear yets go
help! help! evrething is
disapiring yets go to the
police ofes and reort

the end

"Matt! Matt!" "What?" "Time to
get up." "Tough luck. 'Bye. I'm
going to school." "Fine."

Lunchtime. "What are we
having?" "Soup." "Be down in a
second. Did anything disappear?"
"The pot! The table and the stove,
the sink, the floor—everything
(the machine is going crazy).
Let's get out of here, let's go.
Help! Help! Everything is
disappearing. Let's go to the
police office and report it."

the end]

Quite clearly, version 3 became an important and major writing project for Matthew. He declared his intention to write a ''long story'' and (apparently) without any assistance proceeded to do just that during the twenty minutes or so of daily writing periods at school—a process that took more than a month to complete. He himself describes his writing process this way: he would open up his journal, scan back a line or two to find his place, and then write. He reported that he had no overall plot outline and that the events of the story unfolded as he wrote. He said that he ''saw'' the story in his imagination and then wrote what he saw. Certainly, too, one big advantage of the familiar narrative genre for a novice writer stems from the way the genre itself provides a momentum and direction of its own (Himley, 1986).

In writing this story, Matthew discovers and manages to take advantage of one powerful and primary feature of written language: the temporal and spatial advantages of the permanence of the text (Stubbs, 1980). Thus, the writer is enabled to take a topic, sense in a half-formed way the imaginative possibilities in it, and develop those possibilities over time and in detail—for himself and for others.

The third version of the story has all the qualities of a good old adventure tale—a mysterious disappearance, the devising of a plan of action, the enacting of that plan, a resolution that turns out to be illusory, and a surprise ending, with the mystery reinstated but now on a larger scale. Populating the story are the almost archetypal figures of young heroes, a wise old woman who provides the initial clue ("call the police"), an evil figure (the robber), and an authoritative representative of justice and order (the policeman). In addition, there is lots of fast-paced action and dramatic excitement.

Yet the adventure is carefully counterbalanced with safety. The one fantastical element—the mysterious machine that makes things disappear—occurs in a highly realistic world, full of concrete details, evidence of an incontrovertible normalcy. The TV's disappearance causes excitement but not fear, possibilities of adventure but not terror. In fact, the sound of excitement is evident in the narrator's voice near the end of the story when he asks, almost with eager anticipation and hope, if anything has disappeared.

The story suggests the writer's interest in questions about the nature of reality. What is real? What lies beyond the edge of our comprehension? These questions especially address a technological reality that may be fully explainable and knowable to others, but that eludes his grasp and thus generates his interest. Though mentioned explicitly only twice, it is the machine that is central to the story and supplies the dramatic fuel for the events. The title page that Matthew drew for the story consists of two parts: the standard television at the top of the sheet and a sunburstlike design on the bottom with the magical word "poof." When I asked him if he would ever like to produce the story as a play, his immediate question concerned how we could make the television disappear, how we could invent such a machine.

Once the disappearance has occurred, however, the quest begins—and, in Matthew's case, a rather communal quest. He invites participation and enjoys working as part of a team, an equal partner with Tom, although he grants himself a crucial and heroic role in the capture of the robber. Thus, the small virtues shine through, such as politeness, cooperation, graciousness, rather than the large virtues of courage and bravery. Matthew graciously introduces everyone, kindly invites a friend to share in the fun, politely has all the characters thank each other.

Feelings remain subdued. Few words are used to express feelings directly, thus leaving states of mind implied.

As the story progresses, the two kids, empowered by the adults, take on a more foregrounded role, while the adults fade into benign presences in the background. Mom initially provides Matthew with the suggestion to call the police and then is never mentioned again until after the capture, when she, too, receives thanks, implying her presence throughout the course of events. The police are called in, validating and lending authority to the kids' power, until the moment of the actual arrest which requires Captain Tom's final authority. Interestingly, this flips in the fourth version, where the background adults' roles are highlighted and the kids fade away.

The general movement in the story is one of spiraling. The action develops by calling in more and more characters, by repeating the story of the disappearance each time, until the climactic capture. Then the story unwinds back down to a normal, mundane afternoon of play. Abruptly, with time now rushing by quickly—as indicated by snippets of lines to show night passing, school, then lunchtime—the mystery breaks open again at an almost frenzied pace, with the whole kitchen disappearing before the characters' eyes. And so on with a new adventure.

Although the basic textualizing device—external action plus related speech act—continues to carry the text forward and to develop the plot, the dialogues or speech acts or "voices" themselves have become denser and longer, as when Matthew explains the situation to his buddy Matt. They also employ more complex syntax (subordination and embedding) and have fuller development of exposition in some speeches, an exposition that goes beyond the earlier, choppier, interactive clauses. Consider this speech:

> Well, first I should introduce these people. This is Captain Tom from the police station. Now this is why he came here. My TV disappeared, and he might know where it is going.

Although not wishing to overmark distinctions between spoken and written language, I might point out that these lines of text are (arguably) more typical of written language, while the lines of versions 1 and 2 are more typical of spoken (Kress, 1982).

Beyond the textual structuring device of external action plus dialogue, however, the story now is generically developed and can be divided in terms of a narrative macrostructure: a crisis, calling upon authorities to devise a plan of action, the successful enactment of that plan, the return to normalcy with its false sense of security, and the surprise ending with an even greater disappearance and mystery. This overall organization integrates hierarchically the events into a story-plot framework.

In many ways, the text is motivated by the semiotic resources of written language itself, by language as hero, in the making and meaning of this story. That is, the text is not in any simple way the result of Matthew's expressiveness or intentionality but emerges dialogically out of the history of texts like this.

First, the semantic richness of the word *disappear* engages Matthew's interest, matters to him in some way, and opens up a provocative network of meanings and questions and imaginative possibilities.

The permanence of written text—the way a writer can return to a text and its world across time, make changes, carry the text forward, reanimate events, and so on—enables this writer for the first time to compose a "long story."

Further imaginative possibilities are provided by the narrative genre itself, of course, such as the requirements of crisis, characters, narrative order and time, and resolution, and by all adventure stories that have preceded this one.

Lastly, and perhaps in this case most importantly, there are the text-elaborating possibilities of voices. The voices of the wise mother, the authoritative policeman, the detached narrator, the angry robber, the excited boys, the "growing up" boys populate and animate the story. And they all bring multiple worldviews, multiple perspectives, multiple relationships and roles. Essentially this narrative consists of a series of sequenced speech acts: the external action establishes the situation in which particular roles are played, particular kinds of words exchanged, particular kinds of meanings made.

It is primarily through the refracting, or opening up, of those voices that the text world emerges, takes on dimensionality and lives.

---

[4]

the day the tV disaperd	[The Day the TV Disappeared
once upon a time I was	Once upon a time I was
playing Atari and my	playing Atari and my
tv disaperd sow I told	TV disappeared, so I told
my mom and my mom	my mom, and my mom
called the police The	called the police. The
police man said	policeman said
he'd be over in a sekent	he'd be over in a second.
So he rong the bell	So he rang the bell
and he came in	and he came in
and said he might	and said he might

now were evre thing is	know where everything is
gonge. so he count	going. So he caught
the rober and put	the robber and put
him in jale	him in jail.
the end	the end]

Matthew wrote a fourth version of the story, shifting from narrative to summary. It is interesting to note what is missing from the summarized version: the role of the kids in capturing the robber, buddy Matt, the magic machine, and the surprise ending. Interestingly, too, the fourth version uses the text-creating resources more typical of written language (Kress, 1982).

The flow of information in the text is developed and organized now more as exposition than dramatic dialogue, more like "real" written language than transcribed spoken language. More of a notion of the written language sentence operates here. In the fifth line, for example, the capitalized "The" suggests a conventional sentential division, as does the period after "gonge" in the twelfth line. All important information is explicitly developed and expressed in the text rather than hinted at by quick references to external actions, by snatches of dialogue.

In stepping back from the action of the story and from the task of creating the story, the writer is able to identify and connect key events in a causal and temporal way, as evidenced in the greater frequency of connecting cohesive ties, such as "and" and "so." There are eight such ties in a 62-word text. In fact, endophoric ties predominate over exophoric ones about 6 to 1, making this text even more internally cohesive than any of the earlier ones (Halliday and Hasan, 1976).

The text is no longer a fully dramatized tale but rather a summary that highlights key events and explains rather rationally (and precisely) how the crisis was resolved. The dramatic and concrete immediacy of the earlier versions is replaced here with a distanced, third-person, rather official reportorial style.

The writer in the fourth version has shifted to the text-creating resources more typical of written language expository discourse: no direct dialogue, fuller and longer sentences, the use of logical or causal connectors, and explicit expository development.

An Anecdote: Creek Play

"I like to play in nature," Matthew explained. "I like especially to play in water. I like creeks, where you can see everything that is going on in them. Sometimes I play at the creek in South Carolina. I dam up one end of it, so nothing can get in or out, and then watch what happens. I like to see the water stop, and get deeper, and stand still. I can see the animals and stuff as they move around. I like watching what happens then."

Emerging Exposition

In second grade, Matthew was required to keep a journal. The teacher provided regular twenty-minute or so writing times, at least every Tuesday, and often gave students actual topics or even sentence starters. She encouraged a kind of self-reflection in these entries, by suggesting topics like why I like myself, what I would do if I were the teacher, how I will punish and reward my children when I grow up, and so on. The journal was a place for casual writing, although some entries were later corrected by the teacher, recopied onto more formal paper, and sent home in the Friday folder.

There are eighteen entries in Matthew's journal, including the disappearing TV story: four fictional stories, a joke, twelve expository "paragraphs," and one letter written for parents' night.

In this section, I would like to explore the patterns of emerging exposition in these entries, the ways Matthew works across time and within this particular genre of written language.

Beyond using description again as a method, I also use here the analytical scheme developed by Newkirk (1987). This section mixes descriptive and analytical language.

Text IV (2nd grade, fall 1981, age about 6 years, 11 months)

I watch to match tv.
I watch 37 hrs. a week
I watch dukes of hazzard

and lots of other stuf
like Tom and jerry.
if my tv disappeared
I would play more.
I watch tv because I like
it and I like it because
its interesting.

The writer straightforwardly and matter-of-factly states that he watches "too much" television, provides precise evidence about the exact number of hours per week, and presents two specific TV shows as illustration. He clearly and definitively establishes his conclusion. This rather mathematical exactness and precision resonate with a similar expressive style when he precisely lists meals and rationally explains damages in the narratives in texts I and II. He turns next to the question called for in the assignment and declares, not surprisingly, that he would "play more" if he didn't watch so much television. Then he switches directions and explains why he watches television, claiming that he likes it and that he likes it because it's "interesting." In fact, this last line sounds like the writer is beginning to mount a defense for watching television.

The writer's use of periods marks the three ideational units in the text, each distinguished by interesting discursive differences. In the first unit (lines 1–5), the writer relies on the same syntactic format for beginning each sentence, giving the effect of a list rather than a paragraph. There is also a lot of parallelism, in the language and even in the misspelling of "match" [much] with "watch." It is as if the text itself, as it evolves, directs the writer's choices about content and spelling, as he repeats key phrases like "I watch" and "I like it."

The first two sentences are short, simple subject-verb sentences that fit exactly into the space on one line, reminiscent of Kress's (1982) observations about possible early line-sentence conflation in children's writing. The third sentence, however, extends to three lines and includes more complex language forms, as if the writer, too, were beginning to extend into the assignment—and into the genre.

This unit reads a bit like short answers on a quiz or like the language called for on certain worksheets, with the student dutifully responding to an assignment. Only the phrase "lots of other stuf" sounds conversational, personal, a bit jarring actually against the rather straightforward, textbooklike answers in the first two lines.

In the second unit (lines 6–7), the writer provides a terse, expected answer to the problem posed by the assignment. He may even be relying on the way the assignment was written on the board. Each clause, or intonation contour, again is given its own line, suggesting an influence from spoken language. The "I would play more" sounds almost like a cliché, the standard response from parents when they complain that they want their kids playing more rather than watching so much television. Again, the writer sounds dutiful and studentlike in his responses.

In the third unit (lines 8–10), however, the voice shifts, the syntax becomes more complex, and an actual argument begins. Perhaps now the writer really has something to say, a difference to mark, a reaction to the ideas embedded in the assignment itself. The writer explains, and begins to justify, his television watching as an "interesting" activity. The text seems to take off here, with a new voice emerging a bit.

The writer demonstrates some knowledge of what exposition as a genre calls for. He employs two rhetorical strategies here: illustration, and cause and effect, both basic to expository and argumentative genres. He adopts a rather formal register, a somewhat public and rational voice, and he moves in the last unit to a higher level of abstraction, when he makes the more general claim that television as an activity is "interesting."

That word itself suggests a move away from casual conversation about TV shows into a more public discourse, a more formal argument, a more rhetorical stance about watching television in general. It anticipates the audience—possibly the teacher, possibly a more generalized one—and makes its claim based on the possible intellectual value of television. The text is addressed. Perhaps this is a voice shaped by the genre itself, by Matthew's nascent understanding of how exposition is done.

As in the narratives in texts I and II there is a refracting of a real-life and a fictionalized Matt, so here, too, in exposition there is a refracting of personal and public voices. He moves into a more public persona.

In some sense, then, even within this one text, there is a movement from merely listing to hierarchically ordering information, and from dutifully fulfilling an assignment to actually responding rhetorically to a situation or idea.

Using Newkirk's scheme,[4] I would say that this text starts off as a reason list, with the writer enumerating a series of statements that are reasons for a particular proposition. But in the last unit it becomes a couplet, or writing composed (typically) of a statement-plus-reason unit (p. 126).

Text V (2nd grade, February 1982, age 7 years, 2 months)

I get nervous when
Im in the chrismas
program beacas I might
messup. but after the
program I don't feale
nervous ony more. but I
have the chrismas prowgram
two times. soo I get
nervous agan and then I got
back to normal.
          the end

Probably in response to a starter sentence, the writer indentifies when he gets nervous: when he is in the Christmas program. He explains that this nervousness results from his fear that he might "messup." But the nervousness goes away, he further explains, after the program. Since he has the program twice, however, he goes through this experience twice, before he can get back to normal.

The text consists of four sentences, clearly and conventionally marked by periods, with "I" serving as the grammatical subject each time. The first sentence takes the (presumably) given topic and completes it with a "because" clause. After that, each clause begins with "but" or "so" or "then"—that is, with formal cohesive ties that emphatically mark the logical relationship of each clause with the next one. The "the end" tag line demonstrates that the writer considers this text, or perhaps the journal entry or composing episode, to be complete and finished.

The text develops through a series of oppositions, with each sentence reacting against the one that precedes it in some way. Having established his nervousness, for example, the writer tempers that claim by saying the nervousness ends when the program ends. But then he quickly qualifies *that* claim by adding that the program takes place twice, so it's not that simple. In all this explaining, Matthew demonstrates yet again his expressive preference for precision, for explicitly working out the details and qualifications of an answer that might not, by itself, be clear or accurate or complete enough.

It is as if the question sets up a bounded semantic space, an arena for thought, in a sense, and Matthew works the ground within that space with care and caution, almost as if he is damming up textual space in order to observe the varied life floating inside it. This text is also bounded in that it has a beginning and end and a sequence of clauses that move chronologically, and causally, toward closure. Each perceived possible rupture in the argument is acknowledged and resolved, as Matthew explains his movement from "nervous" to "normal." The text is tightly structured, tightly rendered, within its own logical terms.

The text ends with the line, "So I *get* nervous again and then I *got* back to normal" (emphasis mine). Matthew shifts from the present tense of exposition to the past tense of narration. The account shifts from a generalized illustration of the concept of nervousness to a particular account of what it was like after the last Christmas program, or from what happens to what happened (Moffett, 1968), revealing thereby tensions between these two different discursive possibilities.

In this text, the "I" refers consistently to the biographical Matthew, to his real-life experiences. Matthew is making a personal statement about the complexities of his nervousness and fears of messing up. Yet there is a public accent to the text, a sense of a more public audience, which calls forth a rather explicit, rather formal register, almost as if this account were (or could be) illustrative of the larger issue of nervousness in general. The text does not sound casual or conversational. Again, the personal and the public blur and blend.

Exposition as a written genre is enacted by Matthew with logical claims, explication, qualifications, explicitness, and a degree of formality, with authority grounded in personal experience, but with a sense of personal experience as generalizable or public.

The text might be located structurally within Newkirk's system as an extended couplet strategy, because each sentence serves as a comment or qualification of sorts on the topic raised in the preceding sentence. Yet there is also an emergent sense of overall structure, both graphically (it's long enough to be a paragraph) and semantically (it covers the basic network of ideas).

Text VI (2nd grade, April 1982, age 7 years, 4 months)

> I'd use a magic wand to
> Make me a King. And I
> would have castle with
> 1,000,000 dollors.
> And I would spend it all
> on Atari and Activition
> cartragis. And I'd turn my
> moms car into a
> convetable
>   the end
>   by
> Matt Himley
>
> teres a pitcher

In this text, the writer again (apparently) takes up a starter sentence and declares that he would use a magic wand to make himself a king. He would then have a castle and lots of money, actually exactly one million dollars. He would spend it on cartridges for Atari and Activision, and he would magically turn his mother's car into a convertible.

This text takes up nine lines of the journal page, and then in much larger, carefully placed letters, the writer announces that this is "the end," that it was written by "Matt Himley," and that there is a picture that apparently accompanies this text, although it is not in the journal.

Several of the expository paragraphs in the journal resemble this one both structurally and thematically. The text begins with a general assertion of some sort (in this case, a fanciful one), and is elaborated through a series of three "and" sentences, each conventionally and correctly punctuated for the most part. The cohesive tie "and" may serve as a sentence starter, too, as it defines both syntactically and semantically the kinds of things the writer might say next—that is, it is a call for more details or examples. This text represents a classic kernel paragraph form—a kind of topic sentence, with three examples. Thematically, these paragraphs tend to focus rather precisely on money, family, and the acquisition of things and abilities. They also tend to set up situations that resist easy closure.

I think this kind of text demonstrates what Newkirk calls a "basic paragraph," in that it has a topic and at least three or more clausal statements that connect coherently, although the order of these three sentences could vary. It has a self-conscious, fill-in-the-blank quality, as if Matthew has now learned what will count as an acceptable response to these starter sentences and is working the formula a bit each time—the voice, the structure, the implied situation. The repeated use of "and" enables him to generate a rather easy paragraph, one with more formal than functional unity.

Text VII (2nd grade, June 1982, age 7 years, 6 months)

> The most important thing
> in my room is My stuffed
> Animals. I like My stuffed
> Animals beacause there real
> furry. And I have over
> 20 of them too. One is so
> small that you could
> hardly hold it. I am going
> to get one of the
> huge ones that holds
> you in stead ove you
> holding it As soon as I
> get enugh money.
>   the end

The writer begins by identifying what is most important to him in his bedroom: his collection of stuffed animals. He explains that he likes these animals because they are "real furry." And "too" he has a lot of animals; he estimates more than twenty. He then describes a small one, so small that you can hardly hold it. Then he states his desire to have one so "huge" that it can hold him, and he asserts to the reader that he will buy that one just as soon as he gets enough money.

This paragraph consists of five conventionally marked and increasingly more complex sentences that cohere both formally and semantically. The claims cluster around those characteristics of Matthew's stuffed animal collection that account for its importance to him, with structural cohesion achieved through semantic repetition and collocation, pronoun reference, and logical connectors such as "too" and "because."

As in earlier expository texts, Matthew provides the almost inevitable three reasons for his opening claim, but in this text the third reason takes on greater elaboration, both through an oppositional play between big and small and through an impulse toward precision in explaining exactly when and how this "huge" stuffed animal will be purchased. The tensions in the semantic network of meanings and associations set off by this topic create for Matthew possible ways to develop the actual content of the paragraph. The text itself, as it evolves, sets up semantic connections and contrasts that Matthew shapes into a tightly rendered and complete explanation.

Again, the "I" refers to the biographical Matthew and his very real stuffed animal collection, with the voices in the text suggesting pleasure, pride, a bit of humor, and scientific exactitude. Yet there is also a public accent in this account, as suggested by the carefully elaborated syntax and the precise rendering of numbers and explanations. The register of the paragraph imagines a formal situation in which this accounting takes place, a rather formal relationship between participants or their roles, and a formal use of language at both the lexical and syntactic and discursive levels. This is not casual or conversational. It is as if the personal voice were refracted in exposition through a public screen, as if the genre (exposition written in a personal journal) promotes a blending of the personal and the public stance, so that the textual "I" comes to be Matthew as well as "the typical kid."

This may be Matthew's first "real" paragraph—that is, one with truly functional unity and coherence, written in a voice that demonstrates a kind of ownership of the genre. Perhaps with ownership comes personal style or voice. He does, after all, play with the last line a bit humorously, as if he has written his way into the assignment now. In Newkirk's terms, the text illustrates an "ordered paragraph," the last developmental "level" (a term he uses loosely) in his system.

The genre of written exposition, as these descriptions suggest, seems to mean to Matthew a kind of text that calls for a logical and ordered explanation, addressed formally and fully to a rather public or generalized audience, with claims based on a personal experience that might also generalize in some way. Within his journal, he moves from loose and listlike sentential claims, sometimes followed with an illustration, to coherently developed, tightly rendered "real" paragraphs.

As such, his understanding of the genre itself functions as an adult mentor might in Vygotsky's (1986) model of the learning that takes place within what he calls the "zone of proximal development." Indeed, the requirements of the genre might be seen as enabling the writer's development, by directing him toward certain kinds of ideas, certain kinds of language use, certain kinds of interpretive and textual stances, certain kinds of subject positions—as the genre draws the writer more and more into the public sphere of meaning-full possibilities.

Yet as he comes to work these expository resources, Matthew also comes to be more particularly and uniquely expressive, as exhibited in his characteristic impulse toward precision, exactness, comprehensiveness, and closure. As the reading of Bahktin suggests in Chapter 4, the ownership of the public resources of written exposition parallels, and actually enables, the personal expressiveness of the writer. The more fully a writer moves into the resources and genres of written language, the more fully he or she can appropriate and individuate those resources.

Through these paragraphs in his journal, Matthew has come to own those semiotic resources a bit, to work the shared territory of written exposition as a genre, to add his imprint and accent.

Anecdotes and Temporality

During first and then second grade, while he was writing narrative and exposition in his journal at school, Matthew also chose to write at home about actual events of the recent past. These brief autobiographical anecdotes, often about trips with his father, were typically composed on sheets of yellow legal paper that were stored in the desk and used for work-related projects. Informally done, perhaps as a kind of solitary play, these texts were shared with his immediate family in the same casual way that drawings and art projects were.

Text VIII (1st grade, February 1981, age 6 years, 2 months)

fishing

once upon a time me and my dad were planning to go to waskason with me. and my
dad said I coude bring any body wiht. and I decided to bring matt stases. so we piked
matt up and went to waskonson it was a long ride but we made it. we got ther at nine
and went to bed. the next day matt and me went fishing and cote a lot. after we went
fishin we ate breakfast

The writer begins in the anytime, anywhere world of the imagination but
then shifts to a specific historical time when his father proposed a fishing
trip to Wisconsin and offered to take one of Matthew's friends with them.
The writer selected Matt Strauss. They picked him up and drove to
Wisconsin. The trip was long, but they finally made it. He reports that
they arrived at nine and went right to sleep. The next day the two Matts
went fishing and caught a lot of fish. After that, they ate breakfast.

That the text begins with an official title ("fishing") and that the writer
uses the "once upon a time" opening line suggest the genre of narrative
and in particular the possibilities of fantasy or fairy tale. It also illustrates
the productive uses new writers make of the requirement of various genre
features as prompts for getting started. In this case, the title and the
standard opening line, combined with the recent memory of an actual
event, open up general textual and semantic possibilities for composing.
And fishing and camping have also always been two of Matthew's
favorite activities. Although the extra "with me" phrase indicates some
difficulty in getting into the text, some awkwardness or confusion,
Matthew eases into the account with a past progressive verb—"were
planning"—and then a smooth shift into the simple past of narration for
the rest of the text.

The text is organized by sentences clearly marked with periods and is
motivated by a topic-comment structure. Topics themselves are organized chronologically and then commented on in some specifying way.
In the first sentence, for example, the writer sets up the proposed fishing
trip to Wisconsin as the initiating situation. The next sentence specifies

the additional complication that the writer can bring a friend along. The third sentence responds to, or comments on, that complication by naming the actual friend Matthew has chosen. These three sentences, linked by the connector ''and,'' introduce and establish the basic situation or event and add a few specific details.

The word ''So'' begins the second section of text and marks the logical and causal working out of nascent plot: given this plan, we picked up Matt Strauss and headed off to Wisconsin. The fifth sentence raises the topic of trip length and ends with the comment about the long ride and (implicitly) the difficulty of making it.

In relating the exact time of arrival, Matthew moves into the third chunk of text or tale by describing three events that take place once they are in Wisconsin, again following a topic-comment structure: arriving at nine—going to bed, going fishing—catching a lot, after fishing—eating breakfast.

After the fairy tale opening and hint of fictional narrative, the language of the text quickly becomes direct, straightforward, reportorial, in a rather factual or factlike rendering of the kernel events in a series of actions and outcomes in direct chronological order. Little emotion is evoked. Verbs refer to a range of intellectual and physical actions involved in trips that Matthew and the others engage in, such as planning, deciding, driving, fishing, and eating.

In composing this text, Matthew begins to explore the possibility of using writing to recount, remember, and refer to events in his life within the conventions of what I'll call anecdote. He locates himself as a distant first-person narrator, reporting on the main topics or kernel events (with comments), recounting and evoking little or no emotion, and then rather abruptly stopping. Motivated by the temporality of events and organized at the level of sentence, the anecdote has little overall focus or direction and no conclusion. It has the texture and register of a spoken conversation that takes place in a somewhat public setting where the speaker recounts the highlights of a trip to someone who has a casual knowledge of the actual situation.

Indeed, there are tensions here between the private or autobiographical content of the text and the distant, public ''I'' narrating voice, between the typically informal nature of the anecdote as genre (with its possibilities of play, humor, and intimacy) and this rather formal, even reportorial rendering of key events.

Text IX (2nd grade, December 1981, age 7 years)

> Once opon a time I was fishing at
> mistr Bolts pond but i did't cath
> any thing so I woked back.
> the next day I ate brekfist and
> then Grampa and me went back to
> mistr Bolts pond Grampa got a
> fuwe bites but no fish we stayed
> ther for 2 Howrs and went home
> then Kathey and Crag and erick
> came erick was so funny I
> startid to laght   time to eat
> OK be ther in a sekint
> the next day was thanksgiving
> I bet I ate the most
> the next day was the Last
> hole day to be ther   Grampa and
> me went fishing but did not
> chach any thing   the next day
> I went home.
>   the end

Again, this anecdote begins with the classic fairy tale line of "once upon a time" and shifts immediately into the specific historical moment when Matthew "was fishing" at Mr. Bolt's pond. And again the main topic is fishing. On the first day Matthew didn't catch anything, so he walked back to the house. The next day he first ate and then returned to the pond with his grandfather. Though his grandfather got a few bites, he didn't catch any fish. They stayed for two hours and then went home. The next event was the arrival of three people: Kathy, Craig, and Erick. Matthew claims that Erick was so funny he had to laugh. The text then moves away briefly from summary and reporting into dramatic immediacy, as someone yelled that it was "time to eat." Matthew apparently responded by saying, "OK, be there in a second." Then on the next day, which was Thanksgiving, Matthew says he ate the most food. On the next day, the last complete day of his vacation, he and his grandfather went fishing again—and again did not catch anything. He explains then that he went home on the next day.

Again, too, Matthew's particular expressive style makes itself felt, in the precise rendering of actual names and times and activities, the careful balance of key events, the subtle evocation of feeling, and the requirement of closure and comprehensiveness.

Yet to a great extent it is temporality, the "I" narrative agent, and the kernel events focusing on fishing that generate and organize the anecdote. Based on the number of times "the next day" is written, this anecdote covers a span of at least five days and seems to account for the entire vacation. Matthew announces the start of a new day and then reports on an apparently key event that took place on that day, typically a trip to the pond for a fishing expedition. Again, this is the topic-comment strategy for developing text at the local level. On the day that Kathy, Craig, and Erick arrive, however, time is slowed down and summary deepens into scene, as Matthew adds description about Erick's being so funny, his reaction to this behavior, and dialogue—narrative devices for extending time.

Thematically, too, temporality draws Matthew's attention and takes on many forms in the text. First there is the magic time of a fairy tale, suggestive of infinite possibility, followed immediately by the daily press of time as the days pass quickly from one to another. Matthew calculates precisely the number of hours he and his grandfather stay at Mr. Bolt's pond and notes specifically that a day is the last whole day he'll be on vacation. Readers get the sense of time moving quickly, and the repetition of the phrase "the next day" suggests alternately both the daily opening up and closing down of possibilities, until it's time again to return home. Even the misspelling of "[w]hole" presents the same ambiguity of richness and emptiness, presence and absence.

It is tempting to read these anecdotes in particular as rather directly self-expressive, because the "I" is clearly the autobiographical Matthew Himley, the events really happened, the text seems realistic, and the medium transparent in the sense that the text does not forcefully draw attention to itself as text, as artifact and work.

Yet it's not that simple. Temporality itself, as a defining feature of the genre, draws the text forward and shapes how and what gets said. The first requirement is to cover in some comprehensive way the whole event, so a writer must select major events in order adequately to recount the whole story, eliminate or minimize extraneous information or much detail, keep things in chronological sequence, develop some kind of momentum to maintain readers' interest, and provide a lot of summary. Yet another requirement is to vary the temporal patterns, to shift from summary to scene, for example, as Matthew does when he adds in a quick dialogic exchange. In view of this, the writer's "decision" to structure the text around the topic of "the next day," his recurrent reference to fishing, and the thematic focus on time may be read as reflecting the requirements of the genre itself as much as revealing "truths" about Matthew.

In writing these anecdotes, Matthew explores the semiotic possibilities of constructing a version of himself and telling his own story by, through, and against the conventions of the genre. Yet this exploration lasts less than a year. Perhaps this apparent lack of interest results from difficulty in adequately containing diffuse and complex experience within the demands of the genre, or from a lack of valorization of this kind of writing in his school experience, especially for boys. Or perhaps temporality as a key resource doesn't lead "naturally" to narrative tension or ideational opposition or to a problem that requries solving—and doesn't therefore lead to the kind of precise, exact, manageable focus that Matthew has demonstrated an expressive preference for in many of his earlier texts. As with the pleasure in damming up creeks to see what will then happen, there may also be pleasure in bounding up semantic and textual possibilities to compose a tightly rendered, logically coherent, "precise" text—and anecdote may not offer that pleasure to this particular young writer.

Fishing

Text X (3rd grade, September 1982, age 7 years, 9 months)

[written at home]

To be a goob Fisherman
1. First you have to be patient
or you wont catch any
fish 2. After you get a
bite you real it in
Right. Wrong not right

then you wait in til
he has it in his mouth.
And you jerk him. That
way you set the hook.
3. Ther are lots of kinds
of fishing. In river fishing
you don't use a bobber.
You put a large sinker
on your line. About
six inches from the
swivel and then a hook.
You cast it out and
wait intil your poll
bounces up and down
4. Lake fishing you
use a bobbor.
you put the bobor on
and you do the same
thing as river fishing.
After you do that
You cast it out and wait
for the bobber to go
down 5. Lewer fishing
is a lot of work you
have to real in the
lewer all the time.
A lewer can be a fish
or a worm the only
difrens is that they
are fake they go
threw the water like
A real fish or worm.
Ther is something
called a weedless worm
that is what I fish with
in South Carolina.
Ther is no fish lewer
that is weedless. Not
that I know of.
6. There are all sorts
of kinds of fish. A catfish
Has 3 Big spins and
sharp teeth. So if you

ever catch a catfish
grab it right. 7. When
you clean a fish
a fish you dont just
chop his head off and
eat it. If it is a small
fish you scale it and
then chop his head
off then gut him
and wash him good.
If it is a large fish
you skin it you cut
a thin line on both side
of his Fins do the
same for the belly
After you are done,
take a nother thin slice
on one side of the head
fin. Then take a
plers. take a corner
of the skin and pull
it on both sids
Pull the fins and
chop the head off
And then your done.
8. When you eat a fish
you never put enything
in your mouth with
it. 9. I have fished in lots
lakes and rivers
but the best fishing
I have ever had is
in a pond in South
Carolina. I have
caught alot of
fish in that pond.
From 3 inches long to
2 pounds.
         the end

Working with Writing Prompts: The School Voice

In third grade, Matthew's instruction in writing became more formally integrated into the curriculum. He wrote weekly and typically in response to structured, rather carefully controlled writing prompts. The teacher, for example, would provide a dittoed story starter, delineating the imaginative situation and providing questions for the students to answer in their responses, or she would provide a set of four cards with vocabulary words on them which students then had to use meaningfully in the story they were to construct around those words. The prompts function semiotically like the opening of a kind of conversation, and, as a result, the majority of the texts Matthew wrote during this year don't stand alone but rather serve as an answer to the possibilities or questions set up in the first half of the dialogic exchange. His texts work within, answer, and at times ignore the parameters set up in the assignments.

In this section, I will briefly describe Matthew's textual exploration with this school genre as a whole, to understand both how he comes to define the demands (and possibilities) of writing prompts and also how he does (and does not) come to own, individuate, and accent them.

I'll provide less of the actual descriptive reading of Matthew's writing from now on, as I try to work with larger questions and dimensions about the collection of texts as a whole.

The first assignment illustrates what I am calling the kind of story starter that was used as a writing prompt in Matthew's school:

Past or Future?

You have volunteered to take part in Professor Past-Future's famous experiment. He has given you a black box with two buttons on top.

If you press the blue button, you will go back in time; the red button, you will go into the future.

What will your choice be? Why? What will you see and do?

In response to this assignment, Matthew wrote the following on the lines at the bottom half of the dittoed sheet:

I Think I will go in the
future. blip Wat is this?

> Some sorta maze. Ah this
> is better. Wow! There
> is a dirt bike rase
> over there. Those arent
> dirt bikes they have
> four wheels. What
> are they? I think I
> will go to a motel
> 25 dollors. here. Rome 38
> heres the key.
>   the end

And on the bottom of the page is a smile face stamp with the word "Super" printed underneath it.

The writer picks up on the first question by saying he will push the red button and head off into the future. The word "blip" suggests pushing the button and Star Trek-like speed of time travel—and moves the text into a narrative about the future. Abruptly readers are in the mind of the writer, who is puzzled by seeing a maze of some kind. It's not clear what this maze is, but it results, apparently, from a problem of focus or vision, almost as if the future were presented on a TV screen. The confusion is immediately fixed. With dramatic excitement, the writer is located within a specific but unspecified future world, where he notes a dirt bike race going on and is startled by the fact that the dirt bikes have four wheels. He wonders to himself what these machines really are. Then the narrator rather abruptly decides to go to a motel, and there is a bit of dialogue from that scene in which the clerk (presumably) requires twenty-five dollars for the room, the narrator responds, "Here," and the clerk tells him it's "Room 38. Here's the key." And there the text (and the trip to the future) ends.

The writer selects the future, and both the maze and the mysterious dirt bikes suggest knowledge just beyond his grasp, where the familiar has taken on futuristic dimensions. Twice the writer raises questions, wondering what these new objects in a defamiliarized world are. He repeats the "I think I will go" line—an act of decision—and makes a choice that returns him to normalcy, to the familiarity of motels and the discourse that goes with that. Whereas the maze and dirt bikes remain an unresolved mystery, the narrator now has the key to the room and is in charge of the situation. Again, we see Matthew's attention to precision against a vague backdrop that raises lots of unanswered questions and brings the writer to the edge of what he knows—and again we see the shift from the potential confusion to restored order.

In a most literal way, Matthew has answered the question of what will you see (dirt bikes) and what will you do (take a motel room), though he doesn't take on the bigger question of why he picked the future. He seems to have defined his task as answering those specific questions, as if he were having a conversation with the assignment/authority/teacher, and now has to provide his half of the exchange. A rather random mixture of language resources and voices results: the dutiful student answering a question; the dramatic voice of the narrator indicating indirectly the scene he has landed in; the inner voice of the narrator thinking about the dirt bikes and deciding to take a motel room; and the dialogic exchange between the narrator and the motel clerk.

Each textualizing strategy enables Matthew to fill up the page and fulfill the assignment at a local level. He does not, however, take up the implied invitation to develop a full-scale narrative or imaginative report or description of the future. The amount of time allotted to completing this assignment, typically about twenty minutes, may have something to do with this. The text remains ragged, rough-edged, a bit random, as if the writer has drawn bits and pieces from his understanding of written narrative, his reading of the requirements of school assignments, and his interests in dirt bikes in order to build up a formally adequate response to the questions he's been asked. Yet the text as a whole doesn't seem to matter to Matthew, to draw his interest, or sustain his engagement in significant ways.

The last story starter assignment that Matthew did in third grade was a response to this prompt:

Ask the Computer

You are a computer. Many people ask you questions. What were the *funniest*, most *ridiculous*, and most *difficult* questions you have received? What were your answers?

The most funniest question was,
Are you sure your right? I
answered yes. I've had a lot

of funny questens but that
was the funnyest. I've had
a lot of difficult questions
to but the hardest one was,
how many avradge snow flakes fall
on the ground each year
I said about a million.

Those are the most funniest
and hardest questions I've ever
got

The End

Again, the only textual response from the teacher was the smile face with "Super" printed underneath it.

The writer converts the language of the question into a declarative sentence that embeds the imaginary question within it. The funniest question was about the computer's accuracy of knowledge. The computer's answer was a simple, straightforward, and confident yes. The writer elaborates on the point by adding that he has heard many funny questions, but this was the funniest. Then the computer states that he has had a lot of difficult questions, too, but the most difficult was about how many snowflakes on the average fall to the ground each year. The answer to that very hard question was calculated to be a slightly qualified "about a million." In a new paragraph, the writer shifts to the present tense of the original question and concludes the text by restating that these were the funniest and most difficult questions he, as a computer, has ever been asked.

This text yet again takes up the context and the questions posed by the story starter, but now in a more textually coherent way. The text hangs together in several ways. First, the writer returns to the exact language of the assignment in developing his answers, so that the repetitions of the words "funny" and "difficult" (or "hard") function as collocative cohesive ties and result in a tightly organized semantic network. Second, the text remains in one genre—an expository paragraph or beginning essay—and doesn't draw on textualizing strategies from spoken conversations or from narrative. Third, sentences are constructed according to an explicit topic-comment structure, where the writer repeats the topics from the questions each time he starts a new section of the text with some slight variation, and again as he concludes it: ''the most funniest question,'' ''I've had a lot of difficult questions,'' and ''Those are the most funniest and hardest questions I've ever got.''

Again, Matthew's expressive choices can be read in the tightly rendered structure or architectonics of the text, in the precision of the snowflake answer, and in the interest in knowledge and its limits.

Yet another voice is also present—a school voice, perhaps—taking up the words of the assignment; repeating and varying them; completing the task in a rather formal or public register; expanding the basic ideas of ''funny'' and ''difficult,'' but not too much; fulfilling the formal and semantic demands of the task; and staying within the parameters of the prompt.

This mixing of voices results, perhaps, from the specificity of the writing assignments: the story starters provide an imaginary context, questions, register, and can be converted into a formula after a while. For Matthew, to negotiate the requirements of these tasks involves entering into the imagined text world; taking up the suggested voice; generating the content through topic-comment elaboration and through networks of semantic collocation around keywords; bringing topics in from daily life (e.g., dirt bikes, puppies, five-speeds); and completing the text within the time and space constraints. To complete these tasks involves a kind of balancing of various school, textual, and expressive demands. As a result, the voices that animate these texts come from the school context, from the genre itself, from the imagined text world, and from the writer's lived life—in varying configurations.

The learning potential of these kinds of assignments for Matthew may lie in their manageable size, in their boundedness, in their opportunity for experimentation and at times play, and in their imaginative starting points for writing. Yet there are some problems, too. First, the question-answer format of many of the story starter prompts tends to work against real textual coherence and development, as if Matthew has defined the task as merely providing answers to specific questions, in a very local and conversational way, and then in translating those ''spoken'' answers into written form. This conflates the resources of spoken and written language. Second, this particular approach draws attention to the parts of the text but not to the overall intellectual and imaginative possibilities of the context or genre set up in the prompt. The text has to answer questions, fill up the space, read coherently, not take too long, and lead to closure. In a sense, Matthew builds these texts up from these questions, keywords, and topic-comment elaboration, as if he were working from temporal and spatial demands rather than generic ones. Third, the specificity of the prompts narrows his range of response and limits the possibility of personal meaning as the ground of literacy learning, providing little encouragement or reason to "own" the assignment. In Bakhtinian terms, the writer "ventriloquizes" the official languages and formal register of the school context. These story starters make writing "easy," in a sense—a mere matter of getting words on paper in response to the demands of the assignment.

All too often, the tasks can become for Matthew exercises, perhaps playful, perhaps dummy runs. The school voice that then emerges layers a mix of personal content within the prescribed parameters of the story starter assignment in a contained, fill-in-the-blank sort of way, with little real dialogic encounter between what matters to a particular child and the semiotic possibilities of fully realized cultural genres such as fairy tales, adventure stories, science fiction, or mysteries. By limiting the child-culture interaction, these writing prompts may lie in a cramped semiotic space that opens up neither into the full range of "engageable" interest in the child nor into the rich ideational, imaginative possibilities of "real" genres.

Only one of these assignments seems to have mattered to Matthew and to have really taken off, based on the following prompt:

> You are home listening to the radio when you hear . . . "We interrupt this program to tell you that an unusual spaceship has landed on the school playground." You rush out of the house and race to school. What do you see? What is inside this spaceship? Where did it come from? Why? Describe in detail what happens!

Text XI (3rd grade, October 1982, age 7 years, 10 months)

It is so big. And so weard.
It landed right in the midel
of the playground.
It has a gun.
And radar it's beeping!
By that time all the children
in the school were out to

see it.
Suddenly A littel man came out
from it.
It asked where he was.
He had two littel entenas
sticking out of it's head.
Agin the littel creachur asked
where am I.
One of the children said earth.
Where do you come from
I asked.
Mars he said!
All of the children backed up
Exsept one.
He got closer to him
He said.
Don't I know you.
The littel creachur said
I don't now.
Then he said.
Are you Matt?
Yes.
I know you.
You came to mars right?
ya!
Can I come back with
you?
yes.
Well yets go.
They climd back in
the space ship.
It blinked a coupel
times then it was gone
We staired at it for
a sekent.
And then we went back
home.
I sat in bed that night
thinking about it.
the end

The story begins in the present tense, with the narrator describing the spaceship that landed right in the middle of the playground as big, weird, with a gun and beeping radar. There is a sense of immediacy and great excitement in the narrator's voice. The writer then shifts into the past tense to say that by this time all the schoolchildren have come out to see it, too. This begins specifying and establishing an explicit backdrop for the story rather than leaving that backdrop implicit and vague, as in earlier texts. The temporal pace then picks up, when "suddenly" a little man comes out of the spaceship and asks where he is. A suspenseful pause in the dramatic action occurs, as apparently no one immediately answers this question. And during that pause the writer provides further description of the visitor by describing the two little antennas sticking out of his head. Again, the writer provides enough detail for readers to reconstruct the event in more specific ways, as he plays with time by holding readers in suspense for a moment.

"Again," another temporal marker, the little creature asks where he is, as the story shifts into dialogue. One of the children as a character in the story says "Earth." The narrative "I" then asks where the creature comes from, and with excitement learns that the creature came from Mars. All the children then back up, suggesting in an understated and indirect way their fear or amazement with this visitor from an alien place. All the children, that is, "except one"—a textual move that creates suspense and heightens the dramatic excitement, especially because at first this child isn't named but referred to mysteriously as "he." This child not only dares to move closer to the creature but, even more surprisingly, claims to know him. In response, the creature says at first that he doesn't know him, but then suddenly recognizes and names this special child: "Are you Matt?" "Yes," responds the child, and the little creature relates a story within the story, recounting that Matt had been to Mars once before. Matt then asks if he can return to Mars with the little creature, and, when his request is granted, they immediately decide to get going.

The story returns to exposition, as the narrator describes how Matt and the little creature climbed into the spaceship, which blinked a couple of times and was gone, leaving the children and the narrator staring at it for a second, before they went back home.

The story ends hauntingly, with the narrator recounting that he sat in bed that night thinking about "it," about all that had happened that day. In contrast with the extraordinariness of the events, the language here is strikingly understated, evocative, and normal.

The texture of this story results from the writer's increasingly varied uses of the resources of narration. The story starts in the present tense of description, takes the reader into the past in order to quickly establish the setting for the events. Time speeds up with "suddenly"—and slows down during the pause in the action while the little creature has to repeat his question and while the narrator provides a bit more description. Dialogue creates a sense of scene and immediacy, broken only with a brief description of the actions of the other children. The story ends with summary, a temporal ellipsis, and then a rather "timeless" moment as the narrator steps out of the action and sits in bed thinking back on the events, surely with the suggestion that he'll recreate those events over and over again in his mind. This variation in the temporality of the story goes beyond the straightforward, direct "and then" chronology of earlier texts and suggests greater crafting of the text, greater understanding of the resources of narrative temporality and their dramatic effects on readers.

Although dialogue continues to be a major narrative device, it is now interspersed with description and exposition and the inner thoughts of the main character. As a result, readers are provided with a more layered text in which more background is specified, more perspectives are offered, and more emotion and interiority are evoked.

Voices are refracted, with characters located in various positions in the text. One is the "typical" child who speaks to the little creature but then (presumably) backs off with the other children out of fear or at least cautiousness. The little creature itself is both alien and friendly, cooperative and communal in its adventures, willing to go off on a shared journey. The main character, named "Matt," singles himself out from the crowd of children both by his exciting history and by his courage in desiring yet another intergalactic enterprise. And finally there is the narrator, located within and without the narrative, a thoughtful observer, taking responsibility for the telling of the tale and for reflecting on the significance or mystery of the events, but not often participating directly in those events. This textual "I" is refracted, far more complicated than the more autobiographical "I" of the anecdotes or even the first person narrator/character in the early adventure stories. So the talk, too, is layered among, within, and about characters, refracting the voices and multiplying the perspectives on the events.

Matthew moved fully into the genre possibilities of this story starter assignment, and even as he uses a richer range of narrative resources, his expressive choices make themselves felt in the tightly rendered structure, the use of dialogue and voice, the interest in moving to the edge of the unknown and unfamiliar but staying ultimately within the known and familiar, the precision of the descriptions and word choice, and the uses of temporality to organize and represent understandings of the world.

Written Texts as Cultural Artifact

During fourth grade, Matthew's stance as a writer becomes more self-consciously authorial, more focused on the crafting of text as cultural artifact or public product. Often engaed in the process of generating text at the local level of topic-comment within some kind of temporal or textual parameters, Matthew seems to have given little attention to the final form of earlier texts during the composing process itself. In contrast, many of his texts in fourth grade are more finished off, bounded, differentiated, and defined by genre, as if Matthew has moved more fully into the cultural knowledge and authorial stance of, say, a mystery story writer. His understanding of a genre is more differentiated, his ability expressively to work and rework the genre more developed.

Text XII (4th grade, February 1984, age 9 years, 2 months)

The stolen PIE!

Mrs. Brown's pie was stolen from her window and tracks were seen around the house!

The next day Mrs. Brown hired a private eye who's name was Rick Tick Zick the famous private eye "The best" he said. Mrs. Brown had never heard of him but she didn't say any thing. He asked her a lot of questions like "What time was the pie stolen and what kind of pie was it ect, ect. She said the pie was stolen at 4:00 pm and it was a cherry pie. He said I'll get right on it after I eat my cherry pie at home I just got. Mrs. Brown felt suspicious about him. He said he just got a cherry pie and thats the kind that got stolen. Then Mrs. Brown remembered the footprints if she could get his footprint she could prove that he took the pie. She went to take a picture of the footprint so she would have it. The next day the private eye came over. Mrs. Brown told him about the footprint she went to show him. Right before he came she put water on the lawn so it would be muddy. When the private eye was walking he put his foot in the mud. Then Mrs. Brown showed him the footprint. When he left that day Mrs. Brown compaired the two footprints they were the same! Mrs. Brown took a picture of the other footprint. Then she called the police. When the police came over she showed them the footprints. They caught the private eye and put him in jail.

The End

This text was prompted by Matthew's reading teacher providing the opening line and thereby setting up the dramatic situation and the mystery story genre. The large capital letters in the title and the exclamation points highlight graphically the intensity and excitement suggested for the writer by this possible adventure—and add a touch of irony.

With the familiar temporal marker "The next day," the writer propels the main character quickly into action, as she immediately begins to solve this problem by turning to the appropriate authority, a private eye. This locates the emerging narrative in the world of law and order, quest, ingenious problem solving, and mystery. The rather humorous name of this "famous detective," the three rhyming words "Rick Tick Zick," plays with language and parodies the potentially serious mystery story genre. In a similar way, the detective's claim to be "the best" not only serves to satirize the authority of the detective (and remind readers of a once famous boxer) but also interweaves the voice of the writer as amused commentator into the text. Readers are then invited into the mind of Mrs. Brown, who has never heard of this famous detective but wisely decides not to say anything. Three voices animate the text: the arrogant detective, the distant but amused narrator, and the wisely skeptical Mrs. Brown.

The detective then does what detectives are supposed to do: he asks a lot of precise questions about time and kind of pie in an effort to solve the mystery. The "ect, ect" parodies detective discourse and allows the writer to keep the pace of the story moving, without getting bogged down in lots of unnecessary details. Mrs. Brown provides precise answers about time and "cherry pie"—and inadvertently sets up the key clue to the mystery. The dialogue is embedded and indirect quotation, which is yet another way to keep the story moving.

The plot thickens when the famous Rick Tick Zick ends the interview by announcing that he will start on the investigation just as soon as he eats the cherry pie he just got. The writer has the mystery set up and solved now—and invites the reader into the playfulness and suspense of the story by telling the reader that Mrs. Brown "felt suspicious" (as should the wise reader!) and then directly explaining the connection between the pie that was stolen and the pie that Rick is going off to eat (just in case it's not clear). Another voice appears: the writer communicating directly with the readers. The pleasure in the story now comes from the writer's careful crafting of the story, his reversing features of mysteries, and his subtly addressing readers and inviting them into the pleasure of composing this text.

The mystery is now solved but the crook not caught, as the story turns to the question not of knowledge (who done it) but of ingenuity (how to prove it) in an Encyclopedia Brown sort of way. The story now takes up the suggestion in the second half of the opening sentence, with Mrs. Brown remembering the footprint and realizing that if she could just get Rick's footprint, she herself could solve the case. With great precision, the writer devises a plan for proving Rick's guilt. In careful order, Mrs. Brown first takes a photograph of the footprint in order to have evidence for later. When the famous detective returns the next day, Mrs. Brown tells him about the footprint and cleverly takes him out to show it to him. The writer adds here that Mrs. Brown has had the foresight to water the lawn thoroughly first so that she could get another footprint. Inevitably, as the plan unfolds, the detective walks through the mud, produces a footprint, looks at the earlier evidence, and leaves. Mrs. Brown, obviously the *real* detective, compares the prints, wisely takes a picture of the second one for further evidence, and calls the police, who then arrest the private eye and put him in jail.

The story ends happily, with the crooked detective put in jail and the mystery neatly, logically solved by the clever work of Mrs. Brown.

Text XIII (4th grade, March 1984, age 9 years, 3 months)

The Jewerly shop

One day a man named Mike Green was walking along a street in downtown Chicgao when he saw a new jewerely store going up that neaded a owner. He decided to look into it. When he got home he called the place. When he got of the phone he had gotten the job.

The next day he went to work. The first thing he had to do is get jewelry. He decided to get = 4 diamonds, 5 rubys, 3 pieces of rose quartz, and 11 pieces of gold, 4 pieces of Amethyst quartz. The next thing he had to do is price them. I'm not going to give you the prices because it will take to long. Mike had the jewerly and the prices but he had no one to sell it. So the next day he put an add in the paper and three people came in for the job. He hired all of them. The next thing mike said was that we have to advitise this place so tonight I'm going to write a commerchial.

The next day at about 3:00 mike and his workers filmed his comerchial and he put it on TV the next day.

Ever since then they made money like never before.

In a twenty-eight word complex opening sentence, the writer straight-forwardly establishes the basic elements of the narrative: character, action, site, and problem or decision which will impel action. This story begins in the anytime world of "one day" but then names the main character Mike Green and locates the action on a street in downtown Chicago. When he sees the sign on the jewelry store requesting a new owner, Mike Green makes a quick decision. He decides to check it out, makes a phone call as soon as he gets home, and gets the job. By the end of the first paragraph, the text world is completely set up—and the rest of the text carries out the logic of that world in getting a business started.

"The next day," Mike Green goes right to work. First he orders gems for his inventory. The writer carefully lists the kind and number of each gem, but tells the reader it would take too much time to relate all the prices, too. Now Mike has the jewelry and the prices but no one to sell it, so he takes the next logical step of placing a help wanted ad and hiring all three people who apply for the job. Then Mike takes on the next problem: getting customers. He writes a commercial, which he and his workers film this next day at about 3:00, and on yet another "next day" the commercial plays on TV.

The whole project becomes a big success, apparently, and Mike and the workers end up making money "like never before."

The story moves quickly through five busy days, with Mike Green taking on the challenges of starting up a jewelry business in logical, problem solving order. Little emotion is evoked, as Mike is constructed as capable, organized, rational, careful, and ultimately successful. The kernel events are deciding to buy the store, getting and pricing the jewels, hiring three workers, and completing a TV commercial. Each kernel event is elaborated in about the same amount of precise detail.

These two texts can be characterized as finished products, easily read, enacting the conventions of the genre, both displaying a knowledge of the resources of narrative and expressing Matthew's particular approach and unique accent. That is, we can read both the conventions of narrative and the hand and mind of the particular maker in a descriptive reading.

The narratives fully realize the basic elements of the genre: setting (Mrs. Brown's house, downtown Chicago), characters (Mrs. Brown, Rick Tick Zick, Mike Green, three workers), crisis of some sort (a stolen pie, a jewelry store), and resolution (solving the mystery, starting up a successful business). There is little or no dialogue, as the stories are both told primarily through summary and scene. Each story covers a span of several days. The writer moves efficiently but with sufficient detail through major events, without meandering or getting sidetracked. The movement in the stories is logical as well as chronological, motivated by the requirements of the problem set up in the text world, resulting in closure and coherence. There are no superfluous details, and each part of the story moves toward the logical conclusion. The writer works from a midpoint between two perspectives: attention to necessary details as well as attention to the big picture of what it takes to get a business started.

The characters are also more fully realized, drawn from the genre and the prompt and not autobiographical persons imported from Matthew's life and implanted into an imaginary setting. The characters enact different positions and interact with each other. The narrative voice has two levels: at one level, the writer tells the story in a direct omniscient way, and at another level, the writer addresses the readers rather directly, drawing them into the act of composing the story itself.

Again, Matthew works these resources in his particular way, with humor, with precision in language use and the logic of plot details, with an interest in problem solving and questions of knowledge, and with a strong sense of a tightly rendered, carefully balanced textual structure. He is interested, too, in processes and procedures for getting things done in the world, a thematic interest revealed in other texts he has written, such as detailed, precise instructions he wrote for building a birdhouse or for fly fishing. This approach to telling a story resonates with Matthew's early interest in damming up creeks to play in. Here, too, he bounds or contains a universe by focusing on one particular problem or decision at a time within an overview of the whole situation, and by working out the details logically, almost inevitably, as they result from that problem or decision. The text world, like the creek, is bounded, contained, and manageable, and within that world a reasoned order, normalcy, and sense of safety can be (nearly) restored.

Yet there is a new ''voice'' or stance in these texts—that of the author, consciously crafting a cultural artifact for readers whom he addresses as if they, too, will take pleasure in reading what he had (apparently) taken pleasure in producing. As Matthew has worked with the resources of written language, he has come to locate himself differently—less the builder formally constructing a text from fragments and bits, more the architect functionally designing a text from the blueprint of genre. And with that knowledge has come greater opportunity to appropriate some of these genres in more individually accented and expressive ways. So it is that mystery stories have taken off for Matthew as a genre that matters to him, that engages his interest and enables him to learn about the conventions of the genre as he works within the genre in particular, expressive, and personally meaningful ways.

Matthew Writing

As I near the end of this documentary account, I would like to step back from Matthew's texts and theorize more broadly about his engagement across time with written language. In particular, I would like to explore the role of genre and style within development.

Genre as Mentor

The Soviet psychologist L. S. Vygotsky argues (1978) that what children can do with the assistance of others is more indicative of their mental development than what they can do alone. He calls this "the zone of proximal development," defined as "the distance between the actual developmental level as determined by independent problem solving and the level of *potential* development as determined through problem solving under adult guidance or in collaboration with more capable peers" (p. 86). He is looking at mental functions that are in the process of maturation, the "buds" rather than the "fruits" of development. His point is to locate measures of development, not solely within the mind of the learner but within the social interaction, or shared territory, of learner and mentor.

This concept leads to a reevaluation of the role of imitation in learning, which can no longer be considered mechancial but formative, because, according to Vygotsky, "a person can imitate only that which is within her developmental level" (p. 88). If a child is having difficulty with a particular mathematical problem and the teacher solves it on the black-board, the child may grasp it in an instant—*if* it is in his or her zone or developmental level. Thus, learning presumes a specifically social nature and process, by which children grow into the intellectual life of those around them (p. 88), and learning that is most effective is learning that is oriented toward what lies just beyond the already known and completely mastered. As a general law, Vygotsky proposes that learning creates its own zone of proximal development, that "learning awakens a variety of internal developmental processes that are able to operate only when the child is interacting with people in his environment and in coorporation with his peers. Once these processes are internalized, they become part of the child's independent developmental achievement" (p. 90). Developmental processes, therefore, always lag behind learning processes, resulting in the zone of proximal development, as external or social knowledge is internalized and sets up new problems or concerns. To learn a new word, therefore, is not the completion of a developmental process but the beginning of one, because that word opens up new possibilities, new complexities, new processes in the child's thinking.

Genres, too, may "mentor" a new writer by inviting a dialogic encounter and thereby defining and redefining a zone of proximal development.

In *Speech Genres and Other Late Essays* (1986), Bakhtin defines *genre* as the link between the social and the individual, as the shared territory that makes speech communication possible at all. He argues that "we speak only in definite speech genres, that is, all our utterances have definite and relatively stable typical *forms of construction of the whole*" (p. 78)—typical thematic content, style, and compositional structure. To speak or write, then, is to take up a particular genre and individuate and contextualize it.

This definition expands our usual use of the word to categorize literary works by defining *genre* more broadly and more theoretically, as Halliday (1978) does when he contends that genre structure "is not simply a feature of literary genres: there is generic structure in all discourse, including the most informal spontaneous conversation (p. 134). Genres emerge, then, in a culture as conventionalized responses to, and representations of, particular and recurrent situations—situations in which language mediates and accomplishes certain social actions. As I have argued elsewhere (1986), as a child comes to appropriate and rework the features of a genre, he or she comes to learn not only typical substance or formal conventions but also situations that typically give rise to this genre, social actions that may be accomplished, interpretive roles that may be adopted. Miller (1984) contends that "what we learn when we learn a genre is not just a pattern of forms or even a method of achieving our own ends. We learn, more importantly, what ends we have" (p. 165). In my documentary account of Samantha, I argue that it is the formal features of genre that initially enage her interest and provide a point of entry into written language. In the beginning, at least, she attends more to making of a product and "acting" like a writer than to telling a tale or engaging deeply in the intellectual and imaginative possibilities of the genre. Yet over time, new choice points and options emerge for her, as her working within the genre creates for her a kind of zone of proximal development.

In this sense, Matthew's early texts are not "expressive" in the sense that James Britton once argued for, but rather highly mediated by the requirements and constraints and possibilities of the genre itself for specific kinds of meaning-makings. These early texts are public, not private, accessible to adult audiences. Matthew is working not from the inside out but rather from within the boarder regions of self and culture, from within the social semiotic systems that make up the world.

Genre has mentored Matthew well. His knowledge of various genres, such as exposition and narrative, has established parameters and possibilities of length, kinds of content, ways of moving the text forward, particular relationships with the readers. The voices are public as well as autobiographical, offering multiple perspectives or positions from which to compose a text and represent a world. In a sense, then, genres have *occasioned* development by opening up space, creating an intensification of feeling, mattering in some way, setting up expressive choice points that have pulled Matthew further and further into the semiotic resources of written language. In particular, devices of temporality, dialogue, the basic requirements of a narrative plot, and the many voices of different characters have drawn Matthew in. Genres also provide an overview or frame for the project, and thus push toward coherence and closure, by identifying key points, providing momentum and direction, offering the pleasure of a finished-off product that is shareable with others.

Genres such as fairy tales or adventure stories or mysteries have drawn Matthew into the public arena of semiotic possibilities, opening up into cultural practices of signification, new words and worlds. Through genre, he has authored text and authored self and been authored by the culture—all at once. It is at the level of genre that Matthew has enacted in his particular ways the transpersonal meaning potentials of language and culture. It is particularly at the level of genre that personal meaning has intersected with the vast semiotic possibilities of culture.

Overall, it has been this structuring power of written language that has most engaged Matthew. The text world that can be created within a genre can be bounded and comprehensive, worked reasonably within the logic of its own terms, moving across time toward some kind of closure. It is a world imaginatively realized at the intersection of the conventions of the genre and the interests and events from Matthew's lived life that matter to him.

Development as Style

The basic argument of this project has been to understand development as a dialogic encounter of child and culture across, within, through, and against the shared territory of actual language use, particularly as organized by the demands and possibilities of various genres. As children engage with the possibilities of written language, and as their knowledge of those resources increases, so, too, are their particular and expressive reworkings of those resources enabled.

Thus, one way to investigate development is to describe and study "style," or a personal aesthetic, the tracing and enacting of that dialogic encounter of a particular child with particular resources of written language and culture.

Throughout the descriptive readings of Matthew's texts across time, his particular style, or kind of engagement, has emerged. Writing for Matthew has been defined as a public activity, so that even when events are drawn from his lived life, the register in which he recounts those events is formal and public. Anecdotes are written in the first person but elaborated as if for a distant audience and on a rather formal occasion. As a result, the texts are often compact, terse, understated, only somewhat evocative of emotion and interiority.

Often in his writing there is an interest in doubleness, or otherness, as when the two Matts go off on an adventure or fishing expedition together, or when the narrative "I" observes and reflects upon the character "Matt" bravely taking off for Mars with an alien creature in a spaceship. Rhythm is used with both structuring and aesthetic effects, as in the "knocked down and bruised up" phrasings and in the tight balance among parts of the texts. This symmetry is both an organizing principle and an aesthetically pleasing use of language.

Matthew has often drawn up bounded text worlds in which some feature of that world has gone amok and requires action, deliberation, reflection, or knowledge in order to be restored to (almost) normalcy. Parents disappear, bombs explode, spaceships suddenly appear, pies are stolen, and business has to get under way. Thematically, then, a crisis often happens that demands the deployment of mental and fiscal resources. Matthew maintains two perspectives at once, attentive both to the details of the situation and to the overall frame. He's not too distant and not too involved, and he always has ideas about gathering up resources and going into action. Matthew presents that crisis with precision—naming the number of days, calculating the kind of airplanes, determining exactly the way to collect evidence, carefully working out the logic of events based on the when/then premise. This precision in early texts is hauntingly set against a large, unexplained, rather mysterious background, but over time more and more background is provided through description and summary. So the text worlds become more contained, closed, and coherent—balanced between detail and overview.

Voices motivate and animate the texts, bringing in the worldviews and multiple perspectives of policemen, robbers, wise old women, aliens, businessmen, detectives, and variously refracted "Matthews." The world is typically communal, a shared project relying on the cooperative work of many people. Matthew shows an interest in rules and procedures both for getting along with people (politeness rules, ways to hire people for a jewelry business) and for finding out how to solve problems (determining how pies get stolen or TVs disappear). Always this is done with humor, an ironic play with the role of author and with the richness of certain words and puns.

Overall, there is a deep interest in knowing: who knows, what can be known, the limits of knowing, what lies just beyond our knowing, and how the process of knowing takes place in different settings. In particular, there is an interest in science, mathematics, and social issues.

It is in tracing Matthew's particular enactment of the possibilities of written language that development itself can be understood as a dialogic encounter between child and culture; that readers can come to know the child (in partial, ambiguous, and evocative ways) and the resources of written language; and that *the child writing* can be investigated and valued as a subject of study.

When/Then Texts

Text XIV (5th grade, December 1984, age 10 years)

Changing The World

If I could cange any one thing in the world it would probaly be to take people from African Countries such a Ethopia and bring them to the United States to live with families and start a new life.

I would do this so the people in Africa would not have to live in poverty and possibly starve to death. And after it was not so dry and the soil is rich enough to plant crops in I would let them move back to Africa if they wanted to.

I will do this by putting them all on about 20 jet planes and taking them here.

This would change the world because there would be more people on the world and there will be more workers so there is more food and more of everything.

Text XV (5th grade, April 1985, age 10 years, 4 months)

If Spring Never Came

One day I was eating dinner and watching the evening news. I had just heard a story that a giant chipmunk had escaped from a laberatory and was destryoying downtown Tokyo. Suddenly, there was a news flash, the sun was burning out and it was getting cold very fast.

My Mother just walked in. She looked cold and was rubbing her hands together very fast. She told me to turn the heat up as high as I could or we would turn into "icycles."

As I was lying in bed that night, under 20 covers, I was wondering what would happen if the sun never started bruning and spring literaly never came. I thought about that for a long time until I looked at the clock and it said 1:00 A.M., so I thought I'd better get to sleep.

Of course, the nex day I didn't go to school Even if I could my Mom wouldn't let me. We lied down in my in my room and watched T.V. all day.

By then some scientists had a couple solutions. One was that we could send a giant capsule filled with some kind of chemicle to the sun, make it rupture, and set the sun on fire. But at the rate of 1.3 miles per second it would take 3 years for the capsule to get there.

Another solution would be to make about 3 billion heat generators and set them in peoples houses. But by the time we made all those generators and got them in everyones houses, everyone would probobaly be permanently forstbitten and would not do any good.

So, about 3 weeks passed, with the same routine every day. I'd get up in the morning, call my dad to make sure everything was all right, lie down with my Mom and watch T.V. all day, and then call my dad again to make sure everything was all right. By watching the news I learned that alot of people had died from a bad cold or something like that.

The next day a miracle occured, at about 11:00 in the morning I went to look out the window and the sun was shining.

Teacher Talk

To conclude this documentary account and to open it up to further dialogue, I invited teachers from the larger Prospect community to do a descriptive reading, or deep talk, of Matthew's text entitled "To Be a Good Fisherman."

During Prospect Summer Institute II (August 1990) in North Bennington, Vermont, about twelve teachers read all fifteen texts from this account. Then they met and talked together for more than two hours about this particular text. Following Prospect procedures, they began by reflecting on a keyword, in this case "fish" and "fishing," as a way of approaching the topic of the text and articulating networks of personal and cultural meanings associated with these words.[5] The purpose was to open up the rich dialogic history and meaning of those words within our culture. Next they went through a series of descriptive rounds, reading and rereading the text, noting textual choices, locating the text in more and more contexts, using language to explore language use. They took their time; they dwelled in the text. And within this arena of collective thought and talk, they came to understand something of what might matter in deeply dispositional ways to Matthew. They also came to enlarge their knowledge of written language, to create a shared intellectual experience, and to explore educational possibilities (and questions) that announced themselves during their work together.

I have constructed here a dramatic reenactment of this summer's conversation. It is a snapshot of the event, reduced from two hours to thirty minutes, from abut twelve to six "composite" teachers. It moves too quickly, leaps too fast to summary and conclusion, but does illustrate the richness and the raggedness and resourcefulness of the process—and suggests the uses of deep talk in other educational settings.

As always in deep talk, the child's text becomes a meaningful space, an abundantly eventful space, where we, as writers and readers, teachers and researchers, can meet anytime, over time, time and time again, and come to know each other and language and culture in certain situated and praxis-oriented ways.

This description was chaired by Patricia F. Carini, whose work with this particular text was enlarged by her careful reading of the entire account over time. I greatly appreciate her participation and leadership in this conversation.

I would also like to acknowledge the insightful responses to the entire account that were written by Rhoda Kanevsky, a first-grade teacher at Powel School in Philadelphia; Lynne Strieb, a first- and second-grade teacher also in Philadelphia; and Alice Seletsky, a fifth- and sixth-grade teacher from Central Park East I in New York. Having worked with the account for several months, these teachers were able to go beyond this reading and to take Matthew up as a thinker in different domains—to speculate about his style of participation in science, in the visual arts, and in social and political science. Their work is integrated into this reenactment, and I greatly appreciate their deep understanding of how to support children as learners in imaginative and dialogic ways.

To Be a Good Fisherman

This text was written at home in September 1982, when Matthew was 7 years, 9 months old

To be a goob Fisherman
1. First you have to be patient
or you wont catch any
fish 2. After you get a
bite you real it in
Right. Wrong not right

then you wait in til
he has it in his mouth.
And you jerk him. That
way you set the hook.
3. Ther are lots of kinds
of fishing. In river fishing
you don't use a bobber.
You put a large sinker
on your line. About
six inches from the
swivel and then a hook.
You cast it out and
wait intil your poll
bounces up and down
4. Lake fishing you
use a bobbor.
you put the bobor on
and you do the same
thing as river fishing.
After you do that
You cast it out and wait
for the bobber to go
down 5. Lewer fishing
is a lot of work you
have to real in the
lewer all the time.
A lewer can be a fish
or a worm the only
difrens is that they
are fake they go
threw the water like
A real fish or worm.
Ther is something
called a weedless worm
that is what I fish with
in South Carolina.
Ther is no fish lewer
that is weedless. Not
that I know of.
6. There are all sorts
of kinds of fish. A catfish

Has 3 Big spins and
sharp teeth. So if you
ever catch a catfish
grab it right. 7. When
you clean a fish
a fish you dont just
chop his head off and
eat it. If it is a small
fish you scale it and
then chop his head
off then gut him
and wash him good.
If it is a large fish
you skin it you cut
a thin line on both side
of his Fins do the
same for the belly
After you are done,
take a nother thin slice
on one side of the head
fin. Then take a
plers. take a corner
of the skin and pull
it on both sids
Pull the fins and
chop the head off
And then your done.
8. When you eat a fish
you never put enything
in your mouth with
it. 9. I have fished in lots
lakes and rivers
but the best fishing
I have ever had is
in a pond in South
Carolina. I have
caught alot of
fish in that pond.
From 3 inches long to
2 pounds.
the end

Descriptive Paraphrase

The writer is giving us advice on how to become a good fisherman, and it's going to be in a series of numbers or directions, the first of which is that you have to be patient, because if you are not patient, you are not going to catch anything.

After you feel a bite, you wait until the hook is in its mouth, and then you jerk him and reel him in. That way you are sure the hook is set.

* * *

There are many varieties of fishing, with different kinds of equipment. You float the bobber, put a weight on the line, separate it from the swivel, cast it out away from yourself, and—this is where the patience comes in—wait for that pole to bounce. Lake fishing is different because you use a bobber, but it's also the same as river fishing—cast it out, wait for the bobber to dip down. Lure fishing, in addition to requiring patience, is a lot of work, because you have to keep moving the lure, winding it in, letting it out.

* * *

Then the writer explains what a lure is—it can be either a fish or a worm—but they're fake and very good at looking like a fish or worm moving through the water. Then he says there is something called the weedless worm, and I assume that's another kind of lure (I don't know much about fishing) and that this is what he uses as a lure when he goes fishing in South Carolina. There is a thing called a weedless lure or weedless worm, and it has to do with how the hook is made, but in fact when you throw it in, you catch weeds anyway. You can't get rid of the weeds.

* * *

Then he says there are all "sorts of kinds of fish," not just kinds of fish, but he sees this in a larger way. He tells you about the catfish, about the particular care you have to take. He is funny as well as insistent upon making sense. "So if you ever catch a catfish, grab it right." You bet I will now!

* * *

Once you have your catch, it's real important that you know what to do next, which means the art of cleaning a fish. You don't just chop its head off and eat it. There's something else here, having to do with size. There is a difference in treatments between a small fish and a large fish. When you eat a fish, you eat it all by itself. You don't mix it with other stuff. Yet after all the aesthetics and guidance, it is ultimately the quantity that matters—"from 3 inches long to 2 pounds." The important thing, when all is said and done, is catching a lot of fish.

*   *   *

The fisherman says that he's had a lot of experience. He's fished in lots of lakes and rivers, but the best fishing he's ever had is in a pond in South Carolina, and at that pond he's caught a lot of fish. They range from three inches long to two pounds.

*   *   *

We have had a difficult time paraphrasing, which I think is partly because of our lack of knowledge and the precision of the work, and that right away says volumes about this piece.

Descriptive Round One

The writer has taken a rather stern instructional stance, which I would think might be the way he was taught and which might be the way fishing *is* taught, with the more experienced fisher people indoctrinating or initiating the new folk. He's going to try to do this for us. But the ground rules are that you have to be ready to be serious about this game. And the sign of seriousness is your patience. This isn't just something to take lightly. This is a pursuit that's going to engage you for quite a while, so don't bother with it if you're not going to be patient.

*   *   *

Following up on that, I think that then he patiently outlines—you have to be patient not only in fishing but in reading the description of what it requires. He's very patient and wants you to be patient with the reading.

I think it's remarkable for his assimilation of the whole procedure or process and his ability to give it back. Obviously, someone has been very explicit that this is not just any old thing, that this is *fishing,* and when you fish, this is how you do it. A student of mine from last year had been trained as a fisherman by his grandfather, and he had this kind of lore passed on to him, and that is something valuable because it's so hard to do things that way today.

I want to go back to the title of this piece. When I first read it, I read it as "How to Be a Good Fisherman," and it wasn't until I got here that I realized it is "To Be a Good Fisherman." So it's almost like a kind of title that would have an ellipsis after it, and each one of the numbered sections would be ways of completing that sentence, even though the actual language of each of those points doesn't work that way. But it sort of suggests to me an ellipsis. The first point is a general rule about the activity of fishing, about the state of mind you have to be in. Then he goes into the second point as specific instruction about reeling the fish in and about what happens after you get a bite, and then he goes on to talk about kinds of fish and more specific things.

* * *

There is so much knowledge underneath all of this, yet it's as if he is having a conversation with the reader. "And you jerk him," he says. The conveying of all this information comes without a lot of words. There's a lot of complexity in thought, in the way he sees the different kinds of fish and the variation within styles of fishing, and it's not all that straightforward, yet it's expressed in very few words.

* * *

There is precision in the language and in his use of the language and in the spareness with which he gets information across. He's also very precise in his terminology and the kinds of equipment that go with certain settings. That's quite impressive for a young child, not only how varied locations are but also how each location calls for different technique and different equipment needs.

There's a solemnity about the tone and a ritual quality to the performing of all these things. You get the impression that it's about knowledge, about what knowledge is. I get the feeling that he's pleased that he can show it off—he's conscious of how much he knows and pleased that he knows so much.

I'm struck, too, with the rhythm and pace of this, and its very "fisherman" style. I have spent lots of time in Maine, and they say just what they have to say, and if you listen hard enough, you can pick up a lot. It seems to be that there is the style of the fisherman that has to go along with the fishing and the retelling of how you do it. There is a lot of precise language, almost like a poem. The timing and the pacing go along with the patience, with everything that happens with fishing.

* * *

Let me talk about the genre thing first, how-to books, right? Except it could also be lecture notes, and I can see him being quite the teacher. And if you study how you're supposed to lecture, you're supposed to start with defining things, and then you go on from there. He does a lot of that. And the other thing that he does, which they teach you to do in teacher education programs, is task analysis—and he's very good at that, at breaking it down into every little part, though there are some places where he makes mistakes and forgets parts, but in general he's very good at remembering every little piece of it.

*   *   *

It says here that this piece was written at home, and that's interesting. The question arises about whether it was homework assigned at school, like writing directions for something, and if it wasn't, then who the audience is for this piece, because it is obviously written for a purpose. There's nothing sketchy about it. It's a complete work that feels like it was done for someone or for some particular reason. The whole line about having to be patient, particularly given the story before this one about fishing with his grandfather, makes me wonder what he has been told about fishing. Being patient and setting the hook are two big lessons, hard ones for kids to deal with, and he carries himself here in a certain way as the writer—solid, step by step, clear.

*   *   *

To summarize this round, I think I'll start with the posture he takes in this, the style of his writing, and what you have said about this so far. He is taking an instructional stance, and this is like lecture notes. It is the vehicle for letting us know the authority with which he speaks, and he does speak with authority. But never with overbearingness. There are asides like "not that I know of." It's conversational. It's not stiff. He is familiar enough with what he knows so that he can afford to be that way.

And he develops it in a very fascinating way. He starts you off with the essence of fishing, that is, getting the fish. In the very first line, you get the fish. And he tells you how you do that in terms of both the state of mind you need to be in, which is a patient one, a waiting one, and also what you have to do to be sure that fish does not elude you at the last moment. That he does first.

And then a very different sort of way other than that essence, he lets you know that we are talking about a big field of activity that he knows, and he gives you a few examples, which also has the "good teacher" quality. He doesn't overwhelm you with too much, and he helps you to divide it up—you talk about river fishing; you talk about lake fishing; you don't mix these things together. The other way he assists himself with that task is to number these. This is to me an astonishing thing, to stay straight in his language. He is a master of ellipsis in the selection power he has in giving us the illustrations and examples, so that compositionally this is superb for his instructional purposes and also superb for somebody who wants to have himself as his own audience and to internalize what he already knows by outlining it. It's a way of learning that's being displayed here as well—it's not everyone's way of learning—but it strongly suggests that it's one he can use to very good effect.

But I want to pick up on something else that was said. Because of the parsimony of the language, because of the precision and spareness of it, and because of the modesty of it, it has also a poetic quality, and I think we don't want to lose sight of that behind the preciseness—that this is minimalist work, and when we look at some of the other work, that may be interesting to keep in mind.

In terms of the stance of the author, words that come up are solemnity, patient, authoritative, solid, step by step, clarity, a lot of control over one's material, strong authorship. This is somebody "speaking a tradition." It is passed-on knowledge, drawn from reservoirs of knowledge he has seen in his own experience and that he has also been told by someone else.

Descriptive Round Two

In thinking of all the knowledge he has, I'm thinking of one area in particular: the knowledge of the tools of the craft and the environment. You get the feeling that this child's been out in nature, in different environments. Also, the texture of the piece and the use of the senses—a lot of feel and touch and handling of the tools, the fish itself, and the taste of it when it gets in the mouth.

And in some ways the piece is about relationships with others, his experience with people who do something and do it well. It's a mental approach to fishing—it's about fishing as a mental and social process.

*   *   *

I'm fascinated that there are nine parables or proverbs. We have used the phrase *working knowledge,* and we have done some talking about the kinds of things you learn how to do that are narrated by the person who is teaching you, that involve or are immersed in a lot of talk, so I have the feeling that he's learned this both by being immersed in the activity and by being immersed in the talk of the lore. It has, in fact, a magisterial quality, the quality of a sermon.

And I love the image of a seven-year-old saying, "I have fished in lots of lakes and rivers, but the best fishing I have ever had is in a pond in South Carolina." I can see Hemingway. He has a real feel for being a fisherman.

*   *   *

I like the way he can bring me, as an outsider, into his piece by giving me some very particular information and speaking to me as an outsider—how to set my hook. And if I were ever so lucky to catch a catfish, I would now know what to do. And the part about the fish and the mouth, as an outsider, I thought that was purely reverence—this is so important, pay attention. He has this knowledge, and he sort of brings in someone else—I can come into it as an outsider to fishing culture.

Then I was interested in some of the verbs he uses: cast, jerk, reel. And the nouns are about terminology: bobbers, lures, sinkers. But somewhere in those words I hear the poetry of it all; they aren't just words like *throw*. There's a sound to *cast* that is both technical and lyrical.

*   *   *

I just want to say that I know nothing, knew nothing, about fishing, and I studied this story, and I have learned so much about fishing. I just realized that when I was ready to answer this question about lures, because I know now what he means. What he's done, in this magnificent organization, in each of these points—listen to this—context, general, river fishing, lake fishing, lure fishing, kinds of fish, cleaning, eating, importance to writer. That's why that lure fishing hangs together—it's like a chapter in his lecture notes.

Yet what I want to say about him in general is that he invites readers into a conversation, that he really is discussing this in general, and that he really invites you to discuss it with him. I kept thinking, why is there a difference between lake and river fishing—because the river is moving, so you need to put a sinker on it, right? To keep it from moving. On a lake, you don't. I never knew that before. The fact that he's organized it like this, that there's such clarity, means that he invites you to have this deep, complex talk with him, so that when I ask why, I can figure out why from his text and from the way he has described it.

The other thing this reminds me of is the John Cage record in which there are long stories and short stories, and the organization is that each story has to take one minute. And when John Cage tells the long story he has to talk fast, and when he tells the short story he talks slowly. It's a wonderful record—"Indeterminacy." Now when you look at number 7, that's the longest part, and it takes a long part to get through it. I can hear him reading fast. To get to number 8, I think he is savoring this all the way through. Somehow, he is savoring every piece of the directions, like a tasting and a telling. There's also humor in this, as he is watching himself doing all that.

* * *

If we think of all the things we said in the reflection about the comtemplativeness of the act of fishing and of the setting and the people, there is none of that here. It has a quality of matter-of-factness, and what draws us in is the particularity and detail. There is another piece in the documentary account about damming up creeks, and that's the other side of this kind of technical, specific, deliberative, authoritative piece. There is a reflective side to Matthew's writing, but I'm not sure that the power of the contemplativeness is as in evidence here.

* * *

This is like a writer who is older, who is bringing someone else into a new territory, who is sharing language, who is imparting knowledge. And there is so much meaningfulness here—like a bridge among generations in this epic of fishing, in its ritualness. There is something about sharing and generosity here. He uses "you" a lot, not "I"—"you put the bobber on."

* * *

Again, in summary, the writer brings himself into our presence only at the very end of what he has to say, which makes it all the more interesting that the authority he cites and the knowledge are not brought from his person, although we see the solidity of the person behind it because we are looking at it so closely, but his actual self-reference comes only at the very end, and it comes with a statement of value, of importance, of fishing's importance to him, which places it in a not altogether personal realm.

This is not a personalized piece, and yet it is not distant. We have noted that it's conversational, inclusive, reaching out to other people and into himself—and then, just at the very end, he says, "and if you want to know how I value this, I do." He's fished lots of places, and he tells us what he considers to be the very best. There is a quality of dignity there.

What we have added to our statements about his stance, along with his authority, are words like *magisterial*. We have brought it into an elaboration of that idea of knowledge as lore that is passed on, with the statement of its being an epic of fishing, having ritual qualities to it, in the telling, and of wisdom. It carries more years in it than he has lived. It is the vehicle for holding memory, so memory enters here in two ways: in the very large realm of memory, lore, ritual, that which is passed on across generations, and you become the holder of the knowledge before you pass it on; and it also has memory in it in the telling of it back to himself in order that he will know what he knows so that he'll be a reliable passer-on of the lore. He's there not so much in the personal sense, but he stands there as the current receiver and passer-on, imparter, and that may have something to do with the dignity of it, the poetic of it, and the reflectiveness of it, although it is also one of his more matter-of-fact pieces of writing.

Part of the authority comes from the attention to detail and the precision of language. It is not required that every single thing be said but he lets some thing stand for larger amounts—and that has bits of mastery in it, too. If you read this piece carefully, there's a lot more being said than there are words on the page, and that's powerful writing when you are able to do that.

The organization is simply superb, especially to begin with the essence of fishing and to end with its value. That has a loveliness to it.

It has as well the sense of a craftsman knowing his tools, and at the same time, right with that, somebody whose approach to things is powerfully intellectual or mental—the teacher is very strong here as well as the fisherman.

One last thing about memory. There is the suggestion of seeking memory, of a line back into the "just past," of the recapturing of summer and other possibilities.

Relating Text to Other Works

Are there other pieces from the collection that are brought to mind by this discussion, that offer another view of the child, or that raise other questions?

*   *   *

"To Be a Good Fisherman" in its solidity contrasts with a theme that appears in a number of other stories, the theme of things not being quite what they seem to be. Text 3, with the TV disappearing, takes up a perfectly ordinary day, and this and this and this happens, and then things come out OK more or less, back to normal but different.

The metaphor in fishing as detecting is certainly there in other texts— puzzling things out, digging out information, all of that is certainly a motif in a lot of his work, like Mrs. Brown's pie and finding a missing Atari. There is the motif of there being a mystery to things, a sense of things beyond the surface, but a mystery that is solvable, that can be figured out if you just know the steps and the pieces and have the right tools. The knowledge of the task is possible.

*   *   *

There is also a lot of precision, precise detail, throughout the works: distances, phone numbers, times, introductions of people by their first and last names, numbers of hours of TV watching, the time the miracle happened. Text 9 is another fishing text, which is also very detailed, very precise—how long they went, they got a few bites, who went, where they went, the exact day, the last whole day. That particular story is filled with precise detail.

*   *   *

The jewelry shop story is a how-to-do-it story. The first thing you do is get the jewelry, then you price it, and so on. However, it doesn't have the expertise the fishing story has, though he's very specific about the jewels. Less knowledge. They all seem to have a very sequential structure. He sets you up in time everywhere.

*   *   *

Many of them have conversations of one kind or another, or some kind of actual exchange. There's a conversational approach with the reader, like when he tells the reader in the jewelry story that he's not going to give them the prices. The awareness of the audience is very strong, and within the stories there are back-and-forths and then also back-and-forths between the reader and the writer. He's so easy with writing this way.

There is also a lot of what's underneath something else. In the one about Mars, at the end, he stares at the creature for a second and then goes

back home. He sits in bed that night thinking about it, with the suggestion
of so much more meaning in that story that is left implied.

*   *   *

Are there things noticeable by their absence?

*   *   *

There aren't the super hero stories, as in the writing I know from first
and second grade. What's also missing are the popular genre stories,
based on TV and movie connections, a common language that other kids
in that time and place often use.

I'm not sure if this holds up for all of them, but it caught me in the
Africa composition that other people's will and choice don't come up
often. It is limited in this text, too, as he's going to do things for people,
he's not going to ask them what they want or need. There's a kind of
assumption that he knows best. I'm not sure that comes up in other stories
or not. There aren't a lot of large groups, like other kids set up in their
stories. Only the text about his cousins seems populated. It's hard to see
from this where he is in terms of group or community.

*   *   *

There is something, too, about the ways settings are implied, not
described in detail, the settings or background, just a little bit and then
with the action in front of it, so I don't think I have a sense of going down
tunnels and through caves and upstairs in houses. I don't get a mapping
sense; it was sketchy background and fairly sharp foreground.

When he has an assignment to do, there's not a lot of embellishing.
He's spare; he answers the question.

*   *   *

I will turn now to summarizing a bit broadly, based on readings of
other texts in this collection as well as this one.

I will begin with how hiddenness, underneathness, and mystery are
present in these works, including the ways things are not what they
appear to be. And a counterpoint to that is great solidity, locatedness,
precision, detail, factualness, a degree of distance, sometimes served by
the third person. Powerful sequence and sense of logic and impeccable
internal or compositional structures. There is a use of number and that
fairly elliptical form that saves a great many words.

Then what comes through as absence is not a lot of attention to the
context or the background detail, with what is happening being right at

the forefront of the page, right up on the surface of it. At times there is the suggestion that more thinking is going on internally than is necessarily being stated. There aren't so many super heroes, because he counts on logic and solution and homework and thinking it through and detecting to get you to where you want to go.

There's a kind of belief in the do-ableness of things that is quite touching to me, and rather wonderful, so that if you keep at it (which to me goes along with the patience and the waiting in the fishing), you get your knowledge, and if you keep working at it, well, then it will work out, and you don't have to bring in large, outside forces. You're adequate to it yourself: you're clever and you're smart and you think hard and you follow the logic through . . . and there's a willingness to do it.

I want to add two things about ellipsis—those little asides in texts, like the "not that I know of" line in the piece we described. Those are elliptical, but there's also a sort of ease about them, like everyday and ordinary conversation, because you can be elliptical and terse so that you don't get that conversational style.

Although he speaks in dialogue within the pieces, the way he addresses audience is altogether inclusive, where he makes these sorts of friendly gestures to us, to invite us in. It also has to do with the modesty of the way in which he presents himself—qualified, not an extremist.

He has a confidence in people and the workableness of things, the ordinary, but nothing that goes right off the edges in extremes in action or in thought.

Let's turn now to the educational issues that emerge from this reading. What educational questions does our reading of Matthew's work raise, both specifically and generally? What kinds of conversations might you initiate, and what are your expectations about what would come back to you? What are things you definitely wouldn't do? What questions are left in your mind, as teacher, not necessarily that you might share with a youngster, but that you would be entertaining in the background as you were attentive to this child?

Educational Possibilities

The anecdote about the creek ("Creek Play") keeps resonating in my mind, as I read and reread Matthew's writing. He says he likes to play in nature, especially water (which is always shifting and changing, alternately revealing and obscuring its contents). I imagined him not only watching but also savoring the transformations in the creek, "where you can see everything that is going on in them." "I like to see the water stop, and get deeper and stand still. I like watching what happens then." In this anecdote, he explains why he is an observer and how strongly he is pulled into what he is observing. No surprise that his stories are filled with rich detail.

This anecdote suggests areas in science that he might find interesting. He moves easily from the general to the specific, interested in details but aware of the overview. He is interested in knowledge and pushing against boundaries in certain ways. There are many kinds of materials or projects that could expand his knowledge of the world in systematic ways, such as planning ecosystems that depend on varying conditions or using mirrors and lenses or studying genetics. I would expect him to enjoy puzzles, logic, and mathematical games of all kinds.

He grounds actions in thought. He wants to understand things, to figure things out. He is clear, precise, serious, conscientious in these efforts. He gives evidence, reasons for things, and uses "so" and "since" and "because" often as he tries to present a scenario that makes sense. Yet he also enjoys ambiguities and enjoys playing with shadowy and unexplained possibilities as well. Many stories explore this double perspective, seeing both the ambiguous and the matter-of-fact.

* * *

There are many examples in Matthew's writing of a preference for closure, wholeness, boundedness. In the short essays, he states an intention, develops his thought, using lots of detail, and completes it neatly at the end—"then I got back to normal" and "as soon as I get enough money."

I'd be very careful to listen to "the underneath" with him, not just to the surface layer of information but to the child that would be so easy to see as *just* a logical person, and to give him enough time and space to trust in those words that would then come up rather than to hurry or push them.

* * *

I think that with the assurance with which he presents himself, his self-knowledge, which is so apparent (that it's all doable, that it's all solvable) on the one hand, I would want to keep in mind that he must have questions, he must have concerns, he must have worries, he must have things in the world that preoccupy him. My concern would be, what are his questions? What are his interests that aren't fishing? Since he's not likely to reveal those easily, one might have to have the third eye open.

One theme in his writing is an active participation in the world. Right from the beginning, in the story of the two little boys, there's a Matt right in the middle of things. And at age ten, he's writing about saving the starving people of Africa. In many of the pieces in between, I find a kind of quiet assurance and steadiness, and a sense that things in the world are manageable and that there is at least the possibility of change. He writes, too, with a public voice, not impersonal, but not deeply personal. He might like current affairs projects, like preparing a weekly newscast video, which demands precision, careful analysis, exploration of issues, and balanced presentation.

* * *

I want to add to that. When he writes about being in the Christmas program, he worries about "messing up," and there was a sort of directness about that that was interesting to me—and a specificness about it too. "I get nervous when I'm in the Christmas program because I might mess up. But after the program, I don't feel nervous anymore. But I have the Christmas program two times, so I get nervous again before I got back to normal." One of the things I felt he was letting us know is how much he prefers the normal, and so being aware that with all this assurance and solidity, things that deviate from the normal are things he can cope with, but they cost him something. I like the manner in which he says that he gets nervous two times: because you've done it once doesn't mean you're going to feel better the next time. It's tough.

* * *

I have a real big question when I look at this work about the whole business of story starters, because I think it's hard for him to get his voice through, that he has such a hurdle to go over, that there have to be better ways to get students to write.

* * *

I see the adult as very important to him. He lives with his mother, he talks to his mother, Mrs. Brown, being a father, and I see the adult as having a very powerful effect on his life, so I would be interested in thinking about the teacher's relationship with him in the classroom and how he would value and accept what certain adults have to say. You might not want to say too much all the time, because he may imitate more than experiment.

*   *   *

I thought Matthew's early use of dialogue indicated a possible interest in plays. But his stated interest in how to make the TV disappear as if by magic made me think he might enjoy using a video camera or animation to enact his stories rather than trying to dramatize them as stage plays. Both animation and videotaping allow seemingly magical events to be depicted as real.

*   *   *

I was thinking about the longer and extended writing that is part of the Donald Graves business, because of the power of the terseness of his writing. I worry about the urge of teachers to always get kids to expand or fill in what's elliptical.

*   *   *

I would just tag on to that, having gone to several meetings this year in Vermont that have to do with this so-called authentic assessment, that there's a standard there. They're not talking about what the standard is, but there is a standard there about what is better and what isn't, and it's very different from the standard we're holding up when we say the first draft is often better.

*   *   *

First drafts are often better; it has to do with roughness and awkwardness, those features that are important if you are going to keep the writing alive.

That's a problem if he runs into teachers who want something of a certain length, because some teachers think length proves seriousness of purpose. I think, since he's respectful, he will do it, but I wonder what form he'll find. It seems that when he's doing writing for himself, he's got just the right length and form he needs.

*   *   *

Books come to mind, like Scott Corbett who writes a series of books for third and fourth graders, that someone who likes to find things out and decode things might enjoy. I can't remember the other name, but he writes stories about a boy who goes on adventures and there is precision and technical stuff involved, so that when things go awry, they are righted. The illustrations are drawn from different perspectives from what we are familiar with.

* * *

It occurs to me, though, that you can't expect just these pieces of writing to tell us more than they can tell us. I don't know what it tells me about what kinds of things he's going to like to read. I don't think I can tell that yet. I have hunches that need to be tried out. Obviously he likes detectives stories, but whether that takes him into mythology and folklore and that kind of mystery or if it takes him into the mysteries of science, I don't know.

* * *

The question that raises for me is, what can you tell from one medium, writing, about what interests he might have in other mediums. I certainly would try out technical drawing, because of the interest in science combined with that precision. But would this idea hold up? I'd be willing to try it.

* * *

In summary, we must be mindful of the aesthetic of the thinking process. With Matt, it's important to remember that there is much below the surface. Where we locate him in the classroom and the point of vantage from which we observe him are important. We know that he's most comfortable with the known and the familiar—he likes things to "get back to normal"—but also that he can make room for new things. He likes to investigate, explore, experiment. What this suggests is that he is eager to explore new ideas but needs to get to them by means of a path that is familiar. We might, for example, lay out a series of books for him to read.

Because he is serious, thoughtful, respecting of adults, it's important to be conscious in his education of the extent to which one intervenes, interferes, directs. His thinking is compact, logical, coherent, elliptical, precise. It is assured but free of arrogance. It would be unwise to tamper too much with Matt's thinking or to interfere with his writing. He doesn't need to be pushed to refine or revise as a conscious process, since he often does that in the course of a piece of writing. His personal aesthetic, like his standards, is clear.

He tends to be most comfortable with the normal, so we can let him know that extremes are sometimes worth exploring. His education should be designed to support that. The themes of futurity and ancientness seem to be present in his thought as it emerges in these written fragments, together with an interest in detecting, decoding, uncovering what's hidden. Some study like archeology might interest him—looking into the earth and into the past, or, to go in an outward direction, moving into the study of astronomy.

What we have in this collection of Matthew's works are fragments. The final question this raises for us is how far such fragments can be trusted to yield useful information about the person, and to what extent we can rely on them to make educational decisions. What one comes to know depends on (1) how closely and carefully the fragments are looked at and (2) how large the collection is. The more fragments there are, the greater the possibility of forming knowledge based on them, remembering always that we can never fully know the person.

Attending to fragments means turning to the risky side, to the experimental side, of education and making tentative hypotheses, fresh starting points, using fragments of our own knowledge to make connections. Looking at fragments slants us in different and new and individual and risky ways. Fragments situate pedagogy on riskier ground by calling forth lots of questions.

Notes

Introduction

1. The focus of this book is on the constituting and the developing of persons by, through, within, and against actual language use. But Carini explores this question from a larger perspective, by looking at children's drawings, constructions, gestures, and so on, and by more fully acknowledging the role of the natural and cultural worlds in this process. Her goal is to understand how to educate children.

Chapter 1

1. The founders of the Prospect School are Joan Blake, Patricia and Louis Carini, and Marian Stroud. Carini notes, too, that Jessica Howard, except with brief interruptions, has taught at Prospect since 1966, has been involved in planning the school, and has exercised an important shaping effect on the school's pedagogy. The Prospect School is organized in multi-age groups, spanning several birth years. In recent years, the groups have included children aged $4^1/_2$–7, 7–11, and 11–14. This practice means that a child typically remains with the same teacher for three or four years.

2. When speaking of her work, Carini consistently calls attention to its collaborative nature and especially stresses the shaping effect on her own thinking of conversations, or what she calls "good talk," that have occurred in and around Prospect. Those influencing conversations have involved several overlapping circles of speakers: the staff and board of Prospect Center; the teachers who regularly attend Summer Institute II; the Archive Scholars and Fellows Program; and the members of the Prospect study group "Adults as Learners." Other forums for conversation Carini regularly refers to include the Workshop Center at City College; the North Dakota Study Group on Evaluation; the Center for Teaching and Learning at the University of North Dakota; the New York State Bureau of Child Development and Parent Education; the Independent Master's Degree Program at Lesley College; the Early Education Group at Educational Testing Service; the Network of Progressive Educators; Teacher and Parent Study Groups in Mamaroneck, N.Y.; the Center for Establishing Dialogue in Teaching and Learning, Tempe, Ariz.; and, in Philadelphia, the Teachers Learning Cooperative, the School in Rose Valley, Friends Select School, and the annual Summer Institute sponsored by these schools and the Springside School. Carini makes special note of the complementarity of her husband Louis Carini's work to her own and especially her indebtedness to understandings of perception, thinking, and language that he has developed in *The Theory of Symbolic Transformations* and *Three Axioms for a*

Theory of Conduct (Washington, D.C.: University Press of America, 1983 and 1984).

3. By the term *works,* I do not mean to suggest artistic or extraordinary achievement or some romantic view of children as naive creators of great art. I am also not trying to invoke the postmodern work/text dichotomy. Rather, the term here refers to that most ordinary way in which products of all kinds bear the imprint of the unique hand and mind that made them, and to those most ordinary activities such as writing letters, jotting notes in a family cookbook, or designing a garden that constitute daily life.

4. In particular, I would like to acknowledge how much this work has benefited from the active reading of Sheela Harden, a member of the Prospect community in Bennington, Vermont.

5. (Everett) is the Prospect method for identifying a child by his or her documentary name and for ensuring the child's privacy.

6. The details and some of the examples of documentary processes come from *The Prospect Center Documentary Processes: In Progress* (1986a).

Chapter 2

1. See, for example, Lynne Strieb's *A (Philadelphia) Teacher's Journal* (Grand Forks, N.D.: North Dakota Study Group on Evaluation, 1985).

2. See, too, *The Prospect Center Documentary Processes: In Progress,* updated and revised June 1986, available from the Prospect Archive and Center for Education and Research, North Bennington, Vermont 05257.

3. Compare this to the reading process described by Loren Barritt, Patricia L. Stock, and Rancelia Clark in "Researching Practice: Evaluating Assessment Essays," in *College Composition and Communication,* October 1986, pp. 315–27.

4. See M. Himley, "Discourse Communities and Quotation Marks," in *Contesting the Boundaries of Liberal and Professional Education: The Syracuse Experiment* (1988), (ed. Peter Marsh, Syracuse, N.Y.: Syracuse University Press, pp. 35–43) for a brief discussion of the way talk happened in a two-year interdisciplinary seminar in which talking together came to be valued as central to the intellectual enterprise.

5. Consider, for example, this brief descriptive account of the "buying a newspaper" genre. There are particular role relationships between the buyer and the seller ("tenor"); there is the ongoing activity of buying the paper, along with expected casual, rather formulaic chatting about the weather or perhaps sports or a major news event ("field"); and there is a kind of short, informal, but impersonal question-answer spoken language exchange ("mode"). It would violate genre rules if the newspaper buyer launched into a deeply personal account of his income tax problems or if the seller ordered the buyer to make certain kinds of purchases. Typically genres are invisible to us unless rules are broken somehow. Yet sociolinguistics (e.g., Halliday, 1978) argue that all discourse has generic structure or patterning that links the actual words to the context of situation (p. 134).

6. Compare this to the epistemological position in *Women's Ways of Knowing* labeled "constructed knowledge": a position in which women view all knowledge as constructed, experience themselves as creators of knowledge, and value both subjective and objective strategies for knowing. The authors also refer to "real talk" as that which taps simultaneously one's inner and outer world, and to "contextual thought" as that which speaks from particulars, contexts, perspectives, not principles.

Chapter 3

This chapter appeared in somewhat different form in *Encountering Student Texts: Interpretive Issues in Reading Student Writing,* edited by Bruce Lawson, Susan Sterr Ryan, and W. Ross Winterowd, pp. 5–19. Copyright 1989 by the National Council of Teachers of English. Used with permission.

1. I would like here to acknowledge and thank again the readers who worked on this project: Elizabeth "Lib" Hayes, Marty Hiestand, Jacki Lauby, Delia Temes, and Don Wagner.

2. This is a reference to Sheridan Baker's *The Practical Stylist* (4th ed., N.Y.: Thomas Y. Crowell, 1977), the required textbook for the course at that time.

Chapter 4

1. I do not intend to enter the debate about the actual authorship of *Marxism and the Philosophy of Language,* and in fact the translation I have read cites V. N. Volosinov as author and argues that there has not yet been compelling enough evidence to challenge that claim. Given Volosinov's close collaboration with Bakhtin, however, I feel comfortable at the very least to include *Marxism* as part of the Bakhtinian argument or theory of language.

2. In fact, writing researchers might be tempted to agree with Stubbs's (1983) observation about trying systematically to study spoken conversation as it actually occurs in real-life settings: "It is easy to get the impression that discourse analysis is at least a foolhardy, if not a quite impossible undertaking, and that expanding the narrow range of phenomena that linguists study to include natural language in use causes all hell to break loose" (p. 15).

3. See Henriques et al. (1984) for a related argument but constructed in the terms of poststructural theory. They want to ground developmental psychology in an understanding of "how a socially produced individual is not merely moulded, labelled, or pushed around by external forces; but is formed by a process which treats neither society nor individual as a privileged beginning, but takes interior and exterior as problematic categories" (p. 9). They, too, look to language: "It is through a focus on signification that it is possible to link the psyche to the social domain" (p. 211), but I do not think that they characterize language as historical or dialogic, or define language use as creative.

4. For Bakhtin, *ideology* refers broadly to any system of ideas, not just to politically oriented ones, as the term often does in English.

5. J. Zebroski (personal communication) asks us to consider, for example, the conflicting worldviews and ideological battles layered for those of us in composition within the word *grammar* as rather richly illustrative of this point.

6. According to Clark and Holquist (1984), the greatest problem Bakhtin poses for his readers is not just assimilating his rather exotic new terminology but rather rethinking those traditional Western habits of thought that value logical analysis and the breaking down of complex phenomena into component and (presumably) more tractable parts: "What is difficult about Bakhtin is the demand [his] way of thinking makes on our way of thinking" (p. 6), because he "makes the enormous leap from dialectical, or partitive, thinking, which is still presumed to be the universal norm, to dialogic or relational thinking" (p. 7).

7. Compare similar problems of textualizing understanding as they are being discussed in cultural anthropology, as in Marcus and Fischer (1986). There is a preoccupation with a

crisis in representation and with various genres of description. Ethnographers want to evoke, not represent a culture, and they have experimented with various textual strategies, such as dialogue, multiple voices, and readings from diverse perspectives.

Chapter 6

1. From the corpus of approximately 160 texts that Matthew wrote both at home and at school during the period from first through fifth grade, I have selected representative texts to work from in this documentary account. By representative, I mean texts that reflect the range of genre, theme, and expressive choice in the entire corpus. I have numbered tests according to their order in the account and coded them according to grade, date, and age. For the early texts, I have also provided conventionalized versions.

2. I would like to thank and acknowledge the following graduate students in English 613 (Fall 1989) at Syracuse University for participating in this deep talk: Susan Bailey, Eve Crandall, Cheryl Doak, Maria Hosmer-Briggs, Laurel Kallenbach, Michael Mahan, and Craig Smith.

3. The concepts of information, intonation contour, textual structure, cohesion, and genre come from the sociolinguistic work of M. A. K. Halliday, especially as developed in *Language as Social Semiotic: The Social Interpretation of Language and Meaning* (Baltimore: University Park Press, 1978).

4. Here is a brief summary of the structural types that Newkirk identified, which he claims are arranged only very loosely in some kind of "general developmental progression" for exposition as a genre:

1. *Label:* one-word or sentence identifications for pictures.
2. *List—basic:* series of names, dates, facts, etc.
3. *Attribute series:* clauses that state facts or feelings about topic.
4. *Reason list:* series of statements about a proposition.
5. *Couplet:* two-clause units, e.g., question-answer, topic-comment.
6. *Attribute series—hierarchical:* statements sorted into categories.
7. *Paragraph—basic:* three or more clauses coherently connected.
8. *Paragraph—ordered:* paragraphs themselves in specific order.

5. *"Fish" and "Fishing"*
This is the chair's summary of the group's reflective conversation on these keywords.
Fish is an immense word, fish and fishing, and there is a tension created between the fish itself and its life and existence and its meaning for existence, which is utterly different from our own, and the thought therefore of bringing the fish onto land is filled with drama, agony, and great excitement, all mixed together in it. It is a mythic word, lending itself to symbolisms, and I would mention particularly there the way the Christian religion is woven through with fish imagery. But also the fish has in it the mythic beginning of where life comes from, and so to be in the water, or to see fish, is reflection back of that beginning, of water as the source of life. Especially those fish that go deep into the water where it is very dark and that can't see themselves and that are shaped by that experience are a reminder of something from the back of beyond. The way the eyes are placed, the way the eye looks when you look into it, all add to the mysteriousness of fish. They are also a symbol of fertility.

As far as having a dark side to the fish itself, there is a way in which the fish stands for the most spiritual element in people, and that's part of the Christian symbolism, but we brought it up in a number of ways—you can go fishing for an idea, go be "fishers of men," the notion of the fish as soul or inward, watery, not yet formed, associated with feeling. And then there is magic, too, in all kinds of books and stories.

When we started bringing up phrases, the word *fish* shows up in a lot of different places. It swims its way through the language in all sorts of ways. Anyplace you look for what is hidden, beneath the surface, the *fish* is there to hold that possibility. One of the places where that came up for us was the notion of the detective, where words like *lure* or *bait* come in—to draw out of the dark and to draw into vision.

That may be one of its great usefulnesses and makes its way into so many language domains and has very strong transformational possibilities, and I'm awfully interested in the figure of the mermaid or merman, who then comes to stand for the amphibian/human, where the fish stands for that which crosses over borders and boundaries, though the boundary is very strong.

The idea of the mysterious beginning and right on the edges of things, and you have to be near the water, near to the boundary, in order to fish. You cannot do it from great distance, unless you turn it into an economical activity, and one of the most appalling thoughts about commercial fishing is covering the globe with nets that catch everything and take out all of the science and art of fishing.

Fisher people who do it as science and art are terribly knowledgeable about how they are going to do it, what they are going to catch, and people who are trout fishing are not at all the kind of people who go for great northern pike. It's a highly differentiated activity, with equipment and knowledge and technique and are associated with each of those. Then if you stripmine the seas and do this on some massive scale, you remove from it all that kind of personalness of the engagement with fish that makes it so strong in poetry and novels, where the fish continues to stand, for the fisher person, for that which lies beyond reach, for what is the bearer of personal treasure and that which allows all kinds of patience to be given and provides all kinds of meditational and contemplative possibility.

Regarding equipment and technique, there is also experience, having lots of experience, and having those experiences build up and keep refining the technique you are using.

The other part of this is that *fish* brought up a lot of fathers and a lot of childhood relationships. The word brought up some other remarkably beautiful words: silvery, quick, elusive, wet, cool, cold, primordial soup, flit, flip, swim, dart, grace, and rhythm both of the fish and (to bring it back where the relationship is strong) of the person fishing. It is a beautiful activity to observe. That has to do with freedom of space, captivity and struggle, meditation and thought.

References

Introduction

Bakhtin, M. M. *Speech Genres and Other Late Essays*. Ed. by C. Emerson and M. Holquist, trans. by V. W. McGee. Austin: University of Texas Press, 1986.

————. *The Dialogic Imagination*. Ed. by M. Holquist, trans. by C. Emerson and M. Holquist. Austin: University of Texas Press, 1981.

Bauer, D. M. *Feminist Dialogics: A Theory of Failed Community*. Albany: State University of New York Press, 1988.

Berger, J., and J. Mohr. *Another Way of Telling*. New York: Pantheon Books, 1982.

Bissex, G. L. *GYNS AT WRK: A Child Learns to Write and Read*. Cambridge, Mass.: Harvard University Press, 1980.

Cairns, R. B. *Social Development: The Origins and Plasticity of Interchanges*. San Francisco: W. H. Freeman, 1979.

Carini, P. F. *The Art of Seeing and the Visibility of the Person*. Grand Forks, N.D.: North Dakota Study Group on Evaluation, 1979.

Dyson, A. H. "Individual Differences in Emerging Writing." In *Advances in Writing Research, Volume One: Children's Early Writing Development*. Ed. by M. Farr. Norwood, N.J.: Ablex, 1985. Pp. 59–125.

Gundlach, R., J. B. McLane, F. M. Stott, and G. D. McNamee. "The Social Foundations of Children's Early Writing Development." In *Advances in Writing Research, Volume One: Children's Early Writing Development*. Ed. by M. Farr. Norwood, N.J.: Ablex, 1985. Pp. 1–58.

Lerner, R. M., ed. *Developmental Psychology: Historical and Philosophical Perspectives*. Hillsdale, N.H.: Lawrence Erlbaum Associates, 1983.

North, S. M. *The Making of Knowledge in Composition: Portrait of an Emerging Field*. Upper Montclair, N.J.: Boynton/Cook, 1987.

Nystrand, M. "The Structure of Textual Space." In *What Writers Know*. Ed. by M. Nystrand. New York: Academic Press, 1986. Pp. 75–86.

Schrag, C. O. *Communicative Praxis and the Space of Subjectivity*. Bloomington: Indiana University Press, 1986.

Schuster, C. I. "Mikhail Bakhtin as Rhetorical Theorist." *College English,* October 1985, pp. 594–607.

Smith, P. *Discerning the Subject*. Minneapolis: University of Minnesota Press, 1988.

Sowers, S. "Learning to Write in a Workshop: A Study of Grades One through Four." In

Advances in Writing Research, Volume One: Children's Early Writing Development. Ed. by M. Farr. Norwood, N.J.: Ablex, 1985. Pp. 297–342.

Stock, P. L. "Rethinking the Discursive Practices of Education: An Argument for Teacher-Research." Manuscript.

Volosinov, V. N./M. M. Bakhtin. *Marxism and the Philosophy of Language.* Trans. by L. Matejka and I. R. Titunik. Cambridge, Mass.: Harvard University Press, 1986.

Chapter 1

Carini, Patricia F. "Children's Strengths: Another Way of Looking at Evaluation and Education." Address for the Progressive Educators' Conference, Cambridge School, Weston, Mass., October 15, 1987.

———. *The Prospect Center Documentary Processes: In Progress.* Prospect Archive and Center for Education and Research, North Bennington, Vt., updated and revised June 1986a.

———. "The Reference Edition of the Prospect Archive: Its Development and Its Implications for Looking at Children and Their Work." Unpublished paper based on an address made at the Harvard Graduate School of Education, February 1986b.

———. "Reflections on Childhood and Change." Address for the Philadelphia Chapter of Educators for Social Responsibility and Teaching in a Nuclear Age, January 24, 1985.

———. *The School Lives of Seven Children: A Five Year Study.* Grand Forks, N.D.: North Dakota Study Group on Evaluation, 1982.

———. *The Art of Seeing and the Visibility of the Person.* Grand Forks, N.D.: North Dakota Study Group on Evaluation, 1979a.

———. "Considerations of the Lifespan." Essay in *The Prospect Papers.* North Bennington, Vt.: Prospect Archive and Center for Education and Research, 1979b.

———. *Observation and Description: An Alternative Methodology for the Investigation of Human Phenomena.* Grand Forks, N.D.: North Dakota Study Group on Evaluation, 1975.

Chapter 2

Bakhtin, M. M. *Speech Genres and Other Late Essays.* Trans. by Vern W. McGee, ed. by C. Emerson and M. Holquist. Austin: University of Texas Press, 1986.

———. *The Dialogic Imagination.* Ed. by M. Holquist, trans. by C. Emerson and M. Holquist. Austin: University of Texas Press, 1981.

Belenky, M. F., B. M. Clinchy, N. R. Goldberger, and J. M. Tarule. *Women's Ways of Knowing: The Development of Self, Voice, and Mind.* New York: Basic Books, 1986.

Berger, J., and J. Mohr. *Another Way of Telling.* New York: Pantheon Books, 1982.

Brodkey, L. "Writing Ethnographic Narratives." *Written Communication,* January 1987, pp. 25–50.

Carini, P. F. *The School Lives of Seven Children: A Five Year Study.* Grand Forks, N.D.: North Dakota Study Group on Evaluation, 1982.

————. *The Art of Seeing and the Visibility of the Person.* Grand Forks, N.D.: North Dakota Study Group on Evaluation, 1979.

————. *Observation and Description: An Alternative Methodology for the Investigation of Human Phenomena.* Grand Forks, N.D.: North Dakota Study Group on Evaluation, 1975.

Carroll, D. "Thoughts on Notetaking: Suggested Approaches." In *The Prospect Center Documentary Processes: In Progress.* North Bennington, Vt.: Prospect Archive and Center for Education and Research, 1986. Appendix A.

Geertz, C. "Deep Play: Notes on the Balinese Cockfight." Reprinted in *Ways of Reading* by David Bartholomae and Anthony Petrosky. New York: St. Martin's Press, pp. 298–335.

Gusdorf, G. "Speaking as Encounter." Excerpted in *Language as a Way of Knowing.* Ed. by M. Nystrand. Toronto: Ontario Institute for Studies in Education, 1977. Pp. 125–32.

Halliday, M. A. K. *Language as Social Semiotic: The Social Interpretation of Language and Meaning.* Baltimore: University Park Press, 1978.

Hartman, G. H. *Saving the Text: Literature/Derrida/Philosophy.* Baltimore: Johns Hopkins University Press, 1981.

Kundera, M. *The Art of the Novel.* Trans. by L. Asher. New York: Grove Press, 1986.

LeFevre, K. B. *Invention as a Social Act.* Carbondale: Southern Illinois University Press, 1987.

Miller, C. R. "Genre as Social Action." *Quarterly Journal of Speech* 10 (1984), pp. 151–67.

Phelps, L. W. "Rhythm and Pattern in a Composing Life." In *Writers on Writing.* Ed. by Tom Waldrep. New York: Random House, 1985. Pp. 241–57.

Ruddick, S. "New Combinations: Learning from Virginia Woolf." In *Between Women.* Ed. by C. Asher, L. DeSalvor, and S. Ruddick. Boston: Beacon Press, 1984. Pp. 137–59.

The Prospect Center Documentary Processes: In Progress. North Bennington, Vt.: Prospect Archive and Center for Education and Research, 1986.

Volosinov, V. N./M. M. Bakhtin. *Marxism and the Philosophy of Language.* Trans. by L. Matejka and I. R. Titunik. Cambridge, Mass.: Harvard University Press, 1986.

Vygotsky, L. S. *Thought and Language.* Trans., newly revised, ed. by A. Kozulin. Cambridge, Mass.: MIT Press, 1986.

Chapter 3

Bartholomae, D. "Inventing the University." *Journal of Basic Writing* 5, 1 (1986), pp. 4–23.

Carini, P. F. *The Art of Seeing and the Visibility of the Person.* Grand Forks, N.D.: North Dakota Study Group on Evaluation, 1979.

————. *Observation and Description: An Alternative Methodology for the Investigation of Human Phenomena.* Grand Forks, N.D.: North Dakota Study Group on Evaluation, 1975.

Geertz, C. "Thick Description: Toward an Interpretive Theory of Culture." In *The Interpretation of Cultures.* New York: Basic Books, 1973. Pp. 3–30.

Nystrand, M. "The Structure of Textual Space." In *What Writers Know*. Ed. by M. Nystrand. New York: Academic Press, 1982. Pp. 75-86.

Patton, M. Q. *Qualitative Evaluation Methods*. Beverly Hills: Sage Publications, 1980.

Zebroski, J. T. "Writing Time." Manuscript.

Chapter 4

M. M. Bakhtin. *Speech Genres and Other Late Essays*. Ed. by C. Emerson and M. Holquist, trans. by V. W. McGee. Austin: University of Texas Press, 1986.

———. *The Dialogic Imagination*. Ed. by M. Holquist, trans. by C. Emerson and M. Holquist. Austin: University of Texas Press, 1981.

Bauer, D. M. *Feminist Dialogics: A Theory of Failed Community*. Albany: State University of New York Press, 1988.

Bissex, G. *GYNS AT WRK*. Cambridge, Mass.: Harvard University Press, 1980.

Clark, K., and M. Holquist. *Mikhail Bakhtin*. Cambridge, Mass.: Belknap Press of Harvard University Press, 1984.

Dyson, A. H. "Individual Differences in Emerging Writing." In *Advances in Writing Research, Volume One: Children's Early Writing Development*. Ed. by M. Farr. Norwood, N.J.: Ablex, 1985. Pp. 59–125.

Geertz, C. "Making Experiences, Authoring Selves." In *The Anthropology of Experience*. Ed. by V. W. Turner and E. M. Bruner. Urbana: University of Illinois Press, 1986. Pp. 373–80.

Henriques, J., et al. *Changing the Subject*. London: Methuen, 1984.

Himley, M. "Becoming a Writer: A Documentary Account." *Written Communication*, January 1988, pp. 82–107.

———. "Disappearing TVs and Evolving Texts." *Language Arts*, March 1986a, pp. 238–45.

———. "Genre as Generative: One Perspective on One Child's Early Writing Growth." In *The Structure of Written Communication*. By M. Nystrand. New York: Academic Press, 1986b. Pp. 137–57.

Marcus, G. E., and M. M. J. Fischer. *Anthropology as Cultural Critique*. Chicago: University of Chicago Press, 1986.

Nystrand, M. *The Structure of Written Communication: Studies in Reciprocity between Writers and Readers*. New York: Academic Press, 1986.

Schuster, C. I. "Mikhail Bakhtin as Rhetorical Theorist." *College English*, October 1985, pp. 594–607.

Stubbs, M. *Discourse Analysis*. Chicago: University of Chicago Press, 1983.

Volosinov, V. N./M. M. Bakhtin. *Marxism and the Philosophy of Language*. Trans. by L. Matejka and I. R. Titunik. Cambridge, Mass.: Harvard University Press, 1986.

Chapter 5

Bissex, G. L. *GYNS AT WRK: A Child Learns to Write and Read*. Cambridge, Mass.: Harvard University Press, 1980.

Calkins, L. M. *Lessons from a Child: On the Teaching and Learning of Writing.* Exeter, N.H.: Heinemann Educational Books, 1983.

Carini, P. F. *Observation and Description: An Alternative Methodology for the Investigation of Human Phenomena.* Grand Forks, N.D.: North Dakota Study Group on Evaluation, 1975.

Clay, M. M. *What Did I Write?* London: Heinemann Educational Books, 1975.

Dyson, A. H. "Individual Differences in Emerging Writing." *Advances in Writing Research, Volume One: Children's Early Writing Development.* Ed. by M. Farr. Norwood, N.J.: Ablex, 1985. Pp. 59–125.

————. "Emerging Alphabetic Literacy in School Contexts." *Written Communication,* January 1984, pp. 5–55.

————. "The Role of Oral Language in Early Writing Processes." *Research in the Teaching of English,* February 1983, pp. 1–30.

————. "Reading, Writing, and Language: Young Children Solving the Written Language Puzzle." *Language Arts,* November–December 1982, pp. 829–39.

Ferreiro, E., and A. Teberosky. *Literacy before Schooling.* Exeter, N.H.: Heinemann Educational Books, 1982.

Geertz, C. "Blurred Genres: The Refiguration of Social Thought." In *Local Knowledge: Further Essays in Interpretive Anthropology.* New York: Basic Books, 1983. Pp. 19–35.

————. "Thick Description: Toward An Interpretive Theory of Culture." In *The Interpretation of Culture.* New York: Basic Books, 1973. Pp. 3–30.

Graves, D. H. *Writing: Teachers and Children at Work.* Exeter, N.H.: Heinemann Educational Books, 1983.

————. *Children's Writing: Research Directions and Hypotheses Based upon an Examination of the Writing Processes of Seven Year Old Children.* Ph.D. dissertation, State University of New York at Buffalo, 1973.

Gundlach, R., J. B. McLane, F. M. Stott, and G. D. McNamee. "The Social Foundations of Children's Early Writing Development." In *Advances in Writing Research, Volume One: Children's Early Writing Development.* Ed. by M. Farr. Norwood, N.J.: Ablex, 1985. Pp. 1–58.

Harste, J. C., V. A. Woodward, and C. L. Burke. *Language Stories and Literacy Lessons.* Portsmouth, N.H.: Heinemann Educational Books, 1984.

Kress, G. *Learning to Write.* London: Routledge and Kegan Paul, 1982.

Mailloux, S. *Rhetorical Power.* Ithaca, N.Y.: Cornell University Press, 1989.

Marcus, G. E., and M. M. J. Fischer. *Anthropology as Cultural Critique: An Experimental Moment in th Human Sciences.* Chicago: University of Chicago Press, 1986.

North, S. M. *The Making of Knowledge in Composition: Portrait of an Emerging Field.* Upper Montclair, N.J.: Boynton/Cook, 1987.

Nystrand, M. *The Structure of Written Communication.* New York: Academic Press, 1986.

Phelps, L. W. *Composition as Human Science.* New York: Oxford University Press, 1988.

Read, C. *Children's Categorization of Speech Sounds in English.* Urbana, Ill.: NCTE, 1975.

Sowers, S. "Learning to Write in a Workshop: A Study of Grades One through Four." In *Advances in Writing Research, Volume One: Children's Early Writing Development.* Ed. by M. Farr. Norwood, N.J.: Ablex, 1985. Pp. 297–342.

Vygotsky, L. S. *Thought and Language*. Trans., newly revised, ed. by A. Kozulin. Cambridge, Mass.: MIT Press, 1986.

Zebroski, J. T. "The Social Construction of Self in the Work of Lev Vygotsky." Paper given at Conference on College Composition and Communication, Seattle, March 1989.

Chapter 6

Bakhtin, M. M. *Speech Genres and Other Late Essays*. Ed. by C. Emerson and M. Holquist, trans. by V. W. McGee. Austin: University of Texas Press, 1986.

Cazden, C. B. "Spontaneous and Scientific Concepts: Young Children's Learning of Punctuation." Paper presented at Conference on English Education, NCTE, Washington, D.C., November 20, 1982.

Halliday, M. A. K. *Language as Social Semiotic: The Social Interpretation of Language and Meaning*. Baltimore: University Park Press, 1978.

Halliday, M. A. K., and Ruqaiya Hasan. *Cohesion in English*. London: Longman, 1976.

Himley, M. "Genre as Generative: One Perspective on One Child's Early Writing Growth." In *The Structure of Written Communication*. By M. Nystrand. New York: Academic Press, 1986. Pp. 137–57.

Kress, G. *Learning to Write*. London: Routledge and Kegan Paul, 1982.

Miller, C. R. "Genre as Social Action." *Quarterly Journal of Speech* 10 (1984), pp. 151–67.

Moffett, J. *Teaching the Universe of Discourse*. Boston: Houghton-Mifflin, 1968.

Newkirk, Thomas. "The Non-narrative Writing of Young Children." *Research in the Teaching of English*, 21, May 1987, pp. 121–44.

Nystrand, M., and M. Himley. "Written Text as Social Interaction." *Theory into Practice*, Summer 1984, pp. 198–207.

Stubbs, M. *Language and Literacy*. London: Routledge and Kegan Paul, 1980.

Vygotsky, L. S. *Thought and Language*. Trans., newly revised, ed. by A. Kozulin. Cambridge, Mass.: MIT Press, 1986.

———. *Mind in Society: The Development of Higher Psychological Processes*. Cambridge, Mass.: Harvard University Press, 1978.

Index